SURVEYS THAT WORK
A PRACTICAL GUIDE FOR DESIGNING BETTER SURVEYS

Caroline Jarrett

Rosenfeld Media
Brooklyn, New York

"Caroline has created a must-read 'one-stop source' for those looking to conduct a survey. Her book guides the reader through all the necessary stages for creating a robust survey, from beginning to end. The book can be used by experienced survey methodologists looking to improve the surveys they run and by those who are new to the survey world. Refreshingly, its clear and simple language makes survey methodology accessible to the masses, and its practical approach supports this. Importantly, it also helps the reader work out whether a survey is indeed the right choice—a step which is all too often overlooked. Helpfully, the book provides suggestions for additional reading for those who wish to explore particular aspects of survey design further. Read this book—and learn from one of the best."

—Laura Wilson, Data Quality Hub Lead,
UK Office for National Statistics

"Caroline Jarrett is the UX community's foremost expert on conducting surveys. Now we have all of her considerable knowledge about surveys in one place. Her excellent book, *Surveys That Work*, covers everything from theory to process to what constitutes a good question to analyzing and understanding people's answers. This practical book will answer all the questions you have about conducting surveys."

—Pabini Gabriel-Petit, user experience expert,
editor of UXmatters.com

"This book is a sharpening toolkit for taking haphazard surveys and making them useful. As research gets faster and faster, this book will help you keep pace with changing landscapes, especially in digital industries."

—Akil Benjamin, Strategy Director, COMUZI

"If surveys are one of the research techniques you use (or might use), you need this book! In an easy-to-read, conversational style, Caroline takes you through the entire process with wonderful examples, helpful stories, and tons of good advice. And where else would you have an adorable 'Survey Octopus' to remind you of all the elements you need for a successful survey and of how to minimize the various problems that can impact the value of your results?"

—Janice (Ginny) Redish, author of *Letting Go of the Words—Writing Web Content that Works*

"Those of us in the user experience design practice have needed this book for a long time. If you have avoided using surveys as a tool for understanding the needs of the people who use your products, shy away no more: Caroline's mastery of method and her encouraging voice come through in every sentence. This book is a delight to read and use."

—Dana Chisnell, Fellow, Belfer Center for Science and International Affairs and Policy Designer, U.S. Digital Service

"All praise for *Surveys That Work* and the Survey Octopus! This is crucial reading for all those who want to deepen their user-centered practice with quantitative research. A thorough exploration of all dimensions of the thinking process behind good surveys, this book will make you a better questioner!"

—Misaki Hata, Service designer, NHS Digital

"This book is delightful; I'm excited to share it with you. Caroline will help you know when to do a survey, and how to do it well. When we do good research, we can make good decisions!"

—Kathryn Summers, Professor, University of Baltimore

Surveys That Work
A Practical Guide for Designing Better Surveys
By Caroline Jarrett

Rosenfeld Media, LLC

125 Maiden Lane

New York, New York 10038

USA

On the Web: www.rosenfeldmedia.com

Please send errata to: errata@rosenfeldmedia.com

Publisher: Louis Rosenfeld

Managing Editor: Marta Justak

Interior Layout: Danielle Foster

Cover Design: Heads of State

Illustrator: Tasia Graham

Indexer: Marilyn Engst

Proofreader: Gill Editorial Services

ISBN: 1-933820-53-5

ISBN 13: 978-1-933820-53-8

LCCN: 2021931291

Printed and bound in the United States of America

For the National Health Service,
especially all the dedicated professionals
who got me through very serious illnesses.
Without them, I would not be here.

HOW TO USE THIS BOOK

Who Should Read This Book?

If you need or want to do a survey but don't know how, then this book is for you. I also hope you'll find value in it if you are already doing surveys but feel that you could be doing better ones.

There are a few ways to use this book:

- Read it—start at the beginning and keep going. It will take you through an entire survey process and a few specialist topics on the way.

- If you're pressed for time and want to know what you can do quickly, turn directly to Chapter 8, "The Least You Can Do™." It has suggestions for things you can do when you've only got an hour to improve a survey, how to do a quick survey in a day, and how to plan your time when you have the luxury of a whole week.

- Read the Introduction to get an idea of the seven steps to achieve an effective survey and then decide which of the steps sounds relevant to you and skip directly to that chapter.

If you're an academic or student and you want or need to dive into more details and follow up on the references, there's a section on the website for that as well.

What Comes with This Book?

The companion website for this book is effortmark.co.uk/surveysthatwork, or equivalently, rosenfeldmedia.com/surveys-that-work.

You'll find extra material, updates, diagrams, slides, and other supporting materials.

If you're a professor and considering whether this book is suitable for your students, there's a section on the website for you, too.

The book's diagrams and other illustrations are available under a Creative Commons license (when possible) for you to download and include in your own presentations. You can find these on Flickr at www.flickr.com/photos/rosenfeldmedia/sets/.

FREQUENTLY ASKED QUESTIONS

I see so many bad surveys—isn't the best survey the one that's not done at all?

Unfortunately, we are all bombarded with bad surveys. For example, someone in an organization decides that constantly blasting out questionnaires to every customer is a great way to get feedback. Their response rate is terrible, but they don't consider that this poor response will simply create lots of errors—and annoyed customers. And since these bad questionnaires go to everyone, you've got a very good chance of seeing too many questionnaires—and many of them will be rotten ones.

A bad survey gets you bad data. A bad application of any method gets you bad data.

What's the best survey tool?

Survey tools change constantly, so I've learned not to make any specific recommendations. But I have written Spotlight F, "Questions to Ask When You Choose a Survey Tool," that has the crucial questions to ask when you're picking one.

When I'm using a Likert scale, how many response points are best?

If you want a quick answer for the number of response points, 5 is good. If you want a more complex answer, skip to Figure H.9, which is a flowchart to help you decide on the number of response points.

And if you want my reasons for those answers, there's Spotlight H, "'On a Scale from 1 to 5' (Likert and Rating Scales)."

You've included a Survey Octopus with tentacles and a smile—don't you know that's all wrong for octopuses?

You'll meet the Survey Octopus in the Introduction—it's a cartoonish representation of Total Survey Error.

It's not a real octopus: they have mouths between their arms and no tentacles. My favorite feature is their blue blood.

I got sent this terrible survey—please can I send it to you?

Of course! I'm always glad to add more examples to my stash. If sharing the pain with me will help, feel welcome—but I won't be able to do anything about it. You'll find my contact details on my website: Effortmark.co.uk.

Is there any chance that I can persuade someone who sends me a bad survey to do something else?

Yes, contact the person or organization who sent it to you and ask them to buy this book.

CONTENTS

FOREWORD

I can remember when—ten years ago!—Caroline first told me that she was going to write this book.

I immediately thought it was a great idea. At the time, I'd never done any surveys myself since I was such a huge fan of *qualitative* UX research methods (especially usability tests), as opposed to *quantitative* methods like surveys.

But even though I'm biased (after all, I did write two books praising usability testing), I like to think that I'm not a jerk about it. I know there's value in quantitative methods, and I always thought it would be great to be able to do a quick survey and get useful answers to specific questions, like "How many people do x?" and "How many like x better than y?"

So I was delighted to think that Caroline was going to make it easy for me by writing the book I wanted to have:

Here's how to do a survey well without all the work of becoming a survey expert

Caroline Jarrett
Author of *Forms that Work*

But as she started describing it, I was surprised to learn that the book she intended to write (or at least the book she *wanted* to write) was:

Here's why you shouldn't do a survey

Caroline Jarrett
Author of *Forms that Work*

I was sure she had to be kidding, and I hastened to point out that the "talking people out of doing a survey" book probably had far less sales potential than the one I was hoping for. But I soon learned she was only half kidding, because when people asked for her help doing a survey, she often ended up feeling that "Don't do a survey" was the best advice she could give them, for two reasons:

1. She'd seen far too many surveys done wrong, and more importantly
2. She'd seen far too many that shouldn't have been done at all.

Fortunately for us, she ended up writing the book that I wanted. But it took her more than ten years of very hard work. Here's what she did:

- Read a staggering number of survey books and research papers (which we don't have time to do).
- Absorbed and understood it all (which we probably couldn't do even if we had the time).

- Attended lots of survey conferences and workshops, and talked to experts and non-experts to learn about their best (and worst) survey practices.
- Combined it all with her own practical experience doing surveys and helping others do them.
- Boiled it down into understandable advice (which she happens to be really good at).
- Made it into a book (which, having written books myself, I strongly advise against, since it's a ridiculous amount of work, especially if you do it well).

Like me, I'm sure you've been on the receiving end of plenty of bad surveys. Personally, the thing that bothers me most is when I want to answer "Other" or "N/A," but they don't let me. For example, how do I answer this question about the place where I've gotten my morning coffee every day for years?

During my most recent visit to [famous coffee chain], the staff went out of their way to get to know me.	Disagree Strongly				Agree Strongly
	1	2	3	4	5

If I answer 1, it makes my friendly baristas look bad, and if I answer 5, it's a lie. The people who did the survey are forcing me to give them bad data, which means they're going to get inaccurate results, so why should I spend my time helping them? I always fill it out anyway, and answer 5 because my baristas are very nice people, and I don't want them to lose any points. But I'm never happy doing it.[1]

In the pages ahead, you'll find that Caroline talks about how to deal with many, many specific issues, like having an "Other" option. But even more valuable is the clarity she brings to big-picture issues, like what kinds of questions to ask (and how to ask them), what kinds

---

1 Usually, I add a note in the "Any Additional Comments?" field at the end of the survey, suggesting that [famous coffee chain] should hire someone better to do their surveys.

of people to ask (and how many of them), and what to do with the results you get.

Thanks to what I learned from reading several drafts of this book over the years, I'm very comfortable doing what she calls a Light Touch Survey: highly focused, just a few questions, where the results you get will help you make an important decision. In fact, I just did my latest one a month ago to answer a few questions about how people use my website, before finally redesigning it after 20 years.

So if you've ever wanted to do a survey—or you want to do better surveys—you're in the right place.

Just be glad that Caroline did so much of the heavy lifting for us.

—Steve Krug
author of *Don't Make Me Think*

INTRODUCTION

What would you do for a dollar? Amazingly, a dollar—yes, just one—can have a big effect on people's willingness to answer questions.

The dollar comes from an experiment by survey methodologists Jeannine M. James and Richard Bolstein. They compared the effect on survey responses of a dollar bill that arrives in the envelope with a paper survey to $50 guaranteed (not a prize) as a reward for sending in the survey. (James and Bolstein 1992) The dollar bill did better.

Is that what you expected? If so, you're ahead of me. I was surprised and intrigued. For many years, I've worked with organizations on making their forms easier, and, of course, that includes understanding how to make questions easier and how to persuade people to answer those questions accurately.

Through reading about questions, I discovered the rich literature of survey methodology. Most of all, I discovered the concept of Total Survey Error.

Have you met "statistical significance"? That's mathematically related to one of the possible sources of error in surveys: sampling error. There are rather a lot of other types of error, unfortunately, and Total Survey Error brings them all together.

Suddenly, a bunch of ideas connected. I became enthusiastic about surveys. Colleagues began to ask me to help with their surveys.

Eventually, Ginny Redish and Lou Rosenfeld persuaded me that it would be a good idea to write a book—and here we are.

We start with a definitions chapter

Although I'm convinced that Total Survey Error is crucial to getting good results from surveys, I have to admit that I found some of the explanations difficult to get my head around at first. So I've started with an opening chapter that says what I mean by a survey and introduces you to my Survey Octopus—a creature with a cheery smile and eight tentacles that represent Total Survey Error in a way that helps me, and I hope will work for you, too.

There are seven chapters for the survey process

One of the ways that people ask me to help with surveys is to lead workshops on survey design. I learned that it's helpful to have a process, so I ended up with seven steps. The first four are about getting from an idea that you want to do a survey to creating a questionnaire:

1. **Goals:** Establish your goals for the survey.
2. **Sample:** Find people who will answer.
3. **Questions:** Write and test the questions.
4. **Questionnaire:** Build and test the questionnaire.

   Then you'll get the questionnaire to the people you want to respond to it.

5. **Fieldwork:** Get people to respond.

   The best part about fieldwork is that you get answers. After it, there are two chapters where you'll turn those answers into useful results.

6. **Responses:** Turn data into answers.
7. **Reports:** Show the results to decision-makers.

Along the way, you'll encounter the tests you can do to make sure that you get accurate results from your survey.

There's a bonus chapter: The Least You Can Do™

Does that sound like quite a lot of work? I'm not going to conceal it from you: a survey takes time, effort, and thoughtful choices. That's the bad news.

The good news is that there are ways to get decent results reasonably quickly. We'll look at them in the bonus chapter—and I'd like to thank Steve Krug, who encouraged me to write it and has allowed me to borrow his trademarked phrase The Least You Can Do™.

There are Spotlights and Case Studies

In between the chapters, you'll find Spotlights and Case Studies. The Spotlights are technical topics that I thought deserved special attention.

I wanted to make sure this book reflected what's practical, so I did a lot of listening to how people use surveys in practice. The Case Studies showcase some stories that struck me as especially useful, and I'm grateful to the people who shared them.

What Is a Survey? And the Survey Octopus

Most days, at least one website will ask me to respond to a pop-up invitation like the one in Figure 0.1.

HAVE YOUR SAY

We'd love to know what you think about our website.

Your feedback is really important to us to help us improve your experience in the future.

No thanks >   Take survey >
(opens in a new window)

FIGURE 0.1

A pop-up survey invitation.

Because of the button "Take survey"—and many others like it—people tend to think of a survey as a list of questions to answer. But a survey is also the entire process of ensuring that you ask good questions to get useful answers.

A survey is a process

To make it clearer which thing I mean when I say *survey*, I'll use these definitions:

A **questionnaire** is the set of questions that you will put to the people you want to answer them.

A **survey** is a process of asking questions that are answered by a sample of a defined group of people to get numbers that you can use to make decisions.

Let's unpack the elements of the definition of a survey.

A survey asks people to answer questions

It's rather easy to ask people questions. The trickier part is getting them to answer those questions. You'll learn about the topic of persuading people to answer questions in Chapter 3, "Questions."

A survey asks a defined group of people

When I talk about a "defined group of people," I mean that you need to make precise choices about the people you want to answer your survey. You'll also need to think about how many of them to ask and how to find them.

In some people's minds, the ideal survey is "to ask everyone." There's a specific type of survey that asks everyone: it's called a *census*.

Even censuses don't *really* ask everyone. They go to a defined group of people and have specific rules about who gets counted. For example, the U.S. Census Bureau administers the Decennial Census of the people of the United States of America. The definition of "people of the U.S.A." includes the 50 states and the District of Colombia.

But what about Guam—administered by the U.S., but maybe not exactly a part of it? Try these three questions:

1. Are people in Guam in or out?
2. What about babies who are born on census day—in or out?
3. Foreign nationals on a visit to the U.S.—in or out?

(The answers are: 1: In, as you can see in Figure 0.2; 2: In; 3: Out.)

We'll think about precision in deciding about people to ask in Chapter 1, "Goals."

FIGURE 0.2
People in Guam have been included in the U.S. Decennial Census since 1920. This poster is from 2000.

A survey asks a sample

A reliable survey asks a sample, not everyone. Asking everyone creates all sorts of problems. To mention just one issue: if you sent the questionnaire to everybody and something happens to go wrong technically, then you've got no one left to ask.

You'll learn about how many people to ask and how to find them in Chapter 2, "Sample."

A survey gets a number

A survey is a quantitative research technique. When you choose to do a survey, you're choosing to end up with results as a number (well, maybe several numbers—but definitely at least one).

You can certainly include some questions in your questionnaire that get non-numeric answers, such as asking someone to write their opinion in their own words (qualitative answers). But if your aim is mostly to be qualitative, then maybe you'd be better using a qualitative method. You'll learn about different types of methods in Chapter 1.

A survey helps you to make decisions

If you're working for a national statistical institute (NSI), such as the U.S. Census Bureau, then you'll be using the answers to create reference statistics that are used by a wide range of people for many purposes, such as determining how resources like funding for education get distributed to each state.

Most of us have an easier task: we can focus on the specific decisions that our own organization will make, based on the results of the survey.

If you don't want the answers for some purpose, why bother?

Total Survey Error focuses on reducing problems overall

My aim is to help you to get results from your survey that are valid and that accurately measure what they claim to measure. And that are reliable: for example, if you did the exact same survey again, you'd expect to get the same results (assuming nothing much else had changed). To do that, you'll have to tackle all sorts of issues, many of which are connected.

Let's look at one: "How many people do you need to ask?" It's important and one of the main topics for Chapter 2.

Do you answer every survey invitation you receive, or do you make choices about who gets your time?

If you answer every single survey—respect! I did it for a while for research purposes, but mostly I'm firmly in the "make choices" team, and that's much more the norm. If it's an interesting topic, a greater percentage of the people you ask will take the time to answer, so the number of people you ask also depends on the reason you are doing it (see Chapter 1) and the questions you ask (Chapter 3). It turns out that you'll be exploring connections between the issues all the time.

Flip that around, and you'll find plenty of pitfalls to avoid. Too many irrelevant questions, and you'll get more people dropping out, so you'll need to send more invitations to get the same number of eventual answers. One error can create another and another. Overall, the aim is to keep all the errors to a minimum and in balance with each other.

Total Survey Error combines many errors

Because of all the dependencies and related errors in surveys, survey methodologists look at all the choices you make when doing a survey and aim to achieve the least possible error overall, wrapping them up like this:

> Total Survey Error is the consequence of all the individual survey errors.

Meet the Survey Octopus

The survey process sits between:

- What you want to ask.
- Who you want to ask.
- What the final result is—"the number."

To help me to keep track of all the survey choices throughout the process, I combined them into a Survey Octopus in Figure 0.3. Although I'll be talking about the surveys separately, the Survey Octopus also acts as reminder that they are, in fact, somewhat connected.

FIGURE 0.3

The Survey Octopus has tentacles about the choices you make in surveys.

We'll focus on the top half of the Survey Octopus as we prepare and test the questionnaire (see Figure 0.4) in the first four chapters.

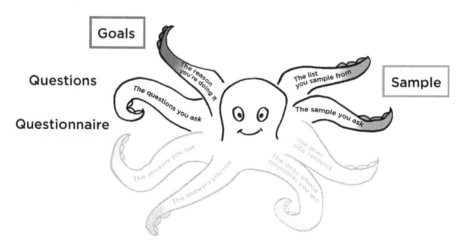

FIGURE 0.4

The preparation is about goals, sample, questions, and questionnaires.

Then we'll be thinking about the ones who answer when we're in Fieldwork: run the survey from invitation to follow-up (see Figure 0.5).

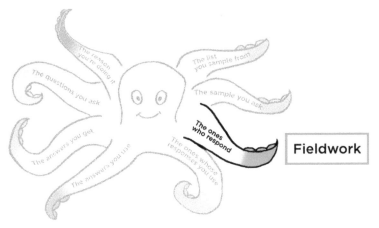

FIGURE 0.5
Fieldwork is about getting your questionnaire to the people who will answer.

And we'll focus on dealing with the last three tentacles when we're looking at Responses and Reports (see Figure 0.6).

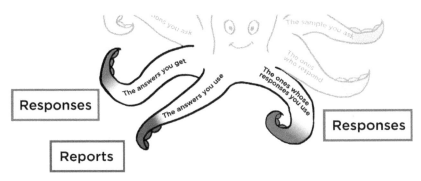

FIGURE 0.6
When you have some answers, it's time to consider the answers you get and turn them into insights.

For now, the important things to know about the Survey Octopus are:

- All the issues are connected.
- You'll meet them along the way.
- If you make good choices for all the issues, you'll get solid results.

We'll aim for Light Touch Surveys

How can surveys be a lot of hard work, but then I claim that you can get a better survey quickly?

Let's step back into history for a moment.

The 1940's mindset was Big Honkin' Surveys

In the 1940s, when the U.S. Bureau of Census took the picture of a census interview in Figure 0.7, the fieldwork for surveys was hard. An army of interviewers would head out, armed with their clipboards, to ask people questions face-to-face—admittedly, usually in homes or offices rather than their rose gardens. Telephone surveys were time-consuming. Even mail surveys took a lot of planning when printing had to be sent to a specialist shop.

FIGURE 0.7
Taking a break from gardening for a census interview.

COURTESY OF WWW.CENSUS.GOV/HISTORY/WWW/ GENEALOGY/DECENNIAL_CENSUS_RECORDS/

Because fieldwork was laborious, it was important to do it infrequently, which meant packing as many questions as possible into each questionnaire. And because surveys were infrequent, organizations looked for large sample sizes to support every possible analysis.

So the Big Honkin' Survey became the norm.

The problem is that each extra question adds to the burden of your survey:

- Harder work for your respondents means that fewer people will respond, so you have to ask more of them. A larger sample is more expensive.
- When you get all those responses, you've got a lot of work ahead of you because you asked a lot of questions.

Big Honkin' Surveys are a challenge. But if you have to do one, we'll get you through it.

The 21st century mindset: Light Touch Surveys

Technology has moved on since 1940. With the convenience of the internet, it's now possible to do lots of very tiny surveys. Instead of a long telephone call, you can ask questions by text message. Even printing is much simpler now.

All this means that you can now do short, sharp surveys—but lots of them: Light Touch Surveys.

The ideal Light Touch Survey has just a single interesting question that you really want to know the answer to. You test the question to make sure that it's one that the people you send the questionnaire to want to answer.

Insights from Mailchimp

Mailchimp's tagline is "Send Better Email." They help people manage contacts, send emails, and track the results of email campaigns—and they have a great user experience team.

They use surveys as one of their research methods, so I asked them to describe one of them. Laurissa Wolfram-Hvass and Fernando Godina from Mailchimp answered my questions.

Q. What was this project about?

Based on past research, we already knew that many customers import subscriber data into the Mailchimp app from other systems. What we *didn't* know, however, were the specific problems customers have during this process.

Q. What made you decide to go for a survey over a usability test?

We pick whatever research method is right for the questions we have at the time. We'll look at the data we already have and then decide on the best method to move us forward.

This time, when we reviewed the data we already had from our past research about importing, we couldn't see any real trends and needed to talk to more people. Usability tests are great for understanding workflow details and user interface problems, but we weren't at that point yet. We needed to first get a handle on the broader issues that people have during the import process before we could begin drilling down to problems with the user interface.

We wanted to reach as many customers as possible in a short period of time, so we opted for a survey. Within a day or two, we could identify a targeted list of recipients, write our survey questions, get feedback on those questions from our team, build and send the survey to a small pilot group, and then make refinements before sending it out to the recipient list. Within a week, we would have a body of data that we could mine for information.

While we may begin with surveys as a research method, we rarely end with them. We are often unable to solve a specific problem or answer all of our research questions through surveys alone, but they do help us quickly establish a baseline and identify areas that need further exploration.

Q. Did you follow a particular approach or work it out for yourselves?

We developed our survey methodology ourselves. The first stage, "goals," was probably the most significant stage for us. Once we had a set of clearly defined goals, we let those goals drive the research process and guide our decisions. This helped us stay focused as we moved from one stage to the next. We, of course, wanted to gather answers and come to a conclusion as quickly as possible, but we didn't force ourselves into a short timeframe that wouldn't allow us to experiment or self-adjust in the middle of the process.

Q. Did you do any interviewing when you developed the survey?

We actually held interviews twice during this project: once before we sent out the survey, and then again after we had tallied and coded the responses. At the start, we talked to over a dozen customers about how they import information into Mailchimp. The interviews gave us our starting point for the survey questions by helping us identify the kind of feedback we needed to gather from our customers.

Our second round of customer interviews took place after we had gathered all our survey responses. These interviews helped us take the survey data and turn it into a story—a qualitative narrative we could use to provide context to the survey's quantitative data.

Q. How did you find the customers to survey, and what sample size did you choose?

We had a list of 5,150 customers who told us that they imported subscriber lists regularly. We wanted a personal touch in our survey invitation, so we decided to use each person's first name. That limited us to people who had a first name saved in their Mailchimp profiles, which left us with 2,626 people—roughly half of our original list. It's a smaller sample, but we felt that we'd get a better response rate.

Then we randomly selected 100 of those folks to receive our survey as a pilot—just to test it and work out any kinks before sending it to everyone else. A pilot of 100 seemed large enough to uncover issues with the survey but small enough that if we had any problems to address, it wouldn't drastically affect our data.

continues

Q. I call that "narrowing down from a list." So finally: What are your top tips for people doing a survey?

We learned so much. We'll start with three tips about thinking about your goals and audience:

- **Narrow your target audience.** Be specific in choosing users who match the survey goals.

- **Be specific and direct.** Be clear about your goals and communicate those goals to your users.

- **Revisit your goals/objectives.** It's easy to lose focus when you're working on a project. We had four key questions we wanted to answer, and we returned to those questions many, many times. If we had a good idea but it didn't help us answer those four questions, we put it aside for later. This helped us keep our scope narrow and allowed us to move quickly.

These tips are about building your questionnaire:

- **Keep it short.** We had seven questions in our survey (and we would have had fewer if we could have managed it). The only way we were able to keep it short was to focus on one particular customer action/behavior we wanted to understand.

- **Use checkboxes (multiple choice/multiple answers) if you can.** This is something we would do differently another time. Most of our questions were open-ended because we wanted customers to explain their processes to us. But tagging and analyzing all that data, answer by answer, was a lot of work. Another time, we'd work out the most common answers and then let respondents select from them or fill in an "other" option for any that we'd missed.

And maybe these last two are the most important:

- **Be human.** Send the survey from a real named person, write like a human, and respond like a human.

- **Move fast.** Do any follow-up activities quickly: respond immediately to technical problems and do follow-up interviews within a week.

Q. Thanks so much.

Four Different Types of Surveys

In this book, I'm focusing on a survey as a process that results in numbers that you can use to make a decision.

A **survey** is a process of asking questions that are answered by a sample of a defined group of people to get numbers that you can use to make decisions.

Perhaps you're thinking: "I'm not sure about that—is it really true that we can only use surveys in that way? I'm sure I've seen other types of surveys."

Busted! Of course, you are right. I think that surveys can be roughly divided into the four types shown in Figure A.1.

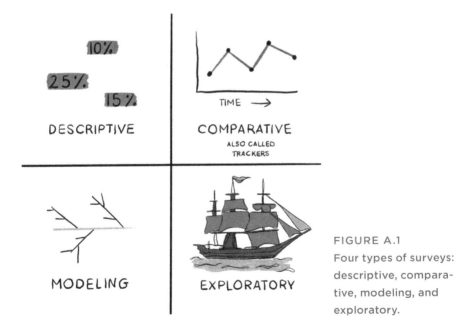

10% 25% 15% **DESCRIPTIVE**	TIME → **COMPARATIVE** ALSO CALLED TRACKERS
MODELING	**EXPLORATORY**

FIGURE A.1
Four types of surveys: descriptive, comparative, modeling, and exploratory.

A descriptive survey gets a number that tells you something

In this book, I've chosen to focus mostly on the *descriptive* survey:

> A **descriptive survey** obtains a number that describes something about your defined group of people.

The number might be something like "17% of our customers have a child under 10 living with them at home," or "12% of people who purchase yogurt at least once a week have tried 'banana' flavor within the last year."

A comparative survey tells you whether a number is changing over time

What if you want to measure something before an event and after it? Or to find out if your descriptive number is changing over time for some other reason? If so, you're looking at a *comparative survey*—also known as a *tracker*.

> A **comparative survey** obtains a number that describes something about your defined group of people, and that will be compared to a number obtained in the future using the same method, or that will be compared to a number already obtained using the same method.

Market researchers do a lot of comparative surveys. For example, their client might want to know the impact of an advertising campaign for banana yogurt, so they'll run the survey before and after the campaign.

If a brand wants to assess its position in the market over a longer period than around a particular campaign, the comparative survey becomes a tracker. There's another fascinating subspecies of the comparative survey:

> A **longitudinal survey** is a comparative survey that is repeated regularly over a long period.

What counts as a "long period" depends very much on the context: it might be every hour for a week for a fast-moving website. The longest survey I have heard about is CH-X, the Swiss National Survey of Adolescents that started in 1854 and is still going, as noted in Figure A.2.

FIGURE A.2
Pädagogische Rekrutenprüfungen, a history of the Swiss National
Survey of Adolescents, and Entre mobilité temporaire et ancrage local:
portrait de la jeunesse Suisse, a recent publication using survey data.

I've mentioned "using the same method." If you need two surveys
to be truly comparative, then they need to be exactly the same, apart
from the time they go out. If you've thought "that question doesn't
seem relevant anymore" when responding to a survey, you may have
encountered a tracker where the researchers have had to stick to
exact comparability.

Clearly, over the long life of CH-X, many of their questions have
changed, so key considerations for comparative and longitudinal
surveys are "What can we keep the same?" and "What must we
change to keep this useful and relevant?"

This can be challenging, as even what can seem like a minor change,
such as swapping the order of two questions, can affect the results.

One example that struck me, because I'm lucky to be very happily
married, was an experiment by survey methodologists Howard
Schuman and Stanley Presser. They compared two groups on their
answers to two questions:

- "Taken altogether, how would you say things are these days: would you say that you are very happy, pretty happy, or not too happy?" (General happiness)
- "Taking things altogether, would you say that your marriage is very happy, pretty happy, or not too happy?" (Marital happiness) (Schuman and Presser, 1981)

Group A got the general happiness question followed by the marital happiness question, and 52% of them reported their general happiness as "very happy."

Group B got the marital happiness question before the general happiness one, and only 38% of them reported their general happiness as "very happy."

Interestingly, the results on the marital happiness were much closer: Group A had 70% who answered "Very happy," and Group B had 63%.

As it happens, I have not yet had a client who wanted to ask questions about marital happiness in any of their surveys, but this is one of the results that has made me rather cautious around happiness and satisfaction—something that clients want to ask about so often that I've created Spotlight C, "Satisfaction," specifically to talk about it.

In practice, you'll see that I tend to favor "keep this useful and relevant" over "make sure that we can compare the results of this survey to the last one," and I'll be urging you to keep iterating your surveys.

A modeling survey finds factors that influence an outcome

Our third type of survey is the *modeling survey*:

> A **modeling survey** asks a variety of questions on topics related to some outcome with the aim of discovering the factors that are associated with the outcome.

For example, a group of Spanish academics wanted to investigate the interplay of gratitude, bullying, and suicide risk in teenagers. They got 1,617 adolescents to complete a questionnaire that covered the three topics; then they used statistical methods to model whether (for example) higher gratitude might be associated with lower suicide risk in people who were bullied. The answer is: yes for girls, no for boys. (Rey, Quintana-Orts et al., 2019)

These modeling surveys are often Big Honkin' Surveys, because you need to ask questions around several factors to give the statistics program something to work with.

An exploratory survey gathers whatever information it can

Our last type of survey is the one that many of my clients ask me to help with:

> An **exploratory survey** gathers whatever information it can about a defined group of people.

The clients, typically, don't have any clear decision that they need to make. Often, they haven't worked out who is or isn't in their defined group. They see a survey as a way of getting their research efforts started.

And, of course, that's perfectly OK. I'd much rather that organizations tried to find out anything about the people they interact with than ignoring them altogether.

On the whole, though, a key message of this book is that a survey isn't my first choice of method when you really don't know much about the people you want to hear from. You'll be much better off starting with some interviews or finding a way to observe people doing whatever you are interested in, and then maybe consider doing a survey later when you know more about what you need from it.

Sometimes surveys start as a mixture

I started this Spotlight by saying that "surveys can be roughly divided into the four types" that I've been talking about.

In practice, I've learned that my colleagues or clients can be delightfully enthusiastic about the idea of a survey and begin by wanting to ask people about all sorts of different things—all at once, with the aim of doing all of the things described in this Spotlight—straight away.

I've also learned that they will get better results when they think carefully about exactly what they need from this specific survey and what they can postpone until a later one—the topic we'll come to next, in Chapter 1.

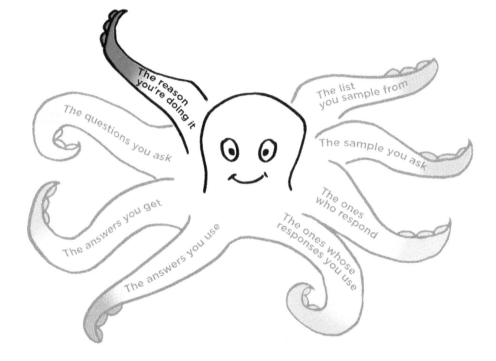

The reason
you're doing it

The questions you ask

The answers you get

The answers you use

The list
you sample from

The sample you ask

The ones
who respond

The ones whose
responses you use

CHAPTER 1

Goals: Establish Your Goals for the Survey

In this chapter, you're going to think about the reason why you're doing the survey (Figure 1.1).

IT'S EASIER TO HIT A TARGET
WHEN YOU KNOW WHICH
ONE YOU'RE AIMING FOR.

FIGURE 1.1
It's easier to hit a target if you know which one you're aiming for.

By the end of the chapter, you'll have turned the list of possible questions into a smaller set of questions that you need answers to.

Write down all your questions

I'm going to talk about two sorts of questions for a moment:

- Research questions
- Questions that you put into the questionnaire

Research questions are the topics that you want to find out about. At this stage, they may be very precise ("What is the resident population of the U.S. on 1st April in the years of the U.S. Decennial Census?") or very vague ("What can we find out about people who purchase yogurt?").

Questions that go into the questionnaire are different; they are the ones that you'll write when you get to Chapter 3, "Questions."

Now that I've said that—don't worry about it. At this point, you ought to have neatly defined research questions, but my experience is that I usually have a mush of draft questions, topic titles, and ideas (good and bad).

Write down all the questions. Variety is good. Duplicates are OK.

Give your subconscious a chance

If you're working on your own, or you have the primary responsibility for the survey in a team, then try to take a decent break between two sessions of writing down questions. A night's sleep gives your subconscious a chance to work out what you really want to find out. If that isn't practical, then maybe try a walk in the fresh air, a break to chat with a friend, or anything else that might provide a pause.

Get plenty of suggestions for questions

If you're working with a team or you're in an organization, then often when word gets out that there's a survey ahead, colleagues will pile in with all sorts of suggestions for their questions. This can feel a little overwhelming at first, but it's best to encourage everyone to contribute their potential questions as early as possible so that you can carefully evaluate all of them, focus on some goals for this specific survey, and have a good selection of other questions available for follow-up surveys and other research.

If I'm too restrictive at the very beginning, I find that everyone tries to sneak just one little extra essential question into the questionnaire a day—or even an hour—before the fieldwork starts. By then, it is too late to test the little extra questions properly, and they could sink my whole survey.

But while you're still establishing the goals for the survey? Great! Collect as many questions as possible. Encourage everyone to join in—colleagues, stakeholders, managers, whoever you think might be interested. If you're running a workshop, give the introverts some space by having a bit of silent writing where everyone captures their individual question ideas by writing them down.

Create a nice big spreadsheet of all the suggestions, a pile of sticky notes, or whatever idea-gathering tool works for you.

Ideally, make it clear that there's a cutoff: suggestions before a particular date will get considered for this survey; miss the date, and they'll be deferred until the next opportunity. This helps to encourage the idea of many Light Touch Surveys.

Challenge your question ideas

When you've gathered or created question ideas, it's time to confront them with these four detailed challenges in Figure 1.2:

- What do you want to know?
- Why do you want to know?
- What decision will you make based on the answers?
- What number do you need to make the decision?

What do you want to know?

Why do you want to know?

What decision will you make based on these answers?

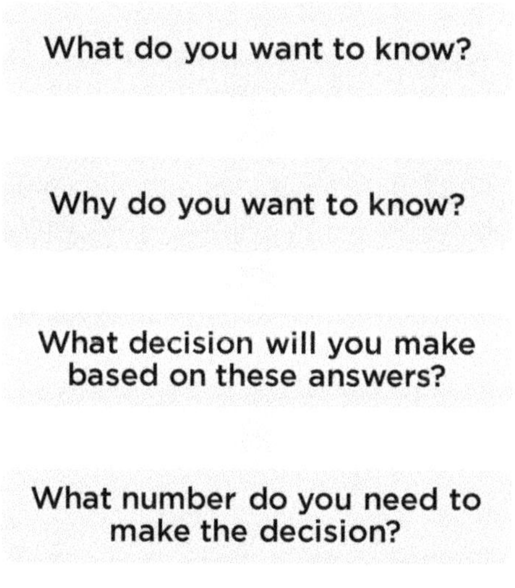

FIGURE 1.2
What decisions will you make based on the answers?

What number do you need to make the decision?

Ask: What do you want to know?

Surprisingly, I find that the question suggestions that I create or collect from colleagues often do not relate to what we want to know. Many times, I've challenged a question by saying, "OK, so you're thinking about <xxx question>. What do you want to know?" and it turns out that there's a gap between the question and the reason for asking it.

Probably the most common example is the question: "Are you satisfied?" The question is OK but very general.

Ask: Why do you want to know?

I'm usually working with someone else when I'm doing a survey. To help narrow down from "every possible suggestion" to a sensible set of goals for the survey, I ask "Why do you want to know the answers to these questions?" and we then go on to challenge ourselves with the three questions in Figure 1.2.

If I'm on my own, then I find it helps to add "this time" or "right now"—to help me focus on the practical matter of getting my ideas down to something manageable. Come to think about it, that's not a bad idea for a team, too—it helps all of them realize that they don't have to ask everyone everything all at once.

Ask: What decision will you make based on the answers?

If you're not going to make any decision, why are you doing the survey?

Look very hard at each of the suggested questions and think about whether or not the answers to them will help you make a decision.

Don't worry at this stage about the wording of the questions or whether people will want to answer them. You'll work on those topics in upcoming chapters.

But if the answers to a question won't help you make a decision, set that question aside. Be bold! The question might be fascinating. You might be looking forward to reading the answers. But you're trying to focus really hard on making the smallest possible useful survey. You don't need to waste the question—it can go into the possible suggestions for next time.

At this point, you'll have some candidate questions where you know what decisions you'll make based on the answers.

Ask: What number do you need to make the decision?

In the opening chapter, "Definitions," I emphasized that a survey is a quantitative method and the result is a number. Sometimes you'll realize at this point that although you have candidate questions, you do not need numeric answers to them in order to make the decisions. That's fine, but it also means that a survey is probably not the right method for you. Your work so far will not be wasted because you can use it to prepare for a more appropriate method.

Choose the Most Crucial Question (MCQ)

If you were only allowed answers to one of your candidate questions, which would it be?

That's your Most Crucial Question (MCQ).

> The **Most Crucial Question** is the one that makes a difference.
> It's the one that will provide essential data for decision-making.

You'll be able to state your question in these terms:

> We need to ask _____.

> So that we can decide _____.

At this stage, don't worry if it's a Research Question (in your language, maybe even full of jargon) or the question that will go into the questionnaire (using words that are familiar to the people who will answer).

Test your goals: Attack your Most Crucial Question

Try attacking every word in your Most Crucial Question to find out what you really mean by it. Really hammer it.

Here's an example: "Do you like our magazine?"

- Who is "you"? Purchaser, subscriber, reader, recommender, vendor, or someone else?
- What does "like" mean? Admire? Recommend? Plan to purchase? Actually purchase? Obsessively collect every edition? Give subscriptions as gifts?
- What do you mean by "our"? Us as a brand? A department? A team? As a supplier to someone else?

- What do you mean by "magazine"? Every aspect of it? The paper edition? The online one? The Facebook page? The article they read most recently? Some parts, but not others? Does it matter if they've read it or not?

I found a great attack on a question by Annie Pettit, survey methodologist. She starts with the question:

"When was the last time you bought milk?"

Here's how Annie attacks "bought" and "milk":

Wait, do you care if the milk was purchased? Or could it be that we have an arrangement whereby we don't actually pay for milk? Perhaps people who live on a farm with dairy cows, or people who own a convenience store?

Do you mean only cow milk? What about milk from goats, sheep, buffalo, camel, reindeer? Or what about milk-substitutes from nuts or plants like soy, almond, rice, and coconut that are labeled as milk? Were you really trying to figure out if we put a liquid on cereal? (Pettit, 2016)

(And she added a whole lot more about topics, like whether or not chocolate milk counts.)

Decide on your defined group of people

When you've really attacked your MCQ, look back and think about your "defined group of people"—the ones who you want to answer.

Add them to your statement like this:

We need to ask _____ (people who you want to answer).

The question _____ (MCQ goes here).

So that we can decide _____ (decision goes here).

If your defined group of people is still vague—"everyone" or something equally woolly—then try attacking again. A strong definition of the group you want to answer at this point will help tremendously when you get to the next chapter, "Sample."

But before you proceed to Chapter 2, let's pause for a moment and think about your plans.

Check that a survey is the right thing to do

Is your research question something that you must explore by asking people, or would it be better to observe them?

Do you want to know "why?"—qualitative—or "how many?"—quantitative?

Let's look at this definition again:

> A **survey** is a process of asking questions that are answered by a sample of a defined group of people to get numbers that you can use to make decisions.

I'm going to contrast that with this definition:

> An **interview** is a conversation where an interviewer asks questions that are answered by one person to get answers that help to understand that person's point of view, opinions, and motivations.

Both of them rely on asking: the interview is about "why"—qualitative—and the survey is about "how many"—quantitative, as in Figure 1.3.

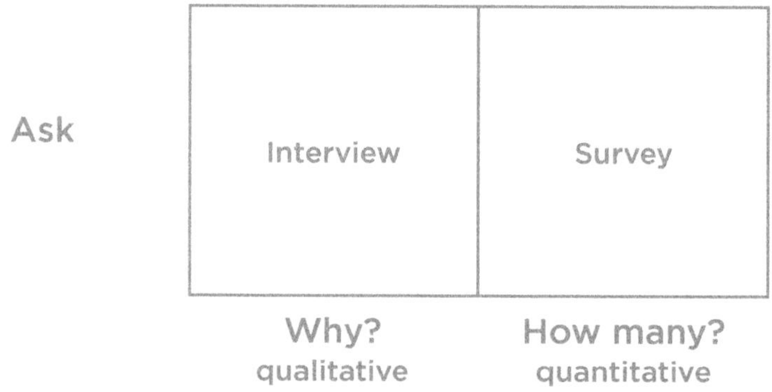

FIGURE 1.3
Contrasting interviews as qualitative and surveys as quantitative.

Must your MCQ be answered by people?

One of my favorite questions was on a printer manufacturer's survey:

"How many pages do you print in a month?"

I had no idea. I knew the answer was more than one and less than a full box of paper because I hadn't bought a box of paper that month—but I didn't feel sufficiently motivated to work out how many pages are in a full box. I guessed, wildly. Very poor data.

The real irony, though, was that my printer was connected to their customer feedback program and was giving them the exact figure all the time: their analytics should have told them.

Here's another example that arrived in my inbox recently:

We need to ask visitors to our website
whether pop-ups make them feel less like buying from us
so that we can decide whether to remove pop-ups.

I'm sure that client must have some good business reasons for using pop-ups that make them hesitate about removing them, but asking people whether they "feel like buying" is a notoriously unreliable thing to do. They may feel like buying, but not actually buy, or feel unlike buying, but buy anyway. (We'll return to this topic in Chapter 3 when we look at the "Curve of Prediction.")

There's a much better quantitative method for questions like this: A/B testing, where you publish two versions and use analytics to decide which one contributes better to the desired outcome.

A/B tests and the many other different types of analytics silently observe what people do without bothering them with questions. These are contrasted with surveys in Figure 1.4.

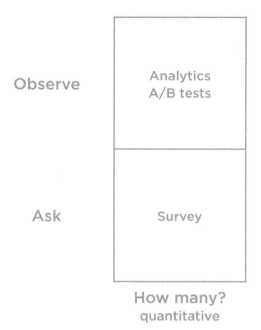

| | Observe | Analytics
A/B tests |
| | Ask | Survey |

Observe

Ask

Analytics
A/B tests

Survey

How many?
quantitative

FIGURE 1.4

Analytics and A/B tests are ways of observing how many people do something without asking them.

Do you want to find out "why"?

You may have spotted that we're sneaking up on the four-way matrix in Figure 1.5. The quadrant we haven't yet looked at is the top-left corner: observing to find out "why."

It's not always obvious why people are doing something. For example, if people tell you they can't find things on your website, then search log analytics will tell you *what* they are searching for—but not *why* they are searching. Did they try searching straight away? Did they try a few clicks without success? Did they see your term for what they're searching for but not recognize it because they had something different in mind?

Here's another MCQ that I see quite often:

> We need to ask visitors to our website
> the question: "What do you dislike about our site?"
> so that we can decide what to improve.

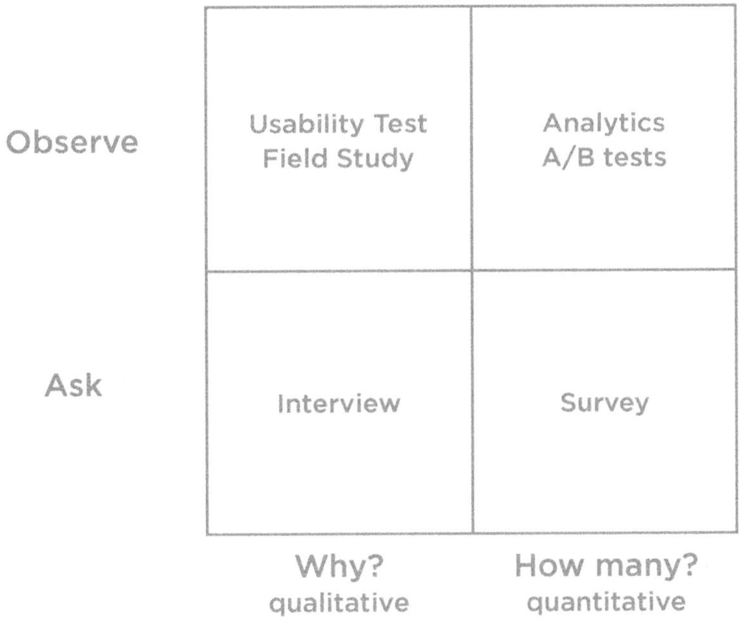

	Why? qualitative	How many? quantitative
Observe	Usability Test Field Study	Analytics A/B tests
Ask	Interview	Survey

FIGURE 1.5
A matrix for choosing the right method.

Leaving aside the problem that "What do you dislike" doesn't have a numeric answer, you've got the more fundamental problem that there isn't a direct connection between "What do you dislike" and "What should we improve?" You need to know why people dislike something in order to get ideas about how to change it.

You might turn to interviews, but it's unreasonable to expect most people to retain all the little details that made something easy or difficult. Observing them as they use the thing is much easier for them—and much richer data for you.

In a usability test, you can observe a participant who is tackling some tasks—often in a research facility. Or you can go out to observe people in their natural setting, a field study.

Consider "why" alongside "how many"

A four-way matrix always makes it look as if the ideas are separate, doesn't it? Of course, in reality, the techniques complement each other.

The route in Figure 1.6 is one that I took around the matrix for a client recently.

- Analytics showed that sales of one product had dropped.
- Usability tests revealed that people thought the website was no longer maintained, so the product must also be out-of-date.
- Interviews at the same time revealed that people often left a long gap between deciding to buy the product and actually using it.
- A survey told us that the out-of-date problem was affecting more people than the wait-to-use problem.

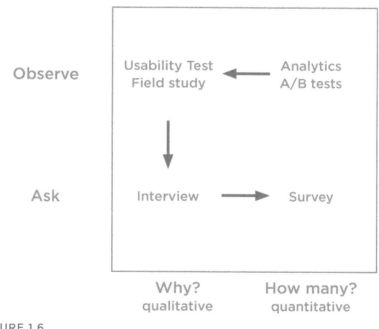

FIGURE 1.6
One of many possible routes around the matrix.

I would love to encourage you to try some triangulation.

> **Triangulation** is when you use a mixture of research methods and compare the results to improve your overall insights.

A draft presentation can help you decide between "why" and "how many"

A couple of years ago, I was chatting about surveys with user experience consultant Natalie Webb. Her tip was:

> "Create a draft of your presentation, based on the results you expect to get from your survey."

It seemed a strange idea to me at first, but the more I've tried it, the more I like it as a way of testing whether I've really thought enough about what I want to ask and whether the number that I will get as a result of my survey really will help me to make a decision—the "so what" of surveys in Figure 1.7.

FIGURE 1.7
A draft presentation helps you to think about the "so what?" of your survey.

I worried that by drafting the presentation first, I'd be somehow constraining the direction of the research—preventing my team from thinking freely about what they were doing, closing down what they might learn.

Gradually, I realized that this is part of the power of surveys. Because you're finding out "how many" of something, you need to understand the "why" before you start. If you don't yet know enough about "why," then you should be choosing to start with observation and interviews.

Think about what sort of number you need

Thinking about the "so what" and the number that you'll need for the decision you'll make also helps with another point to consider now: what sort of number do you need as your result? It may seem early, but statisticians will tell you that you must work out your statistical strategy before you collect the data, not afterward.

Do you need to know the actual number of people who answer a question in a particular way? For example, when I helped with a survey about planning an office move, I wanted to know how many people said that when the office moved to the new location, their commute would become excessively long.

Is it the proportion who answer one way rather than another? For example, I wanted to compare the proportion of people who claimed they would leave if the office moved to a new location to the proportion who said they would be likely to accept the change.

Are you looking for a mean (the arithmetical average)? For example, I might have considered whether increasing the mean commute by more than an hour would kill the idea.

Are you looking for a median (the value right in the middle when you place them all in order from largest to smallest)? Means can get easily distorted by one or two outlandishly large values. If one person's commute suddenly became nearly impossible—10 hours or more—that would greatly increase the mean, but the median wouldn't be affected very much.

And for design, I'm often looking at ranges and modes. The range is the difference between the largest and the smallest values, so with a 10-hour commute and another commute that's zero because the person lived in an apartment above the possible new location, my range would be 10 hours. The mode is the most frequent value, and something that I find I have to consider very carefully for many design challenges—both to design for the people who answered with the most frequent value and to make sure that I'm not accidentally excluding people who don't fit "the norm" for any reason.

Or something else? You may be doing a comparative survey so you'll be considering what you want to compare from this survey to the next, or a modeling survey where you'll do all sorts of advanced statistical manipulations, or something quite different.

Whatever you're planning to do with the answers to your survey, some careful thought at this stage about those statistics will be well worth the time you put into it—and may send you back to have another review of your Most Crucial Question and how you plan to use it.

Determine the time you have and the help you need

So, you have a Most Crucial Question, you know the decision you'll make, and you've thought a bit about the type of number you need to make that decision. It's a good moment to think about timing and who needs to be involved.

First, think about the time available:

- When do you need to have a result, and how much time can you put into it?
- If you're lucky enough to have team members to work with, how much time can they spare?
- When will you deliver the report from the survey?

Next, think about the tools:

- Do you or your organization already have a survey tool?
- Do you know how to use it?
- Will you need to buy or subscribe to one?

Finally, and perhaps most importantly, who else is involved?

- Who needs to be involved in the survey but isn't part of your team, such as the privacy or legal people?
- Who will get the results from the survey?
- Who is involved in making the decisions based on the results?

Interview first, survey later

A common mistake is to think that you'll do a survey first and then do follow-up interviews with some of the people who answer.

The rule is: interview first, survey later. Two especially useful types of interviews are:

- Interviews to find out what your defined group of people think about the topic of your survey (covered in Chapter 2)
- Cognitive interviews—a special type of interview just for survey questions—to help you discover whether the questions are working (Chapter 3)

And, in fact, to get the best results from your survey, you'll complement these interviews with two other techniques from the matrix, as noted in Figure 1.8:

- Usability tests of the questionnaire (Chapter 4, "Questionnaire")
- A pilot test between the usability test and the survey itself (Chapter 5, "Fieldwork")

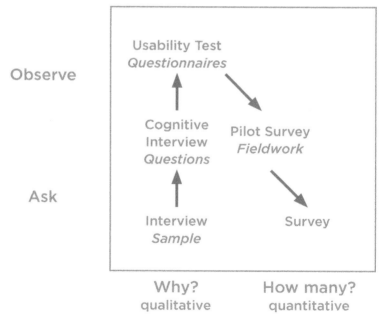

FIGURE 1.8
We'll use techniques from other parts of the matrix on our way to the survey.

If you want a couple of ideas for how to fit all those activities into the time you have available, then skip ahead to Chapter 8, "The Least You Can Do™." A recent survey where I worked hard to get a single Most Crucial Question took me four days—spread out over a month, admittedly, but only because I had a week's vacation in the middle.

What could possibly go wrong with the goals?

For many years, I was quite a purist about surveys. If you'd asked me "What can go wrong when choosing a goal for your survey?" I'd have answered, "Insisting on doing a survey when it's the wrong method for the research problem."

These days, I've mellowed. I know that sometimes colleagues or clients will carry on with a survey for all sorts of reasons, good and bad, when it's not the ideal thing to do. If that's happening to you, don't worry. Keep making good choices, aim for a Light Touch Survey, and iterate as much as possible. No matter what the outcome is, you'll definitely learn a lot about how to do a better survey next time.

Strictly between you and me, I've also become more relaxed about some of the other aims of this chapter. Couldn't get down to exactly one Most Crucial Question? If you still have dozens of MCQs: definitely not. But five or six candidates for MCQ? Not so bad—you can whittle them down when you start working on them in Chapter 3. Not entirely clear about the decision you'll make? Have a go, and revisit it when you've done some more steps. You can iterate, after all.

But I wouldn't often admit that to the team or the client because I know that when we can agree on one Most Crucial Question with a clear decision to be made, the rest of the survey process is going to be much easier and quicker. So I try pretty hard to persuade them to get there.

To be valid, the goals and questions must match

This brings me to the first of the challenges that you'll meet through the steps of the survey process. In this chapter, you've been looking at the first tentacle of the Survey Octopus: "The reason you're doing it," as shown in Figure 1.9.

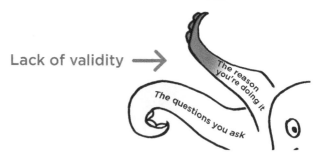

Why you want to ask

Lack of validity ⟶

FIGURE 1.9
Lack of validity.

There's always an error between each tentacle and the next one. In this case, it's "lack of validity."

> **Lack of validity** happens when the questions you ask do not match the reason why you are doing the survey and what you want to ask about.

Or in other words:

> A survey is valid when the questions you ask are a good match to the reason why you are doing the survey and what you want to ask about.

So work really hard on the reason why you are doing it, the decision that you'll make, and that Most Crucial Question.

At this point, you will know

To have an easier ride with the next steps in the survey process, it helps a lot of at this point if you know:

- The resources you have for the survey
- Who you want to answer your question—your defined group of people
- The decision you'll make based on the results
- The Most Crucial Question to help you make the decision
- Whether the Most Crucial Question needs to be answered by people or not
- Whether a survey is the right thing to do

The Net Promoter Score® and Correlation

Possibly the questionnaire I see most often is the "tell us how we did" follow-up that many organizations send us relentlessly. Many of these use the Net Promoter Score®, or NPS®, a well-known single question—there's an example in Figure B.1.

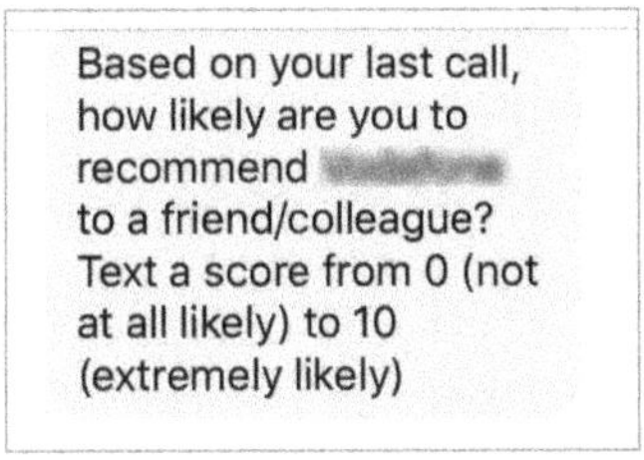

Based on your last call, how likely are you to recommend ▓▓▓▓▓ to a friend/colleague? Text a score from 0 (not at all likely) to 10 (extremely likely)

FIGURE B.1

An example of NPS® delivered as a text (SMS) message after a call to a mobile phone operator's help line.

NPS® aims to measure "loyalty"

The originators of NPS® wanted to measure "loyalty," which they defined as a combination of whether a customer either purchased again or referred someone else who purchased.

They collected a huge variety of questions that looked at different aspects of loyalty, such as "How strongly do you agree that Company X deserves your loyalty?"

All the questions went into Big Honkin' Surveys sent to several thousand customers, and at the same time, they collected actual purchase and referral histories from the same customers. Some customers got the questions first and then had their loyalty tracked; others had their loyalty tracked first and then had the questions.

NPS® chooses a Most Crucial Question using statistical correlation

The team used statistical modeling tools "to determine which survey questions showed the strongest statistical correlation with "loyalty" to find "at least one question that effectively predicted what customers would do and hence helped predict a company's growth." (Reichheld and Markey, 2011)

"Correlated" means that changes are related.

If you compare two things that vary with each other, you can calculate their correlation:

> **Correlation** is the extent to which two things vary in a way that is related.

The amount of correlation is often shown as the Greek letter ρ and is illustrated in Figure B.2

- If ρ is +1, then as one gets larger, the other gets larger according to some exact relationship.

- If ρ is –1, then when one gets larger, the other gets smaller, also exactly.

- If ρ is 0, then the only thing you know is that there's no way to tell about what will happen to one thing when the other changes—also called *no correlation*.

FIGURE B.2
Exact correlations +1, –1; no correlation 0.

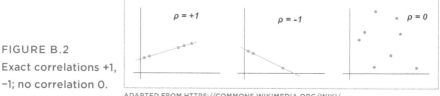

ADAPTED FROM HTTPS://COMMONS.WIKIMEDIA.ORG/WIKI/
FILE:CORRELATION_COEFFICIENT.PNG

In the real world, you rarely find correlations that come to an exact number. It's much more typical to get correlations that fall somewhere between 0 and 1, where if one thing changes, then another changes somewhat in the same direction, or between –1 and 0, where if one thing changes, then another changes somewhat in the opposite direction, illustrated in Figure B.3.

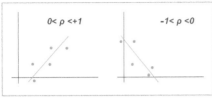

FIGURE B.3

Typical correlations are more messy.

ADAPTED FROM HTTPS://COMMONS.WIKIMEDIA.ORG/
WIKI/FILE:CORRELATION_COEFFICIENT.PNG

Causation creates correlation

Sometimes, things are correlated because one event causes another:

> **Causation** is the extent to which variation in one thing causes a predictable variation in another.

If I see that my husband has placed lettuce, tomato, and cucumber onto our kitchen table, then I'm pretty sure that he is preparing salad for our next meal (causation), but the correlation isn't exact because he also shops, and the veggies may be on their way into the fridge rather than out of it.

Let's have another look at "loyalty." If a customer has already referred someone, then possibly the customer will give a high number as the answer to "How likely are you to refer a friend/colleague?" It's not exact, because the prediction of future behavior is never exact—but the customer may reflect on past behavior and use that to gauge the answer. Plus, a few people may fall into one of these categories:

- I used to refer people, but I've had a bad experience since then and don't want to refer any more.
- I referred a colleague, but I've changed jobs now, so I won't be referring any more.
- I only have one friend/colleague who might ever be interested, so I've run out of people to refer.
- The person I referred is an enemy and has nothing to do with any friend/colleague.

And I'll leave it to your imagination to think of some more.

Correlation does not create causation

It doesn't work the other way around. Some unrelated things can be strongly correlated. For example, in Figure B.4, "per capita consumption of mozzarella cheese" is almost perfectly correlated with "number of civil engineering doctorates awarded" $\rho = 0.96$ from 2000 to 2009.

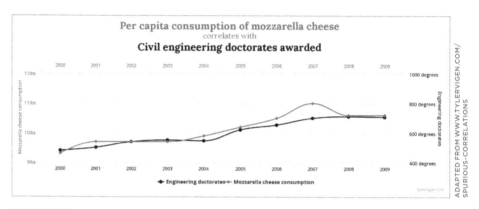

FIGURE B.4
A spurious correlation.

These spurious correlations are the reason why every single statistics book will tell you that "correlation does not mean causation."

For "loyalty," I might say today that I would recommend your product to a friend—but will I actually buy it myself in the future? Is the one thing likely to cause the other?

NPS® uses correlation as ordinary prediction

The theory behind NPS® is that the customers for every business can be divided into three groups, according to their answer to the "recommend to a friend or colleague" question (see Table B.1).

TABLE B.1   THE NET PROMOTER GROUPS AND BEHAVIORS

Group	Expected future behavior	Answer
Promoters	Loyal customers who will keep buying and refer others	9 and 10
Passives	Satisfied but unenthusiastic customers who are vulnerable to competitors	7 and 8
Detractors	Unhappy customers who can damage your brand through negative word-of-mouth	0 to 6

NPS® has an unusual scoring method

NPS® has a specific, and somewhat unusual, calculation method shown in Figure B.5:

- Ignore Passives
- Work out the percentage of Promoters
- Work out the percentage of Detractors
- Subtract the percentage of Detractors from the percentage of Promoters to find the Net Promoter Score®

Although Passives appear in the overall total when working out the percentages, their mildly positive views do not appear in the eventual total.

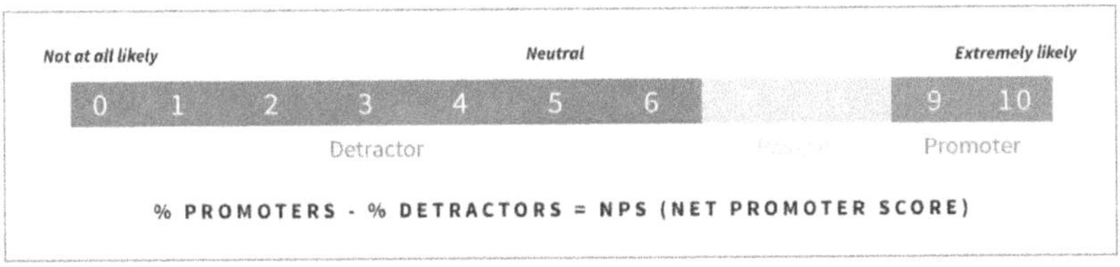

COURTESY OF WWW.NETPROMOTER.COM/KNOW/

FIGURE B.5
The NPS® method of calculation.

Make sure it's appropriate to focus on brand

If you're selling consumer products where brand is everything, then the Net Promoter Score® may work for you. The Net Promoter Score® website mentions quite a variety of big-name brands that have used it, including Porsche, Verizon, and Apple.

Be wary of situations where brand is not really the issue. If you're a cancer ward, is the brand really that crucial? And yet, I've actually seen the question "Would you recommend this ward to a friend or family member?" It's at best, awkward, and at worst, for example after a bereavement, deeply upsetting.

If you must use NPS®, then read Reichheld's book

The decision to use Net Promoter Score® may be out of your hands. Many stakeholders believe that it is the Most Crucial Question and will insist on it.

The Net Promoter Score® was first proposed by Fred Reichheld as part of an overall improvement method where you do surveys at long enough intervals—Reichheld suggests quarterly—so that you have time to understand any major shifts in the score and take action to sort out any problems (or to continue to do more of the things that are creating improvements).

If you are seriously considering using it in your questionnaire—or for anything at all, really—then I think you'll find it well worth your time to read one of his books on the topic, as he clarifies how it is meant to be used.

Satisfaction

Satisfaction is a topic that many of us want to ask about in our surveys, but it can be a tricky one. For example, try this thought-experiment:

> *Picture yourself after a wonderful trip to a tropical hideaway like the one in Figure C.1. Refreshed, you're flying home on a flight that's been trouble-free so far.*
>
> *What's your level of satisfaction with the trip?*
>
> *Now picture yourself chatting with the person in the next seat. Their family has just enjoyed the same break but paid half as much with a different travel company.*
>
> *Would your level of satisfaction be the same?*

COURTESY OF ROWAN HEUVEL IMAGES.UNSPLASH.COM/ PHOTO-1468413253725-0D5181091126

FIGURE C.1
Tropical beach.

Most people report high levels of satisfaction before the chat and much lower afterward. Same experience, but the rating changes. It's an example of how slippery "satisfaction" can be.

And yet "Are people satisfied?" is a frequent Most Crucial Question. It's a Burning Issue. And it's a topic that's especially challenging for the survey researcher. That's why we're going to look at it in this Spotlight.

Satisfaction is all about comparisons

Satisfaction depends on the comparisons that people make. In this little thought experiment, here are two examples of the comparisons I've heard:

- This trip compared to some sort of ideal trip (excellence)
- Whether other people were offered the same trip at a different price (fairness)

Here's an example of another type of comparison around satisfaction that really struck me: a study of bronze and silver medal winners found that on average, athletes who won bronze were happier with the result than those who won silver. (Medvec, Madey, and Gilovich, 1995) It seems that the typical silver medalist compares the result to gold, whereas the typical bronze medalist is happy to have won any honors at all (see Figure C.2). Both are comparisons of "what might have been."

FIGURE C.2
Bronze medal winner.

PHOTO CREDIT: PETERCIPOLLONE WWW.FLICKR.COM/PHOTOS/PETERCIPOLLONE/2796897440

I learned about the importance of comparisons for satisfaction from Professor Richard L. Oliver's book *Satisfaction: A Behavioral Perspective on the Consumer.*

Three of the possible comparisons are "excellence," "fairness," and "events that might have been." He also mentions:

- **Expectations:** What we envisaged might happen compared to what actually happened. ("I thought I was going on a dream vacation, but the hotel was a disaster.")

- **Need:** Whether the experience or product met our needs. ("I bought the t-shirt in my usual size, but the one you delivered was far too big.")

And finally, there's what I think of as the "meh" or the "Who cares?" comparison: where an organization asks me about my satisfaction with something I haven't thought about for a second. Example: a client once asked me to comment on a survey about deodorants, so I had to answer 45 *minutes* of questions on a topic that I hadn't considered for much longer than 45 *seconds* before or since. Tough gig, but it helped me to recognize that sometimes there's nothing to compare to—and the resulting feelings are indifference, as in Table C.1.

TABLE C.1 COMPARING EXPERIENCES CAN CREATE DIFFERENT RESULTS

Compared experience to what?	Resulting thoughts or feelings
(Nothing)	Indifference
Expectations	Better/worse/different
Needs	Met/not met/mixture
Excellence (the ideal product)	Good/poor quality (or "good enough")
Someone else's treatment	Fair/unfair
Events that might have been	Vindication/regret

Adapted from (Oliver, 2010)

When I put that table together for myself, I could see why satisfaction was such a slippery concept. So now, when I'm helping a team to create a questionnaire around "satisfaction," I ask these questions:

- What comparisons are they thinking about?
- What comparisons will be meaningful to the defined group of people they plan to ask?
- What decisions do they plan to make, and which comparisons will help those decisions?

Think about the emotion you want to measure

Sometimes teams say:

> *"We want to ask about satisfaction."*

when what they mean is:

> *"We want to know whether people love us."*

Or maybe there's some other emotion involved. Are people likely to be delighted? Thrilled? Angry? Indifferent?

If you decide that measuring an emotional response is your Most Crucial Question, then it's a useful first step to find out what emotions you're dealing with.

One method is to ask your respondents to type "a word or phrase that describes your feelings right now." Be prepared for a wide range of responses—and often, some surprising ones.

Do you think the responses will include "Satisfied" or "Dissatisfied?"

If you'd prefer to offer some suggestions, have a look at the Microsoft Product Reaction Cards (Benedek and Miner, 2002) There are 118 cards with adjectives, and the first few are

- Accessible
- Advanced
- Annoying
- Appealing
- Approachable
- Attractive

Think about which experience you want to measure

Ever had an encounter with customer service like this one of mine?

I needed something from an organization and couldn't figure out from their website why it wasn't working. I called customer service. The polite person who answered explained that it was the organization's policy *not* to offer what I needed.

My emotions: grateful to customer service, angry with the organization. Shortly after, I got an email invitation, as shown in Figure C.3.

> We'd love to hear what you think of our customer service. Please take a moment to answer one simple question by clicking either link below:
>
> How would you rate the support you received?
>
> **How would you rate the support you received?**
>
> Good, I'm satisfied
>
> Bad, I'm unsatisfied

FIGURE C.3
Invitation to a satisfaction questionnaire that lacks focus.

What was I going to answer? "Bad," because they couldn't help me do what I wanted, but possibly causing a problem for the person who answered my call? Or "Good," since the person answered my question, but ignoring the bigger picture of sorting out my issue?

If you must ask about a specific recalled emotion, then design that question very carefully, as in Table C.2.

TABLE C.2 SOME AIMS AND APPROACHES TO CONSIDER

If your aim is...	Consider....
To learn about a detailed part of a service...	Working extra-hard on the actual Most Crucial Question and the likely Burning Issues
To understand emotional reactions but you aren't sure which ones apply...	Asking for an adjective or using the Microsoft Product Reaction Cards
To learn about the brand as a whole and see if your organization is the type where "recommending to a friend" is a sensible concept...	Asking the question from The Net Promoter Score,® the recommendation-based emotional reaction measurement that you met in Spotlight B

If you must ask for a rating, offer an open box, too

There are times when only a rating question will do. Perhaps the decision you'll make as a result of the survey depends on how much the average rating has changed over time. Perhaps you must fit in with a corporate edict. It happens.

So if you must ask a question where people have to rate their emotion on a scale from something to something, then make sure that you also offer a question with a plain, open-box comment. Many people will skip it, but you'll probably learn a lot from those who take the trouble to fill it in.

Satisfaction is a name for an attitude

The term *satisfaction* is a convenient shorthand for a complex blend of feelings and thoughts about expectations, experience, and outcomes. Survey methodologists call these things *attitudes*.

I've tried to convince you to drill into exactly which aspect of that attitude you're most interested in and to use that focus to create a Most Crucial Question.

Truth is, I know that you're often faced with stakeholders who want to keep track of a summary score for a complex attitude, and they can't be dissuaded from a Big Honkin' Survey to do it. Satisfaction is one of these, and two other common ones are:

- What do staff think about working here (often called a *people survey*)?
- Did attendees like this conference/training event (sometimes called *happy sheets* by trainers)?

When you create a series of statements about an attitude and you combine the answers in a single score, you are building a "Likert scale." They're fascinating and deserve a Spotlight of their own, so if that's what you most need to tackle, by all means skip ahead to Chapter 4's Spotlight H, "'On a Scale from 1 to 5' (Likert and Rating Scales)."

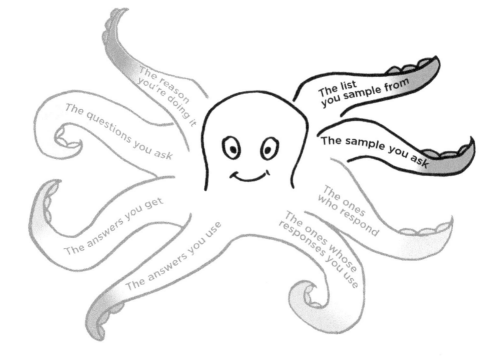

CHAPTER 2

Sample: Find People Who Will Answer

In the last chapter, we thought about "the defined group of people"—the people you want to ask in general.

This chapter is about turning that definition into your "sample," the people whom you actually ask. We'll also think about including a question or two that will help you assess the representativeness of the people who decide to answer.

If you look down the right-hand side of the Octopus in Figure 2.1, you'll see four tentacles. We're going to start by thinking about getting some people to answer this questionnaire: "The ones who answer." Then we'll work back to think about how many people you actually want to answer— "The sample you ask." And finally, we'll think about how to find those people—"The list you sample from."

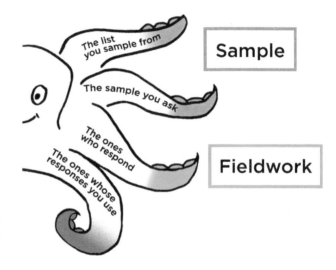

FIGURE 2.1
The right-hand side
of the Octopus is all
about the people you
ask and whether they
answer.

Some of the people you ask will decide not to answer

The number of people who answer is usually lower than the number of people you ask. For example, if you've got 10 people trapped in a conference room after a training event and you politely ask each of them to complete a questionnaire before they leave, you have a possible maximum number of answers of 10. People have been known to sneak out of conference rooms early for reasons like "I have to catch a flight," or "I feel faint," so you may be one or two short, but on the whole the response will be good, and you'll get about 8 to 10 answers.

The **response rate** is the ratio of the number of people who answer to the number of people you ask.

In our training room example, we've got a response rate between 0.8 and 1, or if (like me) you prefer to think in percentages, then it's 80% to 100%.

But if we sent out the questionnaire later when it's easier for people to ignore the request, that response rate might drop to maybe only one or two people answering—a response rate of 0.1 to 0.2 or 10% to 20%.

Response rates vary by the way you deliver your questionnaire

Here are my own rules of thumb for response rates to various types of surveys (see Table 2.1).

TABLE 2.1 MY RULES OF THUMB FOR TYPICAL RESPONSE RATES

Type of survey	Rule of thumb	Rate
Major survey from a national statistical institute, such as the U.S. Census Bureau, delivered by postal mail	1,000 invitations to get around 850 responses	60% to 95%
Academic survey using all the survey methodology best practices delivered by postal mail	1,000 invitations to get around 300 to 600 responses	30% to 60%
Email invitation to a select group of customers with a link to a well-designed web survey	1,000 invitations to get around 100 responses	5% to 15%
Invitation placed carefully in the main reading area of the website text	1,000 people visiting the site to get around 1 response	0.01% to 0.5%
Banner invitation at the top of a website	10,000 people visiting the site to get around 1 response	0.01%

These are a starting point. The response to your survey will vary considerably, and you may be able to do much better—or you may find your response is even worse. The best way to determine your actual likely response rate is by doing a pilot test with the smallest possible sample.

Response depends on trust, effort, and reward

In the Introduction, I described my surprise when I read some years ago that tucking a dollar bill into the envelope with a mail survey can improve response rates—and beat even a guaranteed $50 reward for a completed survey. More recently, survey methodologists Eleanor Singer and Cong Ye did an extensive analysis of dozens of experiments across different types of survey delivery and incentive (Singer and Ye, 2013), confirming that:

- Monetary incentives beat other types of gifts
- Incentives in advance beat promised incentives later
- Prize draws have little effect on response rates

They also remind us that there are other rewards, such as a feeling of being helpful, enjoying doing surveys, or wanting to see the results.

Among the theories about the effect of incentives, the one that has helped me most in practice was Dillman's application of Social Exchange Theory to surveys (Dillman, 2000), which I think of as the diagram in Figure 2.2, a triangle pitting perceived reward against perceived effort, balanced on trust.

Perceived effort   Perceived reward

FIGURE 2.2
People will respond to your survey if they trust you and if the perceived effort is appropriate to the perceived reward.

Trust

Let's think about those prize draws. Most people don't expect to win the prize: no perceived reward. Some people don't believe you'll award the prize: no trust. Either way: no effect on response.

I heard about an example where response rates to a questionnaire sent to students at a relatively small university were definitely improved by the prize of an iPad. That draw worked, because the students knew that the prize would be awarded (good trust) and that the pool of people they were competing against for the prize was limited (an acceptable perceived reward).

Trust, effort, and reward need to balance

A few years ago, someone complained to me: "We got really poor response to this survey even though we offered a $1,000 reward to each person who completed it. Why?"

Looking at the trust/reward/effort triangle shows that the reason is obvious: the reward was so big that it gave the impression that either the effort was going to be incredibly onerous (excessive perceived effort) or that the organization couldn't be trusted to deliver the reward (undermining trust).

Trust is about what people think you might do with the answers

People might trust you in general but not trust you enough to answer the specific set of questions that you want to ask.

Example: Many questionnaires say, "Your feedback will help us to improve our service." People may trust you enough to buy something from you but don't trust that you'll really act on the answers to the feedback questionnaire. So there's no perceived reward.

The staff survey is another example. A lot of people trust their employer in general but are not sure that the employer can be trusted with honest answers to a staff survey. "It's anonymous, but it's not anonymous enough."

Trust is also about respecting privacy

"Not anonymous enough" is a worry about respecting privacy. If someone is going to trust you with their answers—especially if those answers might be tracked back to them—then they want to know that you will look after them properly (see Figure 2.3).

We'll return to the topic of privacy in Spotlight E later on, as it's not enough to reassure people when they decide about the survey invitation—you actually have to look after their answers in practice.

FIGURE 2.3

You can't use answers for anything you like. You must be clear about what you will do with the information you gather.

Response depends on perceived effort

When you ask someone to respond to your survey, you're expecting them to give you some of their time and to think about their answers. That's effort.

For a paper questionnaire, they may flick through to assess how much work will be involved. For an email invitation, you're competing with the rest of their inbox. For a pop-up invitation to a web survey, the effort includes deciding whether the pop-up is a genuine question or some advertisement or other intrusion. All of these things are effort before they've answered a single question.

And if the questionnaire requires too much effort, people will drop out of it. Kantar Panels (formerly Lightspeed Research), a major provider of market research respondents, analyzed why people drop out of surveys, using their database of over three million market research surveys. As you'll see in Figure 2.4, they found that up to 60% of the drop-outs related to effort: survey length, media downloads, large grids (those questions where you're expected to answer a series of rating statements), and open questions.

Reasons why people drop out of surveys

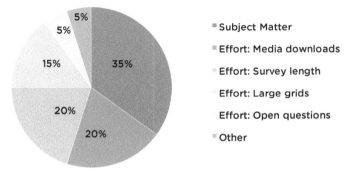

- Subject Matter
- Effort: Media downloads
- Effort: Survey length
- Effort: Large grids
- Effort: Open questions
- Other

FIGURE 2.4

Up to 60% of drop-outs from market research surveys are related to the amount of effort.

Response depends on perceived reward

I vividly recall a particularly grim government questionnaire where only my interest in the gender pay gap kept me going. I'm not alone. Passionate about a cause? You'll answer questions on it, and the perceived reward is the chance to share your views.

Don't care one way or another? All of a sudden that "perceived reward" switches over to be "perceived effort"—with a bad effect on your response rates. Just look at the 35% of people who dropped out of Lightspeed surveys because of subject matter.

> **Non-response error** happens when the people who answer your questionnaire are different from the people who do not answer in a way that affects your decision.

Sometimes, the "perceived reward" is the opportunity to share an opinion. That brings us to the distribution of the response:

> The **zone of response** is the number of people who answer compared to the possible answers.

If all the opinions are indeed shared evenly, then you'll get a zone of response that looks something like the one in Figure 2.5.

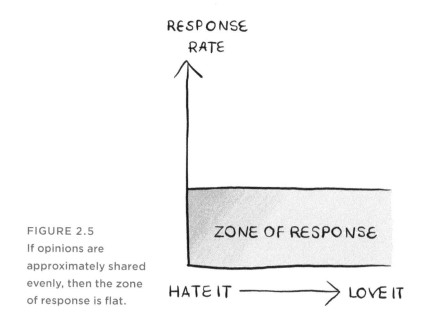

FIGURE 2.5
If opinions are
approximately shared
evenly, then the zone
of response is flat.

Let's think about another possibility that may be more likely, which
is that people with strong views such as "hate it" or "love it" may be
more likely to answer so that you get a higher response from them
and your zone of response has two peaks, as in Figure 2.6.

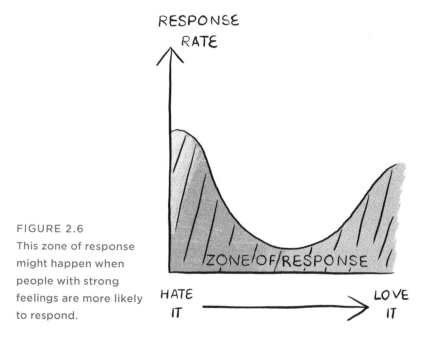

FIGURE 2.6
This zone of response
might happen when
people with strong
feelings are more likely
to respond.

There's also the possibility of a matching problem. You may be in danger of over-representing people with extreme views and under-representing the majority in the middle who aren't that bothered either way, the people in the zone of indifference in Figure 2.7.

The **zone of indifference** has a lower response from people who don't care much about your topic compared to people with strong feelings about it.

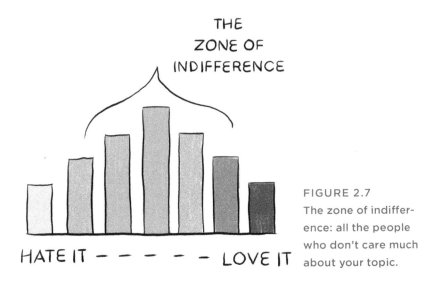

THE
ZONE OF
INDIFFERENCE

HATE IT − − − − − LOVE IT

FIGURE 2.7
The zone of indifference: all the people who don't care much about your topic.

If these problems apply to your survey and you need to know about the extremes, the zone of indifference doesn't matter too much. The people in the zones of response have strong feelings and are more likely to express them. But make sure that you do look at the zone of response, because you don't want to average out a large number of very positive views and a large number of very negative views and end up reporting that, on average, everyone is neutral.

If these problems apply to your survey and you want to make decisions based on people in general, the zone of indifference matters. A lot.

We've met an example of our first error in this chapter, as in Figure 2.8:

Non-response error happens when the people who answer your questionnaire are different from the people who do not answer in a way that affects your decision.

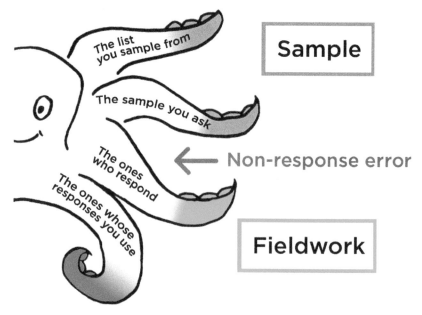

The list
you sample from

Sample

The sample you ask

← Non-response error

The ones
who respond

The ones whose
responses you use

Fieldwork

FIGURE 2.8
Non-response error happens in the gap between sample and fieldwork.

Non-response error can happen because of the example we just met: strength of feeling. It can also happen for many other reasons, such as when some people:

- Differ in whether they trust you with their answers.
- Have more difficulty than others in understanding your questions (a topic we'll return to in the next chapter).
- Consider that a question is irrelevant to them, whereas others consider that it is relevant.

You can also be afflicted by non-response error for some questions but not all of them. For example, people in your organization may be willing to trust you with their opinion about a recent decision to grant them an extra day of paid vacation each year, but less willing to tell you if they've faced bullying or harassment in the workplace. If the decision you need to make is about employee benefits, then you're OK; if you need to assess the level of workplace bullying, then you may well be facing considerable non-response error.

Discover the Burning Issue to avoid indifference

The things that organizations want to ask people about often do not match up very well with the things that people want to tell organizations.

A typical experience is a recent one of mine: I'd called an organization and the support person was lovely, but she couldn't fix the problem. I remained annoyed about the problem, but the feedback questionnaire only allowed me to express my views about the customer support person.

One way to avoid the Zone of Indifference is to find out what people care about. What do they want to tell you?

> The Burning Issue is the topic that people want to talk to you about.

Listen first, ask second

An easy way to find out about the Burning Issue is to interview some of the people you want to ask. If you like, you can also ask them about the topic of your Most Crucial Question—and even try the question on them. I go into these interviews with the motto "Listen First, Ask Second" in mind, as in Figure 2.9, to remind me to let the interviewees tell me about their Burning Issues before I start asking them about my Most Crucial Question.

FIGURE 2.9
This "Listen First, Ask Second" poster is a collaboration with Julia Allum.

After a few interviews—usually, five to eight are enough—you'll know:

- What the Burning Issue is
- A better view on what you really wanted to ask
- Whether you need to refine your Most Crucial Question

Can't interview? Then you can also try:

- Investigating your search logs
- Listening to what people are already telling you when they contact your call center, write to you, or talk about you on social media

Decide how many answers you need

There are two ingredients in the calculation of how many people to ask:

1. Your response rate
2. The number of answers you need

The calculation is:

- Find out, or estimate, your response rate.
- Decide on how many answers you need.
- Divide the number of answers by the response rate, and you've got your sample size.

For example:

Your estimate of your response rate is 25%.

You need 100 answers.

100 divided by 25% = 400.

Your sample size is 400.

We've already thought about response rate, so let's dig into three methods of deciding how many answers you need:

- Consider opinions.
- Use a sample size calculator.
- Iterate up.

Consider opinions—face validity

Often, stakeholders have asked for a survey because "we need numbers." They'll have some sort of feeling or opinion for how many answers they need. This is an example of face validity.

> **Face validity** is making a choice that looks sensible to your stakeholders.

Face validity is a crucial type of validity that can make or break your survey. It applies throughout all your survey choices and is especially important when thinking about the number of answers.

Sometimes, stakeholders get inspired by the apparent simplicity of sending out invitations on the internet and ask for thousands of answers. Sometimes, I can reduce the number by pointing out how much it will cost to process the responses.

Often, though, these views are expressed as a statistical argument: "We need 10,000 answers because we need statistical significance," so that brings us to the next method.

Use a sample size calculator

A sample size calculator will work out the number of answers that you need to achieve statistical significance. First of all, it's important not to confuse statistical significance with significance in practice. Here are my definitions, adapted from statistician Paul D. Ellis's book *The Essential Guide to Effect Sizes* (Ellis, 2010):

> A **statistically significant** result is one that is unlikely to be the result of chance.

> A result that is **significant in practice** is one that is meaningful in the real world.

Statistical significance relies on a combination of assumptions and mathematics, whereas significance in practice happens when you make good choices throughout the survey process.

If you definitely need to be sure that the result is unlikely to be the result of chance, then reach for a sample size calculator. There are plenty online. Choose one that mentions that you need a random sample for the calculation to work, as they all assume that it will be a random sample whether they mention it or not.

Your calculator will ask you for:

- Confidence level
- Population size
- Margin of error

And you may have some other questions, too.

If you are comfortable with those topics, then go for it—you don't need my help.

If you'd like to know more about them, then there are some highlights in Spotlight D, "Statistical Significance," after this chapter.

"Iterate up" to decide on a sample size

I'm going to let you in on a secret: I've had many discussions with stakeholders who have asked for statistical significance, but when I start talking about "What margin of error are you comfortable with?" their eyes glaze over.

This is where I turn to the "iterate up." The easiest way, by far, is to do the survey with the smallest possible sample size that you can persuade stakeholders to accept. The words *pilot, response rate estimator,* and *decision investigation* may help, depending on what works for them.

Find out what answers you get, and then work out whether those answers are good enough or whether you need to try again with a larger sample.

Don't ask everyone

All this discussion of how many people to ask brings us to the second error of this chapter, illustrated in Figure 2.10:

Sampling error happens when you choose to ask a sample rather than everyone.

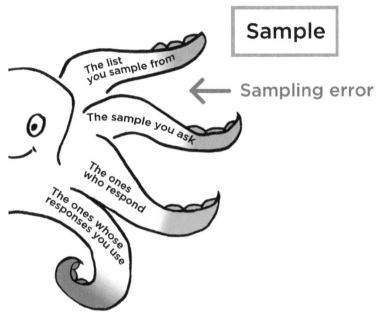

Sample

← Sampling error

FIGURE 2.10
Sampling error happens when you choose to ask a sample rather than everyone.

"Ask everyone" looks like a simple strategy to avoid sampling error:

- Everyone gets the chance to respond.
- You have no worries about who got left out.
- By definition, you have no sampling error.

But the strategy comes at a cost:

- When everyone knows that everyone gets asked, then as in Figure 2.11, "everyone" tends to leave it to "someone else" to respond, whereas if you let people know that they are only one of a few who were asked, they feel special and are more likely to respond.
- It's the most expensive option, especially with a large list.
- There is no opportunity to iterate because you've already asked everyone.

Also, unless your goal for this survey was specifically "to take account of every single person's opinion," then you don't actually need to get all those opinions anyway—only enough opinions to make a reasonable decision.

The smaller the list that defines your group of people, the more careful you need to be about choosing the smallest possible sample to ask. Ask too many too soon, and you'll run out of opportunities to iterate.

FIGURE 2.11
If you ask everyone, no one feels special.

"Enough answers" are better than "too many"

Processing an excessive number of responses is time-consuming, expensive, and may not add any extra information. The aim eventually is to get just enough of the right people, and a few of the right people is a great start, as in Figure 2.12.

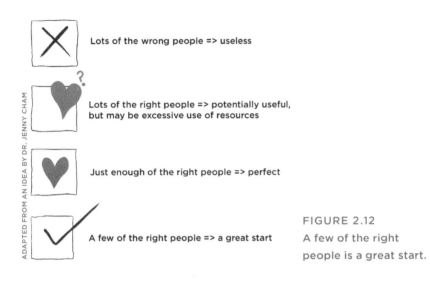

Lots of the wrong people => useless

Lots of the right people => potentially useful, but may be excessive use of resources

Just enough of the right people => perfect

A few of the right people => a great start

FIGURE 2.12
A few of the right people is a great start.

Notice that that the whole sample size thing depends on getting the right people—so now we'll think about finding them.

Find the people who you want to ask

Now that you've decided how many people you want to ask, the next step is to find the right people to ask—and those are the people who are in your defined group. "Just anyone" will not do. It's time to think about "The list you sample from," as in Figure 2.13.

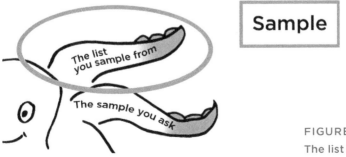

Sample

The list you sample from

The sample you ask

FIGURE 2.13
The list you sample from.

The name of the tentacle comes from the narrow down method of finding people to ask, starting with a list that ideally includes everyone in your defined group of people.

The second method of finding people is to catch people in the moment. A typical example: the feedback sheets handed out at the end of a training course.

If you've ever had a survey invitation that asked you to "forward this to anyone you know who might be interested," you've seen an example of our third method: snowball up (also known as snowball recruitment, chain sampling, or send and hope). The idea is to find some people in the defined group and then ask them to suggest other people in the group—the list grows like a snowball rolling and gathering more snow.

As you might expect, all of them have their merits and problems.

Coverage error happens when the list you sample from isn't perfect

It's rather unusual to get a perfect list of people in your defined group. I've personally never met a list without some amount of coverage error, a mismatch shown in Figure 2.14.

> **Coverage error** happens when the list that you sample from includes some people who are outside the defined group that you want to ask or excludes some people who are in it.

FIGURE 2.14
Coverage error happens when there is a mismatch between those who you want to ask and the list you sample from.

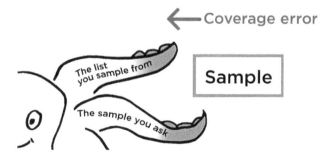

For the surveys I work on most often, the defined group of people is usually relatively easy: "current customers." Often, there's a customer list. Frequently, that customer list also includes:

- Customers who bought a couple of years ago but haven't purchased for a while
- Staff who happen also to be customers
- Test entries created by people working on the systems that have been left live for a variety of reasons
- People who get their products for free, maybe because they are influential people or journalists
- Customers who have moved who are listed with both the old and the new addresses
- Sensitive problems, such as customers who have died or have become unwell and can't deal with their affairs permanently or temporarily

And it may exclude:

- Customers who are so new that they aren't yet on the list
- People who buy through a special bulk purchasing agreement for exceptionally large customers

And no doubt there are other possible inclusions and exclusions that I have forgotten or not encountered yet.

To help reduce coverage error:

- Be as precise as possible about who is in the defined group. ("We want customers who pay for their products and have purchased in the last 12 months.")
- Double-check any list that you use. ("We will cross-check this customer list with our list of 'do not contact' addresses.")
- Expect to ask some questions, usually called *screening questions,* to check whether the person who is answering your question-naire really is within the defined group of people.

Find people by "narrow down"

To narrow down, choose a list and then choose who to ask—a sample—from that list. The perfect list is an exact match with your defined group. Survey methodologists call the list a sampling frame.

Let's assume that I managed to convince you to keep your costs in check and to preserve the goodwill of the people in your defined group, so you've decided to ask a sample rather than everyone.

To do that, you need a **sampling method**. The sample size calculators expect you to do this by picking a simple random sample.

> In a **simple random sample**, every person on the list has a known, non-zero probability of being included in the sample.

There are many ways to do this. If I've got a list that I think is a match to my defined group of people, then I use a random number generator like this. Let's say I want 100. (These instructions work for Excel and for Google Sheets; other spreadsheets are likely to have something similar.)

- Add an extra column called Random.
- Put =RAND() as the formula in each entry in the column.
- Optional extra step: Copy the column and paste it back where it was using "paste special – values." This freezes the random number. It's not essential, but I find it less weird than when the Random column changes all the time.
- Sort the spreadsheet according to the Random column.
- The first 100 rows are my random sample.

But hang on a moment—did you spot the mentions of "perfect list" and "exact match"? As always, we have another bit of wrestling with the Survey Octopus to do—thinking about possible coverage error.

Narrow down from a private list

I call this method—starting with a list that's a reasonable match to your defined group of people and then refining it—"Narrow down from a private list."

Two examples of private lists that I have used successfully:

- Students enrolled at a university
- Members of a professional association

The students' list was very well maintained, with up-to-date email addresses for nearly everyone on it.

The professional association was so-so; many of the members only contacted their association once a year at renewal time (see Figure 2.15).

FIGURE 2.15
Many members of professional associations only update their contact details at renewal time.

If your list is patchy, don't be too dismayed. Even a poor list gives you a place to start—it simply reduces your potential response rate and gives you more work to do.

Narrow down from a public list

What if you don't have any list that resembles the defined group of people? That happens a lot with government surveys. They often rely on two sorts of public lists that at one time used to contain everyone:

- Landline numbers
- Addresses

If you've had a mystery "silent call" on your landline, that may have come from a Random Digit Dialer. These automate the sampling by trying potential phone numbers (they aren't quite random; they use lists of area codes to help) until they get a match, with the intention of connecting the person who answers the ringing phone with a call center agent or interviewer. If no interviewer is available when you pick up, the result can be a silent call.

If you are thinking, "Landline? Who has them now?" then you've spotted the obvious problem. If your defined group of people includes anyone who is young or poor, then your chances of reaching them by landline are not good.

Although many of us have abandoned our landlines, we still have to live somewhere, so most of us continue to have addresses. To take advantage of those addresses, you must first take the time and expense to obtain them, and then send mail or arrange for someone to visit that address in person.

There's no hiding it: delivering your questionnaire by phone, by mail, or by sending interviewers to specific addresses is expensive. Despite that, phone or mail can work out to be cheaper in the end because those methods tend to have higher response rates than most types of electronic surveys.

What if you could simply contact someone else who has done all the hard work of putting together a panel of people who are willing to respond to survey invitations?

There are a few panels based on "narrow down" methods, mostly created and maintained by academics working in social research. The LISS panel in the Netherlands was the first one. The best-known in the U.S. is the AmeriSpeak panel operated by NORC at the University of Chicago. If you are doing some types of social research, you may be able to get access to the panel in your country. It's a useful short-cut to narrowing down from a public list.

Narrow down from a purchased panel

For the rest of us, some market research businesses and some survey tool vendors offer the opportunity to purchase a sample from their panel. Depending on the particular vendor, you may be able to specify some of the definition you are looking for ("people over the age of 65"), and from there you will need to include some questions in your survey that help you to decide whether the panel members who answer are indeed in your defined group.

People who join panels tend to be much more willing to answer questions than people who don't join panels and also to have more time on their hands. Many market research questionnaires fall firmly into the category of Big Honkin' Surveys, so panel members may have a level of tolerance for long sequences of questions that are unusual. This may not matter for your survey.

Find people by catching them "in the moment"

Sometimes, you can define the group by catching them in the moment.

The "moment" could be defined by time: "People who visit our website between specific dates."

Or by an action: "Anyone who completes a flight with our airline." (If you travel regularly, that one might be over-familiar.)

Or by a location: "Anyone who comes to our café." Or "People who get help from our center for homeless people."

Or all three: "Anyone who visits our museum (location) to see the exhibition (action) that we're showing in November (time)"—as in Figure 2.16.

FIGURE 2.16
A museum placed this feedback kiosk at the end of a compelling exhibit.

Picking a moment to define your group of people has one big advantage: you've immediately got perfect coverage.

Of course, nothing in surveys comes without a compromise. The first one to think about here is: Will the people want to divert from whatever they are doing in that moment to answer your questionnaire?

The answer often is: No, not really. It's one of the many survey compromises: reduction in coverage error may result in a big increase in non-response error.

And the second thing to think about is: Have you changed your definition of the group you're interested in to allow for catching them in the moment? If so, is that still going to meet your overall goals for the survey?

Find people by "snowball up" (especially for hard-to-find people)

What can you do when there isn't any available list and there's no obvious way of catching people in the moment?

I was in exactly that situation when Steve Krug and I wanted to do a survey of user experience professionals. We used our social media networks and asked people to share the link to our questionnaire—an example of "snowball up," sometimes also called "friends and family."

You can make your "snowball up" more orderly in this way:

1. First, catch anyone at all in your defined group.
2. Think about the people who respond and what you've learned from them.
3. If you can make the decision that you need to make, based on the survey findings, then you are done. If not, keep going.
4. Use what you have learned so far to adjust your ideas about how to find people.
5. Repeat from step 2 until you've made the decision.

When Steve and I were looking for respondents to our survey, the decision was: "Do we have enough responses to give us plenty to think about for our conference presentation?" We got that after our first appeal, so we stopped at step 3.

The biggest problem with "snowball up" is coverage error. It's hard to know who you are reaching or how they compare with the defined group that you want to reach. People closely connected with the first ones you catch may get lots of invitations, and you may entirely miss people outside of those networks, as in Figure 2.17.

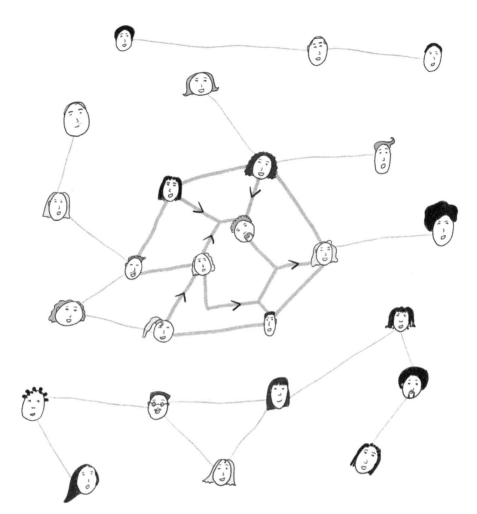

FIGURE 2.17

With "snowball up," people in the same network can get multiple invitations, and you can miss people outside of that network entirely.

The right response is better than a big response

Back in 2010, an internet prank caught my attention (see Figure 2.18). A Justin Bieber fan site asked people to vote for the location of his next concert. North Korea won.

Technology

Prank leaves Justin Bieber facing tour of North Korea

By Daniel Emery
Technology reporter, BBC News

5 July 2010

FIGURE 2.18
BBC coverage of an
internet prank.

The BBC assumed, and I agree, that Justin Bieber didn't have all that many genuine fans in North Korea but that the responses came from people who didn't like him and wanted to tease the fans.

Let's think first about coverage. The fan site opted for "snowball up." If they'd had any way to keep the snowball to networks of fans, then they would have been OK, but in practice it got noticed by people who wanted to make fun of them. This meant that they included lots of people who weren't genuine fans: plenty of coverage error.

In terms of sampling, the fan site didn't restrict the responses at all, and they didn't have any way to estimate the size of the group of people they were sampling from. That means we have no way to calculate sampling error.

What about response? In theory, anyone could answer: fans, pranksters, and people who didn't care (the zone of indifference). We can reasonably assume that the "don't cares" didn't bother to respond, and for this poll that was acceptable—the aim was to get a response from people who did care. So, surprisingly, there probably wasn't much non-response error: the people who didn't respond were different from the people who did, but not in a way that would likely affect the results.

This prank captured for me the perils of getting enough of the right people to respond to your questionnaire—a set of challenges that I'll forever think of as: Have we got any Justin Bieber/North Korea problems?

How, then, will we get enough of the right people to answer? And how does it work with a more realistic example?

A big response may come from the wrong mix of people

There's no doubt that a big response looks impressive. "We got 10,000 responses" sounds good, doesn't it? And surely that would be enough.

Well, no. It's easy to confuse a big response with a good response.

Suppose that 10,000 people respond: if you've got exactly 10,000 customers, then your response rate is 100%—well done. You've got a perfect response. However, there are some negatives: you've still got the expense of processing all 10,000 responses, which may be more than you really needed—and if you didn't ask exactly the right questions, then you don't have anyone in reserve to ask again for another survey.

What if you sent the questionnaire to a million customers and got a 0.01% response rate?

Perhaps the 10,000 who responded all love you and the rest are indifferent? Perhaps the 10,000 people who responded have a particular agenda that they want to push? We don't know. All we can say is that the people who did respond have the potential to be different from the 990,000 who didn't in a way that affects the results of the survey.

A good response rate may not be good enough

For a long while, I was convinced that if I got a good response rate—I usually aimed for somewhere above 50%—that meant I had a good questionnaire. But it turns out that response rate isn't enough. What matters is the amount of non-response error, which we met before:

> **Non-response error** happens when the people who answer your questionnaire are different from the people who do not answer in a way that affects your decision.

Whenever the response rate is less than 100%, there's the potential for non-response error.

Going back to our Big Honkin' Surveys in the 1940s and 1950s, response rates were high, and survey methodologists didn't focus all that much on non-response error. When response rates to surveys started to decline rapidly toward the end of the last century, survey methodologists started to do a variety of experiments to explore the implications for their results. They had to pay higher incentives to maintain response rates, which added costs. Were those costs justified in terms of better results?

The answer is: sadly, no. Or, at least, not clearly enough to justify focusing on response rates as the sole indicator of quality.

To make inferences, you need representative response

The crucial concept that distinguishes "enough of the right people" is representativeness.

> The people who respond are **representative** when they accurately reflect the views and characteristics of the defined group of people.

In an election, we count the votes that we get on the day and announce the result. The definition of "the right people" is whoever turned out to vote.

For your survey, it depends on the decision you want to take. Is the simple vote from the respondents good enough, or is it important to make inferences about the defined group of people as a whole?

If you want to make decisions based on inferences, then you need the responses to be representative of the group.

How do you know whether the responses are representative? That's a very tricky question to answer.

FIGURE 2.19
A few pictures of birds in a sample.

Look at this sample of bird pictures in Figure 2.19.

It's quite impossible to know whether this sample is representative unless we know something about the underlying structure of the group that it came from. If the sample came from the selection in the next illustration, it's clearly unrepresentative (see Figure 2.20).

FIGURE 2.20
If our sample came from this selection, it's clearly unrepresentative.

That's why it's tricky to know whether the response you get is representative or not: you need to know about your defined group of people to be sure that the people who respond to your survey are representative.

Demographics describe representativeness

"Demographics" are statistics that describe a defined group of people, and "demographic analysis" (slightly confusingly usually shortened to "demographics," too) is the science of deciding on demographic statistics and measuring them.

Even more confusingly, you'll often hear the word *demographics* applied to the familiar questions about age (such as in Figure 2.21), marital status, gender, and so on that appear in many surveys. These are some of the "screening questions" that we met earlier when considering how to narrow down from a list to find our defined group of people.

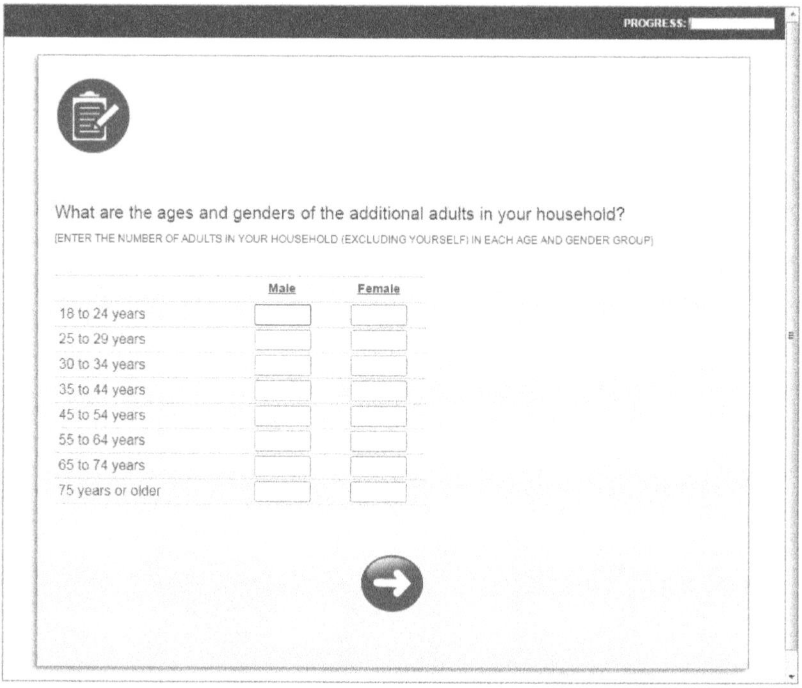

FIGURE 2.21
A market research questionnaire that I did recently started with nine demographic questions. This one, on age, is one of them.

If your defined group of people is "everyone who is resident in the country we work in," then comparing demographics that you get from the people who answer your questionnaire to the demographics of the residents of your country as published by your National Statistical Institute (NSI) can be quite a handy way to check representativeness.

Most countries only have one NSI. If you're in the U.S., then you have several of them. For working out demographics of who is a resident in the U.S., go to the Census Bureau. For typical occupations in the U.S., go to the Bureau of Labor Statistics.

Use representativeness questions that are relevant to your defined group of people

Most of us are doing surveys where the defined group of people is much more tightly specified than "everyone in a particular country." We might want "people who buy yogurt," or "our customers," or "visitors to my website." Of course, you can ask them the familiar age, gender, and suchlike questions—but will that really help you know whether they are or are not truly part of your defined group?

Also, many people find these questions boring or intrusive.

Boring questions may lower the response rate from busy people. If "being busy" doesn't make much difference to the answer to the Most Crucial Question (maybe: the flavor of juice you prefer to buy), then that won't create a non-response error. But for other MCQs (maybe: choices about how to spend leisure time), there is a lot of potential for non-response error.

Intrusive questions lead to break-offs. Do you want to accidentally increase your non-response error because people abandon your questionnaire? I think not.

The answer is to find questions—not too many—that help you to work out whether someone who answers is or is not within your defined group and whether you are accidentally getting too many answers from some types of people and too few from others.

Let's think about a survey for a professional association that wanted to find out whether or not business owners in their membership were interested in purchasing some types of insurance through the association. Their draft questionnaire started with these questions:

- Gender
- Age range
- Country you live in/country you work in
- City/town
- State/province
- Typical activities of the business

The "typical activities of the business" was the most useful question for deciding whether they got a representative sample, followed by "state/province." We could forget about the other four.

It can also be handy to look at the details of the definition of your group of people. For example, if you're looking for people who are customers, you might ask about how recently they bought something from you or their level of experience with the product you offer.

Use triangulation and iteration to understand representativeness

There are two strategies available to understand representativeness:

1. Compare the responses you get to other sources of knowledge about the defined group of people ("triangulation").

2. Start small with a tiny sample to learn something about your defined group of people. Gradually increase the samples as you know more. Keep checking back along the way as you increase your knowledge of the defined group ("iteration").

I mentioned using published data from the Bureau of Census or a similar National Statistical Institute as one sort of triangulation. You may also have other sources available, such as data on your customers. For example, I used a type of triangulation on a survey of students for a large university. We checked that the proportions of respondents from each subject area, their ages, and the number of credits they'd completed were in line with the proportions across the whole student population.

I used iteration on a survey of front-end developers. We started with a tiny sample and used it to challenge our ideas about the defined group of people, as we learned more about how the developers worked with their designer colleagues on the topic we were interested in. Then we gradually increased our sample size as our knowledge improved and we learned more about how to find them.

Representativeness matters more than response or response rate

Table 2.2 shows a comparison that includes a North Korean flag to represent the "Justin Bieber problem."

TABLE 2.2 A COMPARISON OF RESPONSE, RESPONSE RATES, AND REPRESENTATIVENESS

Concept	Definition	Example	Main use
Response	Number of people who answer	10,000	Impressing stakeholders
Response rate	Number of people who answer divided by the number of invitations sent out	87%	Calculating sample sizes
Representativeness	Whether the respondents you get are typical of the defined group of people		Getting solid results

What can possibly go wrong with sampling?

The errors in this chapter are quite complex, so let's recap. I've illustrated the different overlaps and gaps in Figure 2.22.

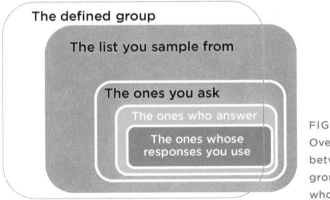

FIGURE 2.22

Overlaps and gaps between the defined group and the ones whose answers you use.

Problem: coverage error

If the list that you choose to narrow down from isn't perfect, or if you choose to iterate up or to catch people "in the moment," then you'll almost certainly have some coverage error:

Coverage error happens when the list that you sample from includes some people who are outside the defined group that you want to ask or excludes some people who are in it.

If you think hard about your defined group of people and try your best to match the list you sample from to the group as closely as possible, then you can keep your coverage error to a manageable level.

Problem: sampling error

If you decide to ask everyone in your defined group of people, then you may have other problems, but you won't have sampling error.

Sampling error happens when you choose to ask some of the people rather than everyone.

Sampling error gets a lot of attention because it's the only one that can be described easily using statistics. It's the source of concepts like "statistical significance" and "confidence intervals." If you'd like an introduction to them, it's coming up after this chapter in Spotlight D.

Problem: non-response error

If everyone you ask decides to answer, then you have a perfect response and zero non-response to consider. In practice, people have reasons why they do or don't answer, so non-response error is important.

Non-response error happens when the people who respond are different from the people who don't respond in ways that affect the result.

The errors build on each other

All these errors build on each other. For example, if you've got coverage error because the list you sample from isn't very good, you can't solve that problem by increasing the size of the sample you ask.

If you ask too many people too often and the people who are indifferent stop responding, you've got non-response error, and you can't solve that problem by asking even more people. You can see all three errors together in Figure 2.23.

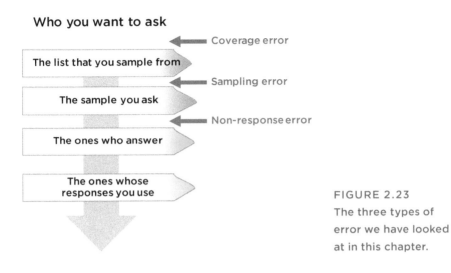

Who you want to ask

The list that you sample from ← Coverage error

The sample you ask ← Sampling error

The ones who answer ← Non-response error

The ones whose responses you use

FIGURE 2.23
The three types of error we have looked at in this chapter.

All the sampling methods have compromises. Sometimes, creating a great survey can seem like negotiating a tricky path through a series of compromises—and deciding on the list you sample from is exactly that. Table 2.3 sums up the choices.

TABLE 2.3 FIVE METHODS FOR OBTAINING A SAMPLE

	Coverage	Calculation of sampling error	Potential for non-response error	Cost
Narrow down from a private list	Good	Relatively easy	Depends on the quality of the list	Depends on the quality of the list
Narrow down from a public list	Good	Possible	Manageable	High
Narrow down from a purchased panel	Not very good	Might be possible	Manageable	Medium
Catch in the moment	May be OK	Possible	Depends on the type of moment	Depends on the type of moment
Snowball up	Poor	Impossible	Possibly very high	Low

At this point, you will know

You've added a lot to the planning of your survey in this chapter. You have:

- Thought about the factors that will influence your response rate.
- Investigated whether your defined group of people has a Burning Issue.
- Worked out the number of responses that you need.
- Decided on whether to find people to ask by narrowing down, iterating up, or catching them in the moment.
- Thought about the representativeness of the people who answer.

In the next chapter, we'll move on from these big, difficult topics and start to focus on the details of writing good questions.

In between, there's Spotlight D. If you have a stakeholder who is insisting on a particular sample size because "we need results that are statistically significant," but you don't happen to be a stats person yourself, this is for you. For everyone else, see you in Chapter 3, "Questions."

Statistical Significance

Back in the Introduction, I talked about how the result of a survey is a number that you can use to make a decision.

Sometimes, you'll find that people ask whether this number is "statistically significant." This Spotlight is a quick introduction to significance.

Statistical significance is different from significance in practice

My definitions of significance are based on statistician Paul D. Ellis's book *The Essential Guide to Effect Sizes* (Ellis, 2010):

> A result that is **statistically significant** is one that is mathematically unlikely to be the result of chance.

> A result that is **significant in practice** is one that is meaningful in the real world.

Statistical significance is worked out by using one of the many statistical tests for significance. It's closely related to sampling error, and you can achieve it by doing things like getting a big enough sample of people to answer your questionnaire and choosing a statistical test appropriately.

In contrast, significance in practice is much broader and is closely related to Total Survey Error. You achieve significance in practice by considering all the possible things that could go wrong during the survey process and making good choices about them.

Statistical significance testing looks for a probability

Here's one more definition:

> An **effect** is something happening that is not the result of chance.

From the point of view of statistical significance testing, any result is either an effect or is happening by chance. The aim of a test of statistical significance is to help to decide which of these is more likely.

The result of a test of statistical significance is always reported as a probability known as a *"p*-value," usually called *"p"* for short. Somewhat arbitrarily, the definition of "mathematically unlikely to be the result of chance" is usually given as *"p* < 0.05," so we get:

> A **statistically significant** result is one where *p* < 0.05.

Something can be significant in practice but not statistically significant

Knowing whether or not a result is statistically significant can be handy when you are aiming for a result that is significant in practice, but you can definitely have a result that is significant in practice but not statistically significant.

For example, a tweet by Professor Sir David Spiegelhalter, a leading statistician, caught my eye in 2019, when he described an academic paper as "Appalling." (Spiegelhalter, 2019)

In the paper (Hernández, Ospina-Tascón et al., 2019), the researchers compared two treatments for people with septic shock. For one treatment, 92 out of 212 patients died, which is 43.4%. For the other, 74 out of 212 patients died, which is 34.9%. That's 18 fewer people who died and a difference in death rates of 8.5%.

You can see from the graph in Figure D.1 that cumulative mortality from the better treatment was consistently lower than cumulative mortality from the other treatment after day 4. Professor Spiegelhalter clearly considers that this is significant in practice.

In this paper, the result of the significance testing (*p*=0.06) didn't quite meet the *p* < 0.05 we met in the definition. The authors said that there was no effect instead of pointing out that their study did not have enough power to tell whether or not an apparently better results might be happening by chance or because of an effect.

If I were a relative of one of the extra 18 people who died on the less good treatment, I'd want to see, at the very least, a recommendation for further research.

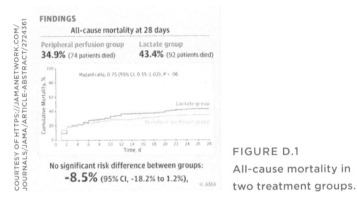

FIGURE D.1

All-cause mortality in
two treatment groups.

Something can be statistically significant but not significant in practice

The more data points that you have for your test, the more likely you are to identify an effect. You will have more statistical power:

> **Statistical power** is the probability that a test will correctly identify an effect. (Ellis, 2010)

Unfortunately, something can be a detectable effect but not significant in practice.

Here's an example from a real experiment on an electronic customer satisfaction survey, aimed at persuading people to switch from completing a survey on their smartphone to completing it on a PC. The researchers (Peterson, 2012), quoted in (Peterson, Griffin et al., 2017), did an experiment with almost 10,000 people, divided into three roughly equal groups. One group got a message in the survey invitation telling them that the survey worked better on a PC than on other devices (invitation). The second group got a similar message in the introductory screen of the survey (introductory screen). The final group didn't get any messages.

The researchers kept track of the proportion of people who answered who switched from a smartphone to a PC.

TABLE D.1 A COMPARISON FROM AN EXPERIMENT ON SURVEY INVITATIONS

	Invitation	Introductory screen	Control
Did not switch device	99.7%	99.1%	99.6%
Switched from smartphone to PC	0.3%	0.9%	0.4%

The sample sizes are so large that the differences between groups are statistically significant, but researchers pointed out that in this context, the effect size—the number of people who were influenced to change device—is too tiny to have any significance in practice. It demonstrates the risk of picking a large sample size without considering the size of effect that is useful for making the decision.

This problem of "too large a sample size to be useful" is a recent one. When Ronald Fisher first started talking about "significance" in the statistical context of the 1920s, data sets had to be small by today's standards because it was really hard to do calculations on big data sets. With the tools available at that time, statistical thinking was dominated by the question of how small a data set you could get away with.

These days, computers do the calculations for us, so we have to think much harder about what size of effect is important. Sometimes, a tiny effect matters—perhaps because you are Amazon, and you sell billions of items every day—and it is appropriate to work with a huge sample size that might detect it. Other times, that great big batch of data might make it seem very easy to achieve a statistically significant result—but does it matter in practice?

Something can look statistically significant because of wrong assumptions

I've pointed out that statistical significance and significance in practice can be very different from each other. It's only fair to point out that quite often an effect that is significant in practice is also statistically significant.

That brings us to a further complication, which is that there are many different ways to test statistical significance. To ensure that you do a statistical test correctly, you have three things to consider:

1. The choice of statistical test (the mathematical manipulation of the data)
2. The assumptions about the data that are required for the statistical test to work
3. The amount of data that you give to the statistical test

For example, statistical tests generally assume that your data set comes from a random sample. If it doesn't—perhaps because you chose to sample by "snowball up"—then the tests will deliver something that looks like a valid result, even though they may not have worked as intended.

If your stakeholders are genuinely interested in statistical significance, it's important to have a discussion with them before you collect the data about which tests they consider to be appropriate for the decisions they want to make, and then you must adjust your data collection methods accordingly so that you fulfill the assumptions for those tests. That's why this Spotlight comes before Chapter 3.

If you are doing a survey on your own and want some advice about choosing tests, then many universities offer advice aimed at their students, such as www.sheffield.ac.uk/mash/statistics/what_test.

Many leading statisticians reject the overuse of statistical significance

You may have noticed that I have a certain skepticism about the overuse of statistical significance. In 2019, I was delighted to discover that many leading statisticians shared my view. Over 800 of them signed a call to put statistical significance in its place as a tool with only limited applications. A summary of their views was published in *Nature* under the headline "Scientists Rise Up Against Statistical Significance." (Amrhein, Greenland et al., 2019 and Figure D.2)

COURTESY OF WWW.NATURE.COM/ARTICLES/D41586-019-00857-9

FIGURE D.2

The cartoon suggests that statistical significance will be put into the dusty room with discarded concepts like phlogiston.

For example, three of the statisticians who contributed recommended an approach based on ATOM:

Accept uncertainty. Be **T**houghtful, **O**pen, and **M**odest.
(Wasserstein, Schirm et al., 2019)

Personally, I treat ATOM as an instruction to focus on significance in practice and think about the whole Survey Octopus.

For example, instead of trying to make claims about the entire defined group of people, I often report what I learned from the people who actually answered and point out that there is always some uncertainty when you're looking at a sample.

You're generally better off with a confidence interval anyway

Sometimes, you may need to explain how much uncertainty there might be about what your survey tells you about the true population value.

> The **true population** value is the result you get when you ask precisely everyone in your defined group of people, and all of them answer accurately.

A confidence interval is a way of quantifying the amount of uncertainty.

> A **confidence interval** is a range that estimates the true population value for a statistic. (Tullis and Albert, 2008)

To get to a confidence interval, you need to decide on a confidence level (how much certainty you are looking for). Most people go with 95%, which is related to the "$p < 0.05$" that we met earlier, but for everyday decision-making where they have no plans to put their results into an academic journal, people often go for 90% instead, which is equivalent to $p < 0.10$.

A confidence interval relies on having a random sample, so you need to have made a decent effort to get a random sample, or at least believe that the sample you have isn't excessively biased.

For example, suppose that you want to get an estimate of the average height of children. If you decide to create that estimate by going to a large school and measuring the height of all the children in the first classroom you find, you might get all 5-year-olds, which would definitely not be a random sample.

Also, you need to think about how spread out the data is—in statistical terms, the "standard deviation" of your sample. The calculation of a confidence interval relies on the standard deviation of your sample being similar to that of the population.

In the example of the height of the children, the spread of heights of 5-year-olds is likely to be a lot narrower than that of children in general. (I've met 15-year-olds who are easily 6 ft. tall, but rarely found a 5-year-old who tops 4 ft.)

To work out a confidence interval, there are plenty of calculators online, and most spreadsheets have them built in or available as a free add-on.

In my next example, I've chosen a calculator that works out a confidence interval when I know the mean (arithmetic average) of my sample (let's say: 42), its standard deviation (5.7), my sample size (500), and the confidence level that I want to use (95%).

TABLE D.2 CONFIDENCE INTERVAL BASED ON 95% CONFIDENCE LEVEL

Mean	Standard deviation	Sample size	Desired confidence level	Confidence interval
42	9.8	500	95%	41.1 to 42.9

In other words, I'm accepting a 5% risk that the true population mean falls outside the range 41.1 to 42.9. I've got rather a large random sample, so I get a lot of precision.

Let's suppose that I could only afford a sample size of 50. Now I get a larger confidence interval.

TABLE D.3 CONFIDENCE INTERVAL ADJUSTED FOR A SMALLER SAMPLE SIZE

Mean	Standard deviation	Sample size	Desired confidence level	Confidence interval
42	9.8	50	95%	39.3 to 44.7

With a sample size of 50, I'm accepting a 5% risk that the true population mean falls outside the range 39.3 to 44.7. With a smaller sample size, I have a wider confidence interval.

The calculations are a bit different when you're trying to determine a confidence interval around a percentage or proportion instead of a mean, so when you search for your calculator on the web or pick one in your spreadsheet, make sure that you are choosing one that matches the type of result that you are working with.

Use your desired margin of error to work out a sample size

Instead of gathering some data and then working out your confidence interval, it's possible to turn the idea around and say: how precise a result do we need to make a decision?

> The **margin of error** is the level of precision that you need in your result.

To use a sample size calculator:

- Guess what your mean and standard deviation are likely to be.
- Decide on the margin of error you need.
- Choose the confidence level you are willing to accept.
- Plug those numbers into the calculator.

The calculator will tell you the sample size you need to achieve your desired precision.

Of course, I recommend that instead of relying entirely on guesswork, you run a pilot study to get an initial estimate of the mean, standard deviation, and response rate.

Statistical significance is also about hypotheses

In this Spotlight, I have talked about the difference between statistical significance and significance in practice, including a mention of the size of an effect and statistical power.

What I haven't done yet is offered an explanation of this crucial definition:

> A **statistically significant result** is one where $p < 0.05$.

So here you are:

> The **p-value** is the probability that the data would be at least as extreme as those observed, if the null hypothesis were true. (Vickers, 2010)

If you would like to read my attempt to explain that definition step-by-step, including a visit to the concepts of "false positive" and "false negative," then please have a look at my website: www.effortmark.co.uk/statistical-significance.

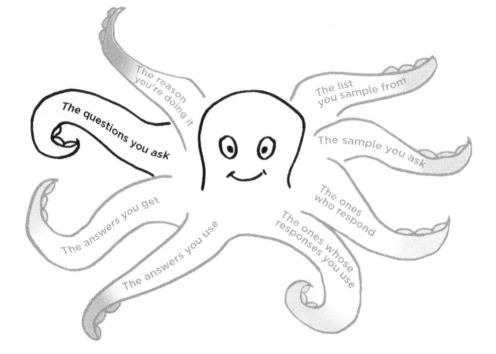

CHAPTER 3

Questions: Write and Test the Questions

In the last chapter, we were looking at the right-hand side of the Survey Octopus, thinking about the people who will answer your survey and how many of them you want to ask.

We are now going to swap over to the left-hand side, looking at the questions you might ask.

Before you tackle this chapter, you need to know:

- What you want to ask—and specifically, your Most Crucial Question.

- What people want to tell you about—and specifically, their Burning Issue.

Understand the four steps to answer a question

Sometimes a question is so quick and easy to answer that you barely notice it.

Question: "Who's there?"

Answer: "It's me!"

Other questions can be trickier. Figure 3.1 has one, Question 25, in a questionnaire that I slogged through in my quest to find as many examples as possible to discuss here.

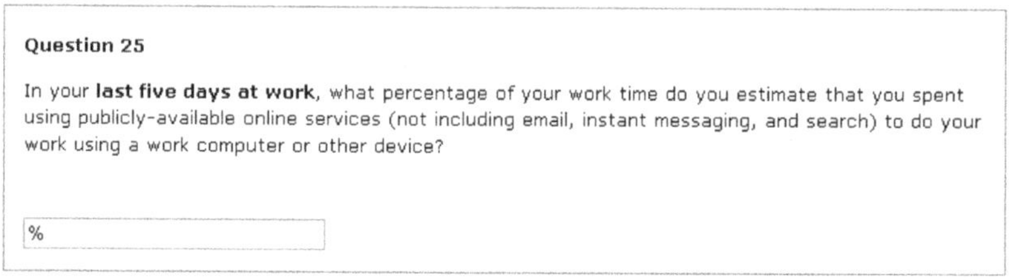

Question 25

In your **last five days at work**, what percentage of your work time do you estimate that you spent using publicly-available online services (not including email, instant messaging, and search) to do your work using a work computer or other device?

%

FIGURE 3.1

A daunting question, especially after I've already answered 24 previous ones.

To provide an answer, I've got quite a lot of work to do.

1. **Understand the question.**

   For example, what is a "publicly-available online service?"

2. **Find an answer.**

   I'll need to think back over my recent activity and work out what I was doing for the "last five days at work."

3. **Decide on an answer.**

   How much of that activity counts toward this question? Am I willing to tell them that?

4. **Respond with the answer.**

   Or maybe guess, perhaps 25%? To be fair to this question, at least it doesn't force me to try to map the answer I have to their views of what an answer might be—so there's no guessing about which option to pick.

And finally, at this point, I might simply feel tired and decide to break off from the questionnaire.

Of course, you don't want people to guess, or to break off, or to feel bemused by your questions.

I've adapted the four steps in Figure 3.2 from *The Psychology of Survey Response*. (Tourangeau, Rips et al., 2000) We're going to look at each step in detail, but first I want to mention that sometimes they blur into each other. When answering a simple question, these steps happen so fast that you barely notice them. Other questions, like Question 25, manage to pose quite a challenge at each step.

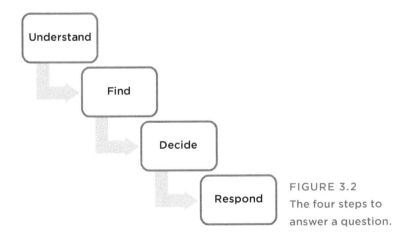

FIGURE 3.2
The four steps to answer a question.

Good questions are easy to understand

To understand a question, people have to:

- Get it off the page and into their heads (perceive).
- Turn it into something meaningful to them.

Perceive the question: see, hear, or sense

Are you reading this by looking at letters on paper, dots on a screen, by listening to a screen reader, or feeling it on a Braille display? Or something else?

Are you sitting in a comfy chair with a tablet, standing on a commuter train, flicking through a paper copy in a shop? Or something else?

Have you set aside plenty of time to absorb every word, or are you rushing through?

The people you are asking have their own idiosyncratic mixture of contexts, technologies, and available time. Note that if they can't perceive it, then they definitely can't turn it into something meaningful.

Turn it into meaning: short and simple

Comparing the easy question "Who's there?" and the hideous Question 25, it's obvious that it's often harder to construct meaning from over 40 words than from two words. On the whole, shorter is better when it comes to sentences.

But short isn't everything. For example, I could make the horrible question shorter by chopping out every other word so that it's only half as long—and, at 22 words, well within typical guidelines for "short sentences" (25 words or fewer).

> *In last days' work, percentage your time you that spend publicly available services, including instant and to your using work or device?*

Doesn't help all that much, does it?

Turn it into meaning: familiar words in familiar ways

We all become accustomed to the words and phrases in our professional environments. To us, they're a convenient shorthand. To people outside, they're jargon: words that are unfamiliar, or (even worse) familiar words that are used in strange ways.

Let me tell you about a time when I was working for a government agency, and we tried this question on farmers:

What browser do you use?

I learned that farmers vary widely in their digital skills. Some farmers gave us a long reply that compared the merits of their preferred web browser and explained why they sometimes chose to switch to others. Others gave us replies like these:

"What's a browser?"

"Oh, do you mean how do I get to the internet? I click on 'e.' I've never understood why it's 'e' for internet."

"Google. Yes, I use Google."

My favorite interview was with a farmer with no digital skills whatsoever. Farming her sheep in a remote moorland farm like the one in Figure 3.3, her skills include breeding and training the sheepdogs she uses to manage her herd, as her land is unsuitable for any vehicles. But with no telephone and no mobile coverage on her farm, she didn't have a computer, so "browser" meant nothing to her.

FIGURE 3.3
Moorland sheep.

On reflection, it's not that big a surprise to discover that a sheep farmer isn't familiar with IT jargon. It can be more of a surprise to discover that people doing the same job as you aren't familiar with the jargon that you use.

For example, I was helping a team of designers and developers asking similar people about details of their work. We didn't expect jargon problems at all.

One of our questions was:

> "What methodologies do you use on this project?"

When we tested it, we found that half of the people we tested the question with didn't know what we meant, and the other half interpreted it quite differently from how we'd intended it: we wanted to know about whether they used CSS methodologies such as BEM, but they answered about using Agile development approaches.

We went back to the question, thought harder about what we really wanted to know, and changed it to:

> "Which CSS architecture do you follow?"

We were now using words that were entirely familiar to our defined group of people, in ways that made sense to them. Familiar words in familiar ways.

> "Of course I can read it," he said. "I know what every word means."
>
> "Well, then?" said Masklin.
>
> Gurder looked embarrassed. "It's what every sentence means that's giving me trouble," he said.'" (Pratchett, 1990)

Turn it into meaning: ask people to focus on one thing at a time

One of the most frequent mistakes that I see in questions written by people who are new to survey research is asking about two things at the same time, such as Question 31 in Figure 3.4.

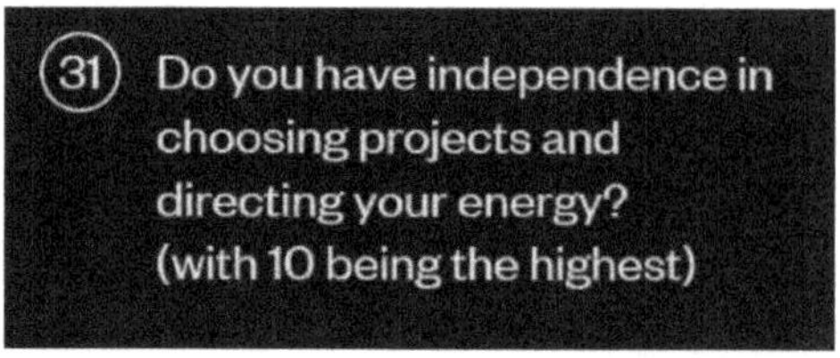

FIGURE 3.4
Question 31: "Do you have independence in choosing projects and directing your energy (with 10 being the highest)?"

> (31) Do you have independence in choosing projects and directing your energy? (with 10 being the highest)

Let's unpack question 31 a little. Maybe you have complete independence in everything that you do: easy. Or perhaps you are entirely at the mercy of a boss or someone else: unpleasant for you, maybe, but at least the question is easy.

What about people who can choose their project at the start but must then commit to it with little control? What about people who must accept whatever assignment they are given but can then choose how much energy to put into different aspects of it?

Survey methodologists call this a *double-barreled* question, borrowing the adjective from the idea that a double-barreled shotgun might fire at you twice at the same time.

Do you think I'm being a bit nitpicky about that example? Try one in Figure 3.5 instead, from an online diagnostic quiz for people suffering from low moods.

Q 18 of 18

If this questionnaire has highlighted any problems, how difficult have these problems made it for you to do your work, take care of things at home, or get along with other people?

FIGURE 3.5
This question includes work, home, and other people.

When we tested the low mood question, we learned that people had different answers for work, home, and getting along with other people: a triple-barreled question, especially unfortunate in this example, given that a low mood tends to have a bad effect on people's cognitive capacity.

Good questions ask for answers that are easy to find

When you've understood the question, you've got to find an answer, as in Figure 3.6.

Consider a question such as "When did you last visit a grocery store?" The answer is probably

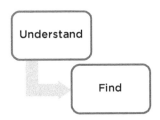

FIGURE 3.6
The next step is to find the answer.

somewhere in your head. You may need to think about it for a while, but for most of us, retrieving the memory will be possible.

A second type of question asks you to gather the answer from somewhere else. For example, in Figure 3.7 a UK supermarket starts a feedback questionnaire by asking for a 4-digit code from a receipt or invitation card. The pictures of where to gather the answer in Figure 3.7 help quite a bit.

FIGURE 3.7
Gathering an answer from a supermarket receipt.

Occasionally, you'll have to ask someone else to get an answer. Maybe another person will remember something that you don't. ("I forgot which room number we had at that hotel. Can you recall it?") Or perhaps it's something that you never knew in the first place. ("Mom, do you know how old I was when I had that immunization shot?") If your questionnaire is going to a business, then one specific person may have to do a lot of asking others to get through it.

There's a final category: an answer that you have to create at the time you're asked. A British newspaper, the *Guardian*, asked me one of those recently, when it asked me in Figure 3.8 to decide how much I agree with the statement "I feel really close to the Guardian." It's not a topic that I'd ever thought about, so I didn't have an opinion conveniently in my head. I couldn't look up an answer on the web, and I think I'd have felt quite silly if I'd asked someone else, so I created an answer by thinking about it.

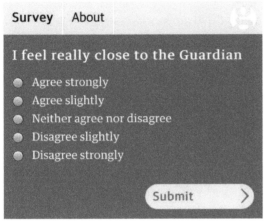

FIGURE 3.8
A question that made me create an answer.

Sometimes, the strategy that a person will use depends on the question and their own circumstances. For example, Figure 3.9 asks about products stocked in a grocery store.

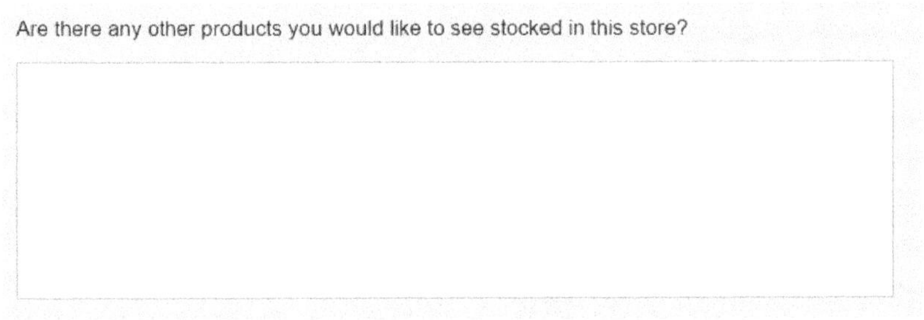

Are there any other products you would like to see stocked in this store?

FIGURE 3.9
Are there any products you would like to see stocked?

One person might need to think back, consulting their memory: "Now let me think. When I couldn't get that cereal—was that this store or that other one?"

If you've just had a frustrating experience in a grocery store, going in with a detailed list of items and failing to find some of them, then you might find the answer to "Are there any products you would like to see stocked?" by gathering your list of missing shopping items from your list.

Another person might, just possibly, ask someone else who went on the same shopping trip. "What was that beer you couldn't get yesterday?"

And yet another person might decide to be creative: "Now that you mention it, we're changing to a more plant-based way of eating so, hmm, let me see, how about tempeh?"

At this point, review your questions and think about the strategies you expect people might use to answer them. On the whole, "in-your-head strategies" are the easiest; if you expect people to gather an answer, ask someone else, or create an answer, then you're increasing the effort, which may stop people from finishing your questionnaire.

There is an approximate curve of forgetting

Let's think about memory for a specific event. You can only retrieve that memory accurately when:

- You noticed something about the event and remembered it in the first place.
- The memory was still there and accessible
- The memory hasn't gotten confused or overlaid with something else.

People remember some things better than others. If it's a major life event such as getting married, a special vacation, or a house move, then probably many details of it will be easy to recall a year later, or even more. Sometimes a distressing life event is so deeply memorable that the memory becomes a burden, leading to unpleasant flashbacks or even Post Traumatic Stress Disorder. Other memories can be a source of continuing joy, a "happy place" that can be revisited at will.

For many of us, there are noticeable, occasional events that we can remember quite well for a week or two, but then they start to fade. For example, I enjoy shopping for materials for quilting. I can easily recall the trip two weeks ago and the fabric I selected, but the details of the one a few months previously have gone, merged in my memory with earlier events.

Then there are unremarkable, repetitive events that we can barely recall an hour later. How many times have I looked at my phone today? No idea. (Although I can probably guess: too many.)

I've compared these different experiences in Figure 3.10.

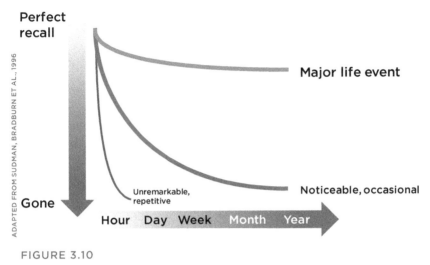

ADAPTED FROM SUDMAN, BRADBURN ET AL., 1996

FIGURE 3.10
The approximate curve of forgetting.

Ask about a recent, vivid experience

Let's take another look at Question 25, this time in Figure 3.11. It's asking about what for many of us—certainly for me—are exactly those unremarkable events that I wouldn't be able to recall. I might be able to estimate how much time I spent looking at a computer yesterday, but there's no chance of a good estimate of exactly what I did when I was using it.

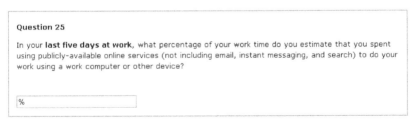

Question 25

In your **last five days at work**, what percentage of your work time do you estimate that you spent using publicly-available online services (not including email, instant messaging, and search) to do your work using a work computer or other device?

%

FIGURE 3.11
Question 25 asks about unremarkable, repetitive behavior.

Be realistic about the practicalities of recall. Choose time periods that are appropriate to the types of event you're asking about. Ask about people's recent, vivid experience to get the best data.

Distinguish between recall and recognition

The market researchers often want to know how people think or feel about brands, for clients who may be looking at their brand positioning or the effectiveness of a recent advertising campaign.

For example, when finding out about chocolate brands, as in Figure 3.12, a good researcher will always ask about recall first:

"Please name three chocolate brands."

and only then move on to recognition (also called *prompted recall*):

"Have you seen or heard anything about these chocolate brands recently?
- *Cadbury*
- *Hershey*
- *Nestle (and so on)*

FIGURE 3.12
If only all questionnaires were about chocolate.

Recall is the harder task: it relies on people caring enough about that product category to have laid down some memories around brands. That's exactly what a lot of advertising is aiming to do: it's trying to get you to focus on a brand for long enough to remember something about it.

Recognition is easier because it creates an immediate experience. But recognition has the disadvantage that it focuses you on the list offered—possibly driving away any other brands that might have been mentioned. Which ones can you think of?

Avoid asking for predictions of future behavior

Did you notice that the chocolate question asked about what you've seen and heard recently, not about which brand you planned to buy next?

That's an example of good survey practice: ask about events in the recent past, or what people think right now—not what they might do in the future.

If you ask someone to predict their behavior, then that's a created answer—and known to be somewhat unreliable. Think about your own behavior: if you've ever skipped a planned workout, eaten something that wasn't quite as healthy as you intended, or missed a deadline purely because your prediction of the time you needed wasn't very accurate, then you've got more than enough examples of your own.

So, sadly, there is not much "curve of prediction" to tell you which of those created answers about the future might be reliable, so Figure 3.13 features a large negative cross.

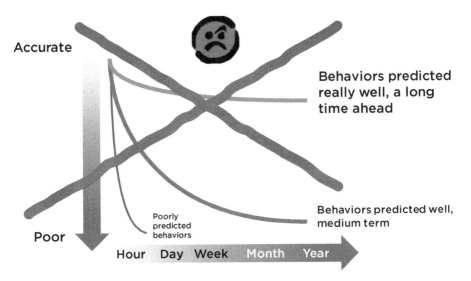

FIGURE 3.13
There is not much "curve of prediction."

The easy recommendation is: Don't ask people to predict behavior.

But I've seen too many MCQs that are exactly about predicting behavior. Three that I see all the time are:

1. "Will you buy this product?"
2. "Will this price make you more likely to buy?"
3. "Are you likely to recommend our product to a friend?" (Yes, that's the Net Promoter Score® that we met in Spotlight B.)

The more nuanced recommendation is:

> *If you must ask people to predict behavior, bear in mind that there is not much "curve of prediction."*

Good questions are comfortable to answer

Answering a question is a social act, and the third step, "Decide" in Figure 3.14, is about the decisions you make about whether you want to reveal your answer, or which answer to choose when there are several possibilities.

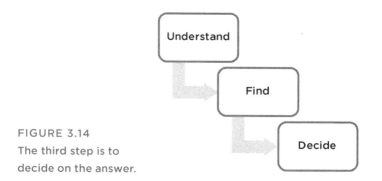

FIGURE 3.14
The third step is to
decide on the answer.

Psycholinguistics expert, Lise Menn, lists a selection of the ways that people use language to do things:

> *"People choose words to have the effects that they want on other people—to be polite, to be understood, to make other people feel like insiders or outsiders, to make them feel good or ashamed, to encourage or console, impress or inform." (Menn, 2011)*

A thoughtless choice of words, or a difference in perspective, can lead to tricky exchanges like this one in Figure 3.15.

FIGURE 3.15
An unconsidered answer can have a bad effect.

For most of us, most of the time, this process of deciding what to say and how to say it is unconscious.

Let's listen to this in an example from Kevin Cheng, illustrated in Figure 3.16:

> Let's say I was in a car when someone called and asked, "Where are you?" Here are some answers I could give:
>
> - "In a car." (It's somewhat useful but doesn't describe much.)
>
> - "In a black Subaru." (It might be completely unnecessary detail or might be incredibly useful if the person is on the lookout for your car.)
>
> - "On my way." (It has similar utility to "in a car" in that it conveys you are in motion but not much else.)

FIGURE 3.16
Where are you?

> - "Almost there." (It's much more useful information, even though it's quite vague.)
>
> - "At 4th and Main." [It's more precise and useful, although not necessarily indicating whether you're staying there or not (Cheng, 2012)].

You might add a few more choices, such as "stuck in traffic, so I don't know yet when I'll be with you."

The "decide" step is all about these little calculations about what sort of answer might be appropriate.

Privacy is important

> "I'm not telling you."

One of the most obvious decisions you can make is about what you're willing to reveal and to whom. A question about income might be impertinent from a business that's trying to sell you a hotel room, but acceptable (albeit onerous) from a government agency that's got a legal mandate to ask. Almost any question can be OK in one context, but unacceptable in another:

> "Where do you live?"
>
> "What's your email address?"
>
> "What's your Social Security number?"

In this internet age, when it's easy to get any question in front of a rich variety of people, we're also becoming acutely conscious that the answers may fall into the wrong hands.

Remember the Survey Octopus, Figure 3.17? The "decide" part of answering a question is deeply affected by the reason why you're asking and the concerns of the people who are answering.

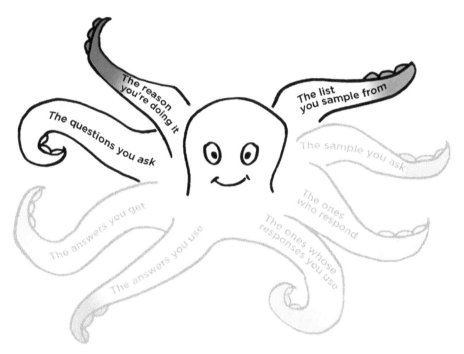

FIGURE 3.17
The acceptability of a question depends on why you're asking and who is answering.

Do they trust you enough to reveal their Social Security number in a survey? Probably not, and why do you need it anyway?

Do they trust you enough to reveal their email address in a survey? Maybe—it depends on what you're planning to do with it.

Do they trust you enough to tell you whether they have an email address or not? Probably—assuming that they know what "email address" means.

The context affects the decisions

Ordinary conversations are based on making inferences about relationships between consecutive statements.

If you consider it entirely on its own, a question such as:

Q: "Can you see the drugstore?"

might have several possible interpretations, including:

Q-a: "If you look around you right now, can you identify any stores that might be a drugstore?

Q-b: "Is this new branding for the drugstore bright enough to be visible in bad weather?"

Q-c: "Is your sight good enough for you to spot a drugstore?"

Does that seem like a stretch? You've recently been thinking about Kevin in his car, so Q-a probably seems like the obvious, most plausible interpretation.

If I change the context, the other interpretations might seem more realistic. For example, I might explain that the context in Q-b was a conversation about repositioning the brand. And the context in Q-c was in an optometrist's office.

Or maybe not—once you've settled on one view of a question, it's harder to be convinced by others.

These shifting sands, where a question can change its meaning depending on what happened previously, are well known to the survey methodologists who call them *context effects*.

> A **context effect** happens when a question changes its meaning according to its position in a questionnaire or in a conversation.

There are countless examples. One I'd especially like to mention is this example from psychologist Cordelia Fine:

Have you, for example, ever filled in a question on a form that looks something like this?

[ ] Male

[ ] Female

Even an innocently neutral question of this kind can prime gender. (Fine, 2010)

"Prime gender" means that questions like this remind women that society has gendered views of women's capabilities, and therefore leads them to reflect those gendered views in their answers. For example, Cordelia Fine describes an experiment where a gender-priming question led women to rate their math skills lower than women who did the same exercise but with a different preceding question. (Sinclair, Hardin et al., 2006)

Learning about gender priming has made me much more careful about whether I really need to ask about gender, and if so, I try hard to put the question toward the end of the questionnaire.

The context of the person who answers is also important

Typically, you create your questions within your world view, and that can be surprisingly different from the world view of the people you're asking. For example, here's an excerpt from a test of questions in the General Social Survey, a survey of contemporary American society run by the National Data Program for the Social Sciences based at the University of Chicago. In this example, the question as written assumes that people would identify with a political party—but this respondent clearly did not. *I* means *Interviewer,* R is *Respondent,* and :: signifies *prolongation of the preceding word.*

I: *Generally speaking, do you usually think of yourself as a Republican, Democrat, Independent, or what?*

R: *As a person.*

I: *As a Republican::*

R: *No.*

I: *Democrat::*

R: *No.*

I: *Independent or what.*

R: *Uhm:: I think of myself as (pause) Christian.*

I: *OK. (writing). But politically, would you have any particular: (inaudible)*

R: *I am one of Jehovah's Witnesses so, you know, when it comes to:*

I: *I see.*

R: *So I'm, I am acclimated toward government, but it is that of Jehovah God's Kingdom.*

(Suchman and Jordan, 1992)

Yes, that excerpt came from a book published in 1992, but I can assure you that difficulties about deciding how to answer are as frequent today as they were then. For example, in the week before writing this sentence, surveys from two different organizations asked me questions about "support for my local community" that I couldn't decide how to answer because the communities that I'm part of are based on shared interests, such as the charity that we support, not on geography.

Deciding on an answer can be painful

Sometimes the process of finding an answer "in your head" can stir up painful memories or bring to mind a topic that's deeply sensitive and that makes the decision about what to reveal or not to reveal a difficult one.

Let's return, briefly, to that frequently seen question about gender. Cordelia Fine described it as "innocently neutral." Here's another view, from s.e. smith:

> *"For some trans* folk, it is a place of endless heartbreak. Every. Single. Time. I fill out a form, I stop here. There is a long pause. A hesitation. A sigh. I am not male. I am not female. On paper forms, I often leave it blank. . . .*
>
> *Think about how it would feel to fill out a form with checkboxes which do not include a space for you.*
>
> *Imagine doing this over, and over, and over again. Imagine dreading the filling out of forms not because it's a hassle and it's repetitive and it's not very fun. Imagine dreading it because you know that you are going to have to lie and erase yourself every time you fill out a form."* (smith, 2009)

Of course, questionnaires are optional, so if any people in your defined group feel like s.e. smith when asked a question about gender, they have the option of breaking off. But the negative side is that you lose their data, you lose their views, and maybe (if this is a survey of customers) you lose their goodwill.

Conscious sensitivity about gender may be relatively rare, but there are many other topics that can stir up difficult emotions, such as bereavement, illness, divorce, or losing a job.

Sara Wachter-Boettcher writes movingly about the emotions and decisions that went through her mind when she had to answer the question:

> *Ich bin das __ Kind meiner Mutter, one form says: "I am the __ child of my mother" (Wachter-Boettcher, 2015).*

For many of us, revealing the birth order in our families would have no particular resonance, but Sara had a brother who died in infancy.

Fortunately for us, Sara channeled her powerful emotions into the excellent book *Design for Real Life*, in Figure 3.18, that she wrote with Eric Meyer.

FIGURE 3.18

Design for Real Life. (Eric Meyer and Sara Wachter-Boettcher, 2016)

Good questionnaires make it easy to respond

Most traditional surveys rely on an interviewer—face-to-face, or more recently, on the telephone. The interviewer reads out the questions from the questionnaire, and the person who answers gives their response to the interviewer. The interviewer must record the response accurately, and sometimes that includes an on-the-spot interpretation of the answer to work out how to record it—the final respond step, as in Figure 3.19.

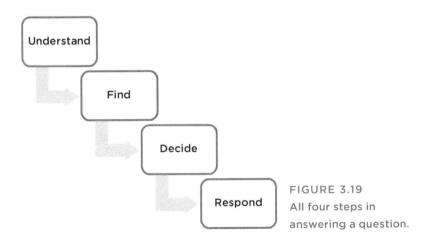

FIGURE 3.19

All four steps in answering a question.

With newfangled ideas, like getting someone to do a web survey, that respond task shifts over to the person who is answering the question. Creating a good questionnaire that makes it easy to respond is such a big topic that we're going to give it an entire chapter, Chapter 4 "Questionnaire," coming up.

Test your questions in cognitive interviews

You'll save a lot of time and effort when making your questionnaire by testing the questions first.

If you did the interviews to find Burning Issues that I recommended at the end of Chapter 2, "Sample," then you'll be one step ahead, because those interviews typically start to reveal any problems of a clash of world views, or issues with privacy and trust.

Even so, now that you have specific questions, some cognitive interviews are definitely worth the effort in order to reveal the detailed problems hidden within.

Try a little cognitive interview

Try this little cognitive interview yourself. Answer this question, and as you do so, think aloud and notice the processes you go through.

"How many windows are there in your house?"

Did you notice any hesitation or confusion? Maybe you live in something other than a house or are currently not exactly living in any fixed location.

Maybe you weren't sure what counts as a window. My friend has some interior windows in the wall between her kitchen and her living room. Do they count? Our front door, pictured in Figure 3.20, has two glass panels in it that could count as zero, one, or two windows.

And what about your answering strategy: did you happen to know the answer for some reason, perhaps because you recently had all the windows replaced, or did you mentally stand outside the house and look at it or take yourself on a walk from room to room? Did you keep a mental running tally, or use your fingers, or write notes?

FIGURE 3.20

I live in an 1896 house with glass panels in the door.

That's a flavor of the rich variety of things you'll find out when you try some cognitive interviewing on your questions.

Do cognitive interviews with people in your defined group

Find a few people in your defined group and invite them to try some questions for you. (I avoid using the technical term *cognitive interviewing* when I'm setting up the sessions.)

If you expect people to work through your questionnaire in a group, then it's fine to test the questions with a focus group.

I invariably expect that people will answer the questionnaire on their own, so I aim to do cognitive interviews with one person at a time—but, of course, that person is welcome to bring a helper, carer, family member, or friend, if they'd usually have that person with them when they tackle a questionnaire.

I usually ask the person to work through the questions one-by-one and to do the following:

- Read the question aloud.
- Explain it back to me in their own words.
- Think aloud to find some potential answers.
- Tell me about the choice of which answer to give.

Meanwhile, I'm listening quietly and taking notes. The "listening quietly" is the hard part—focused listening is fascinating but tiring.

Most of all, cognitive interviewing is far, far quicker and more interesting than sitting in a meeting with stakeholders trying to write the questions in the first place, or (if you're a team of one) trying to second-guess what the people who answer will make of your questions all on your own.

What could possibly go wrong with the questions?

Writing questions isn't easy. There's a risk that the people in your defined group:

- Won't understand your questions.
- Will understand them in a way that is different from what you intended.
- Won't have an answer.
- Will have an inaccurate answer.
- Won't want to give you their answer.

Measurement error happens when questions do not work well

If any of those things happen, you've got "measurement error."

Measurement error is the difference between the true value of the answer and the answer you get.

It's the error that falls in the gap in Figure 3.21 between two tentacles of the Survey Octopus: "The questions you ask" and "The answers you get."

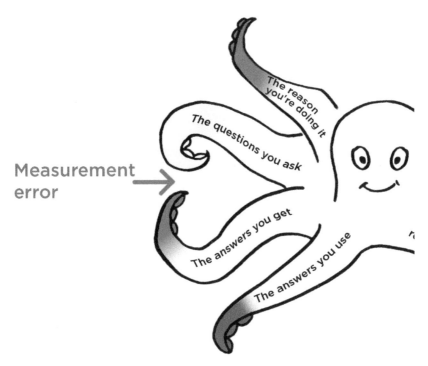

Measurement error

FIGURE 3.21
Measurement error happens in the gap between the questions you ask and the answers you get.

One uncomfortable, but major, potential source of measurement error is a Most Crucial Question that people can't or won't answer. The uncomfortable part comes from this dilemma:

- Option 1: Press on with the survey, knowing that you'll have lots of error in the final result?

  Or:

- Option 2: Iterate, returning to the Goals step to find a new Most Crucial Question?

Obviously, I hope you'll choose Option 2: Iterate, especially as it gives you another chance to include consideration of the Burning Issues that you discovered in your interviews in Chapter 2. But even if you decide to press on, it's better to discover that you might have a problem at this stage when there are still opportunities to help the people you want to answer, maybe by writing a better invitation or wording the Most Crucial Question slightly differently.

At this point, you will know

All this work on questions means that by now you have a set of questions that:

- Include the Most Crucial Question that will help you make the decision.
- Include the Burning Issue, the topic that they most want to talk to you about.
- Can be understood and answered easily by people.

It's time to turn them into a questionnaire, which you'll do in Chapter 4.

On the way, you'll find essential reading in Spotlight E, "Privacy." Please make sure that you read it.

And there are two additional Spotlights:

- Spotlight F, "Questions to Ask When You Choose a Survey Tool," because it's a topic that I get asked about a lot.
- If you are open to consider delivering your questionnaire as something other than a web survey, then have a look at Spotlight G, "Choose Your Mode—Web, Paper, or Something Else?"

Privacy

When you have your questions, it's crucial to think about privacy before you start to build your questionnaire.

Let's think about a couple of examples. On a random day, I put "Data Breach" into my usual search engine and had a look at the "News" results. They included stories of data breaches at a supplier to Boy Scouts of America, Pearson (a major educational publisher), and a supplier to the New Zealand government, as in the news story in Figure E.1.

FIGURE E.1
One of many examples of data breaches.

Another day, another data breach, and another big embarrassment—possibly even a massive fine—for some organization that has failed to deal properly with privacy. It's easy to think "I'm glad that it's not my job."

And you may be right: if you have privacy experts in your organization, then you can skip this Spotlight and go consult them. (But you might want to read it anyway so that you are armed with the key ideas before you open the discussion.)

Or you may be like me and responsible for privacy matters yourself. So I asked Heather Burns, a privacy expert in Scotland, to help us. She works with software projects and developers to help them to improve their approach to privacy.

She's not a lawyer—she says, "That's the whole point of my work, really"—and neither am I, so don't mistake this introduction for legal advice.

Why you need a Privacy Impact Assessment (PIA) for a survey and how to make one

Q: I'm a bit daunted by privacy. Isn't it a lot of legal mumbo-jumbo with the possibility of fines?

A: It's important to realize that good privacy practice isn't scary, and it may not need a roomful of lawyers either. It's about making sensible, proactive decisions that put the user first and protect your work in the process.

Q: By "users" of surveys, do you mean the people who are answering your questions?

A: Correct.

Q: If I've got to sort out the privacy concerns myself for my survey, where do I start?

A: There are two things you need to think of:

- How you protect yourself, internally.
- How you protect your users, externally.

For the first—yourself—you need to anticipate any privacy issues before they happen. I do that by helping clients to develop a Privacy Impact Assessment.

Q: What exactly is a Privacy Impact Assessment?

A: A Privacy Impact Assessment is usually abbreviated to PIA. It is a means of discussing and documenting any privacy risks in the work that you're doing and the information that you're collecting. It acknowledges that you have sat down and thought about these issues, identified any precautions you need to take, and written down your decisions for the record.

Q: Is a PIA the same as the privacy notice that you see on most websites?

A: No. The privacy notice is the public document that you'll do in step 2: protecting your users, externally. A PIA document is strictly internal. Technically, in the event of a data breach or a privacy concern, a data protection regulator can request to see a copy of your PIA.

Q: Does everyone need a PIA?

A: My rule is "If you have to ask if you need one, then you do." A data breach can hit the news in a way that you really don't want it to.

Think hard, and creatively, about what risks are inherent to your organization and the project you are working on:

- Reputational damage?
- Bad media coverage?
- An angry data protection regulator?
- A class action lawsuit from aggrieved data owners?

Even if you are a lone student or a person with a small business, these days the social media can be savage.

Yes, this is something where you'll be thinking about legal matters, but don't necessarily look at it in terms of "comply or die." Think of best practice, creating user trust, and transparency of your work. There's absolutely a legal element to that, but it's about being good people as well.

Q: What goes into a good PIA?

A: Here are the steps I'd recommend.

1. Set up your document. Invest time in making a template you can use fresh on every new project.

2. Describe:
   - The information you're gathering
   - Why you're collecting it
   - What you're using it for
   - Who you're collecting it from
   - Where you will store it
   - Who will have access to it
   - How long you will keep it
   - How you will aggregate it
   - What you will do with your survey data at the end

3. Describe how this information flows:
   - From your users to you
   - From your users to a survey tool
   - From you to your partners
   - From your survey tool to third parties

   Think very hard. It's the information flows that can surprise you, especially ones from your survey tool to third parties. If you have not yet read the privacy policy for your survey tool, now would be a good time.

4. Identify who is doing the work here.
   - Who has access to the data?
   - Who is in charge?
   - Who is responsible?
   - Whose job is it to deal with user concerns?
   - Whose job is it if something goes wrong?
   - Who is keeping an eye on things, such as who is accessing the data?
   - If a data protection regulator wants to raise a concern, who is the point of contact?

5. Identify what privacy and data protection risks are inherent in the data. What would happen if your dataset was:
   - Misused?
   - Compromised?
   - Breached?
   - Aggregated with other information?

6. Identify and list what you're doing to mitigate these risks and prevent them, as much as you can, from ever happening.

7. Record everything you've done in steps 1 through 5 and sign the record. Someone's name needs to be on this sheet.

8. Amend and update the PIA as necessary. Use it in your project postmortem.

9. Rinse and repeat.

And my top tip is: If your PIA process raises questions like "Should we even be doing this?" or "Is this legal?"—you may have bigger issues than a document template.

Q: That looks like a lot of work, but I can see how it will repay the effort to keep the first one and amend it. Please tell me that having a good PIA will make it super quick and easy to write a privacy policy? Please?

A: Yes, absolutely. People want to know what's being done with their data and if they can trust the people asking. If you've done your PIA thoughtfully, then you'll know both of those things.

Here's what I want to see in a public-facing privacy notice:

- What data are you collecting about me?
- Why are you collecting it? That needs to be specific.
- Is that reasoning legally and socially justified, or are you a data vampire sucking my data blood?
- Which third parties are you sharing it with? Are you just a middleman?
- What third-party data are you aggregating it with (even if that's an online ad network)?
- Who else will have access to it?
- How long are you keeping it?
- Is it being aggregated or stripped of personally identifiable information?
- Should I expect any follow-up? What if I don't ever want to hear from you again?
- What if I change my mind later and decide that I don't want you to have my data anymore? How can I get it back from you?

Q: Yes, I can see how those questions look a bit daunting on their own, although I didn't expect the vampire. I can also see that if you've done the work of the PIA thoughtfully, then they are relatively easy to answer. So now I've got my privacy notice, where do I need to put it?

A: The people who answer must be able to read it easily.

- For an online questionnaire, include the privacy notice as an early question ("Would you like to read our privacy notice?") or provide a link to a website plus an easy way to get back to the questionnaire.

- For a face-to-face questionnaire, provide your interviewers with paper copies to hand out.

- For a phone questionnaire, the interviewer must be able to read aloud the privacy notice. Work hard to make it short enough to be comprehensible.

- On an ambient questionnaire (one that's left around for people to pick up, such as the little questionnaires sometime seen on café tables), include a printed link to a website notice.

- On a paper questionnaire, sometimes privacy notices are printed on the back of the invitation letter so that anyone who wants to read it can flip it over.

- Kiosks are a little tricky. It's probably best to have your link printed onto the kiosk itself for the very simple questionnaires with only a single question or button. If your kiosk contains a multi-page questionnaire, then that's more like online, and it's best to build the privacy notice into a question.

Q: Any final thoughts?

A: It's easier when you embrace privacy as part of everything you do for the better. Try not to think of privacy as a scary, negative legal problem to run away from. It's an opportunity for trust and user empowerment that will make you a better professional.

Questions to Ask When You Choose a Survey Tool

It's a Frequently Asked Question: "Which is the best survey tool?"

It's not an easy question to answer because there are hundreds of tools available at all price points. New ones appear all the time, and older ones disappear or change. Also, the best survey tool for me may not be the best one for you. Or even, especially in larger organizations, the best survey tool for one survey may not be the best one for a different one.

So I'm not going to recommend any specific tool, but instead give you some things to think about when making your choice.

Are you familiar with a particular tool?

If you already know one of the tools, why not continue with it? You'll save time on a learning curve, and that's time you can spend on testing your questionnaire and iterating.

Do you care about privacy?

Yes, this is a trick question. Did you read Spotlight E? If not, go back and read it now—it's essential.

The good news is that, so far, every survey tool provider I've looked at has a privacy policy.

The bad news is that those policies are highly variable. My experience is that it is not easy to disentangle what the tool provider expects you to do to safeguard the privacy of the people who answer and what it will do for you.

The other bad news is that some features of online tools that you might want (like: Can it stop someone from responding twice?) rely on tracking people in ways that can easily compromise their anonymity.

Make sure that you set aside plenty of time to read the privacy policy of any tool that you consider. Pack a lunch.

Do you care about accessibility?

Yes, "Do you care about accessibility?" is another trick question. Of course you care about accessibility! It's the right thing to do.

You don't want to make it difficult for people with access needs to respond to your questionnaire. And in these days of widespread use of social media, who wants to be the person who has to deal with angry comments along the lines of "I wanted to answer the questionnaire from organization X, but I couldn't increase the size of the text?"

Unfortunately, accessibility is a badly neglected area in survey tools. Although some of the tools claim to include access features for the people responding to the questionnaire, none of the vendors seem to realize that people with access needs might be trying to run a survey—even though in many countries, it's a legal requirement to ensure that the tools you choose are accessible for current and future employees.

By the time you read this, I hope that tools will be better. Meanwhile, if you have access needs yourself, or any colleagues with access needs might work on your survey, then all I'm able to do is to recommend that you try a small survey with whatever tool you can get hold of—and make a huge fuss if it doesn't work for you.

To find out whether your questionnaire might work for people with access needs, the best thing to do is to choose a tool that at least claims some level of accessibility for respondents and then make sure that when you test your questionnaire, you include some people with access needs in your tests. There's an example of how to do it in Case Study 2, "Doing a Survey with People Who Use Assistive Technology."

Does your organization already have a survey tool?

I've discovered that even the smallest organizations may have subscriptions to one or more of the popular internet survey tools. Any large organization is likely to have a market research or customer insight department that pays big bucks for a full-featured market research tool. Using something that you already have saves money, and often you'll get the bonus of free help from the colleagues who are more familiar with it.

Also, linking up with the other users of your organization's tool means that you can coordinate your survey with other surveys that are happening—and maybe combine efforts, or discover that you don't need to do your survey at all because another team has already asked similar questions.

Do you need panel management as part of the service?

Back in Chapter 2, we looked at three methods of finding a sample: "narrow down," "snowball up," and "in the moment."

One special example of "narrow down" from a public list is using a panel: a list maintained by the survey tool vendor.

If a survey tool or a market research business offers to supply you with a list of people to ask, or to send invitations for you, then they'll be drawing on their proprietary panels that they have nearly always recruited by "iterate up" methods: People opt in to the panel by volunteering themselves.

These panels have their advantages:

- People on the panel have said that they are willing to be invited to complete surveys.
- The panel provider's network is very likely to be different from your own network.

Their disadvantage is that, in common with all "snowball up" methods, they have lots of problems with coverage.

If you need to make sure that your respondents represent people in general for a one-off survey, then panels are not a good way to find a sample for these reasons:

- They recruit panel members online and rely on sending them web questionnaires, so you won't reach anyone with poor or no internet access.

- On some types of panel, the members get constant invitations to respond to Big Honkin' Surveys that are firmly stuck in the 1950's "ask everything" mindset. People who stay on the panel for any length of time must have a high tolerance for answering lots of questions and time on their hands. This is not the place to find busy people.
- On other types of panels, members rarely get an invitation, so they get bored and leave.

If you use these panels iteratively and ask some carefully chosen questions to help you assess the representativeness of your sample, then the first time you do a survey with a panel, you can learn something about the composition of the panel and how people on the panel react to your topics and questions. Then for the second and subsequent iterations, you can judge whether the people who answer those iterations are representative compared to the previous time.

It's important to use the same panel for each iteration, as in Figure F.1.

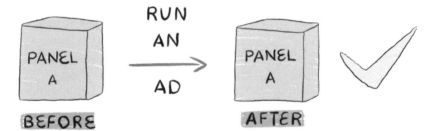

FIGURE F.1

To compare reactions before and after running an ad, you need to get your samples from the same panel each time.

Panels can work very well for market researchers doing comparative surveys. Let's say you want to learn whether existing purchasers of Choco-xx might enjoy purchasing new gluten-free Choco-gf when they have seen the exciting Choco-gf advertising. You could run a sample from the panel to assess how many of them are Choco-xx buyers and ask them about their thoughts on gluten. Then run it again once you've aired the Choco-gf advertising. Now it doesn't matter all that much how representative the original sample was: you're comparing before-and-after results from the same panel.

Because this type of before-and-after comparison relies on using the same panel each time, major brands are very cautious about where they get their samples initially, because changing is expensive. To keep comparability, each change means using both the old and the new panel in parallel for a while (at double the cost) to find out how the old and new compare so that they can calibrate the new panel.

Sound complicated? You're right, it is. And I've mentioned all of this because the apparently "simple" solution of buying a sample from a vendor may turn out to be rather more complicated in practice.

Don't fall into the mistake that I've seen from time to time: choosing the tool first and then deciding to use a purchased sample because the tool offers it. Don't let your choice of tool determine your sampling strategy.

If you choose to set up your own panel rather than relying on one that's offered by your survey tool vendor, then have a look at an article that I wrote with Naintara Land: "7 Questions About User-Research Panels," www.uxmatters.com/mt/archives/2017/06/7-questions-about-user-research-panels.php.

Will the tool let you download the data?

Many survey tools offer a variety of "instant" reports. There's a possibility that these will give you the analysis that you need, but my experience has been that it's much harder to do data cleaning (coming up in Chapter 6, "Response") within the tools. I always prefer to download the data to my preferred spreadsheet. Most survey tools will let you download the data, but be sure to confirm before committing to the tool, especially as this can be an option that is not available in the free or trial version.

Do you need translations?

If you need translations, look for tools that offer support for the languages that you need, such as handling appropriate accents and language-specific conventions for punctuation. Make sure that you test the questionnaire in each language you offer with people who are native speakers of that language.

How much are you willing to spend?

It's always worth asking about costs, but this is an area where "more expensive tool" definitely doesn't always mean "better for your survey." The extra expense may add things that you do not need, such as more respondents, panel management, or different people creating surveys at the same time.

For example, I was doing a survey with a tool that allowed up to 100 responses in the free trial version. I gave in to the temptation to splash the cash for a "paid for" because I thought extra responses would look more impressive. I forgot that I was spending money to give myself more work in analysis and that the extra work wasn't going to make any difference to the decision we made.

Do you have to create lots of Big Honkin' Surveys?

Although I'll continue to urge you to try Light Touch Surveys ahead of the Big Honkin' Surveys, I definitely understand that professional life is a compromise between best practice and what circumstances allow.

If you've got to manage multiple Big Honkin' Surveys, then look for features such as version control, the ability to reuse questions across different questionnaires, and creating access to the tool for more than one survey organizer at a time.

Features of survey tools that you probably don't need

This brings me to the last topic in choosing a survey tool: things that you almost certainly don't need.

I picked out a small selection of features from the marketing blurb of some top-of-the-range tools.

TABLE F.1   A SELECTION OF FEATURES IN SURVEY TOOLS AND WHY YOU MAY NOT NEED THEM

Feature	Meaning	Why you may not need it
A/B test text and images	Running two tests at the same time to compare the effect of a small change (A) with another approach (B) to see which one gets the "best result," usually the most clicks.	You might need to do an A/B test, but that's a different matter from your survey. Don't choose a tool because it offers help with a completely different method.
100+ question types	Some survey tool vendors use the term "question type" to describe ways of presenting a question, such as having an open text box or a slider.	We're about to look at ways of presenting questions in the next chapter. I call them "response formats" and recommend sticking to a small number of simple ones.
Survey review powered by artificial intelligence	A computer program will look at your questionnaire and give feedback about problems, like whether it is too long.	You're applying real intelligence by using this book and doing the testing with people that I suggest.

If you looked at those features and thought "Well, I use all of them"—busted! You've clearly already got survey tools, and that brings me back to my question, "Are you already familiar with a particular tool?"

But for the rest of us: don't be persuaded to buy a more expensive tool purely for the extra features. Get started on building your questionnaire in whatever happens to be convenient and will help you to get testing more quickly with the people you want to answer.

I've done a lot of my question development in Microsoft Word because it's familiar, it is good enough for me to collect my questions for cognitive interviews, and I'm often working with stakeholders who aren't comfortable with anything else. Those advantages are enough for me to outweigh the difficulties of wrangling Microsoft Word, which was never designed as a survey tool, and the extra work of transferring everything into a different tool when I build the actual questionnaire.

A note for people who prefer "build your own tool"

If you have development skills and generally build your own forms and websites, then in my mind that comes under the heading "use the tool that's familiar." Go for it! One advantage of this approach is that you can store all the data on your organization's own servers, so you don't have to worry about the privacy policies of third-party survey tools. Of course, you'll still have to consider your own organization's privacy policy.

An extra suggestion, though: set aside a couple of hours to do a technical investigation of how long it takes you to build your own questionnaire compared to building the same questionnaire in one of the popular survey tools, and have a look at the features offered by the tools, such as management of access from the same IP address. That will quickly give you an idea of whether it's better for you personally to invest your time in building your questionnaire from scratch or to use a tool.

Some developers I know are much quicker and more comfortable with build-your-own; others prefer to get to grips with a survey tool (which they generally do much faster than most people anyway) for the purposes of an occasional questionnaire.

CASE STUDY 2

Doing a survey with people who use assistive technology

Chris Moore is the Digital Accessibility Champion for Her Majesty's Revenue and Customs (HMRC, the UK tax authority). Chris is himself a user of assistive technology, as he is both blind and deaf; the setup he uses is in Figure CS2.1. He collaborated with Alistair Duggin, who at the time was Head of Accessibility for the UK Government Digital Service (GDS), to run a survey for GDS.

FIGURE CS2.1

A selection of devices that Chris uses for accessibility testing.

COURTESY OF HTTPS://ACCESSIBILITY.BLOG.
GOV.UK/2016/07/01/ACCESSIBILITY-AND-ME-CHRIS-MOORE/

GDS is responsible for GOV.UK, the single website for the UK government. The GDS accessibility team wanted to know about the range of assistive technologies used by people accessing GOV.UK and decided that a survey was the best way to find out. You can read more about what they found in Chris's blog post: "Results of the 2016 GOV.UK Assistive Technology Survey" https://accessibility.blog.gov.uk/2016/11/01/results-of-the-2016-gov-uk-assistive-technology-survey/.

I interviewed Chris and Alistair about their experience of running the survey.

continues

CASE STUDY 2 (continued)

Q. Your survey absolutely had to be usable by people who rely on assistive technology, as that was the whole purpose of the survey. How did you choose a tool?

Chris: I started by creating a draft survey in Google Forms. I could use it with my assistive technology, but when I looked at the way the HTML was written, I had some concerns. Also, Google Forms needed to be tied to a single user's account and offered inferior analytical features. My first test was with Alistair, and we agreed we needed to look elsewhere.

Alistair: I had a look at the HTML of the questions created by a number of tools to see if they followed best practice for forms. None of them did, and none of them had what would be considered best practice code for forms. We chose Survey Monkey, as it had the best markup out of the bunch, but it was by no means perfect.

Chris: And we also noted that RNIB, the UK's leading charity for people who are affected by sight loss, uses Survey Monkey for their own surveys so that gave us some confidence that screen reader users would be able to respond to our questionnaire.

Q. Did you do anything special when you created the questionnaire?

Chris: We kept the form very simple by sticking to a single question on each page. There were bells and whistles we could have used in Survey Monkey, but they came with accessibility trade-offs, too.

We also offered alternative ways (Word document or phone) for people to provide the information if they weren't able to use Survey Monkey.

Q. Did you make the right choice?

Alistair: We got 712 responses, and that gave us lots of great information for making decisions about which assistive technologies to use when testing GOV.UK, so the answer must be "Yes."

Chris: We had about 10 people who asked to use our alternative ways of providing information, so we were glad that we provided those options.

Q. Would you do anything different if you were doing a similar survey again?

Alistair: In February 2018, Terrill Thompson published an analysis of how four popular tools dealt with one of the most important question types: "Multiple Choice with Radio Buttons: A Comparison of Online Survey Tools" http://terrillthompson.com/blog/854 and found many problems that might trip up people using access technologies—similar to the ones that we'd discovered in our review.

By the next time we do a survey, we hope that the survey tool vendors will be doing a better job of supporting accessibility standards.

Q. Any other tips for people running a survey?

Chris: Don't forget about making your reports accessible for colleagues who use assistive technology. We published our results on the GDS Accessibility blog, and we know that many people who read the blog use assistive technology themselves.

continues

CASE STUDY 2 (continued)

For example, I used a bar chart (in Figure CS2.2) to show results for people who can use images and an accompanying table (Table CS2.1) with the same results as text for people like me who don't read images.

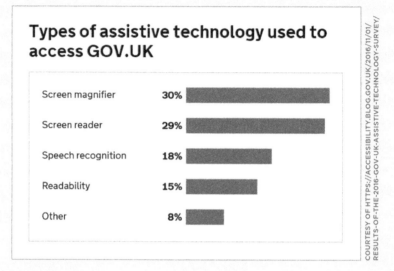

FIGURE CS2.2
A bar chart of results.

TABLE CS2.1   THE PROPORTION OF RESPONDENTS WHO USE
                VARIOUS TYPES OF ASSISTIVE TECHNOLOGY

Assistive technology	Proportion of respondents
Screen magnifier	30%
Screen reader	29%
Speech recognition	18%
Readability	15%
Other	8%

Choose Your Mode: Web, Paper, or Something Else?

Most of the surveys I see these days pop up at me when I visit a website, and many of the remainder arrive by an email invitation. So just as a wild guess, I'm going to assume that when I say "Build your questionnaire," you've got a web questionnaire in mind, and you plan to invite your defined group of people through a web method such as a pop-up, banner, or email invitation.

But let's pause for a moment to consider whether something else might get you a better response rate and, even more importantly, a more representative response.

To explore this, try collecting some data yourself: over the next week (or whatever length of time you feel able to devote to it, try counting the number of times you receive:

- A pop-up, banner, or other web-based invitation to a web questionnaire
- An email invitation to a web questionnaire
- A questionnaire sent to you on paper in the mail
- And maybe even, if you're willing to accept some calls from unknown numbers for the length of your experiment, a phone call asking you to respond to a questionnaire

Survey methodologists talk about mode, and they're usually referring to questionnaires:

1. Delivered in a face-to-face interview.
2. Sent in the mail on paper.
3. Delivered in a phone interview.
4. Sent as an email invitation to a web questionnaire.

And there are two more modes that I'd like to throw into the discussion:

1. A questionnaire placed somewhere handy, like the ones that are located next to a cup of coffee in a café. (I call these ambient.)

2. A dedicated kiosk placed where people might answer as they walk by, as in Figure G.1.

FIGURE G.1
A "happy face" kiosk has buttons with faces.

Let's ignore the complication of using more than one mode or a mix of modes, and instead try a showdown on the benefits and challenges of each mode based on a few of the key ideas from the previous chapters.

Mode showdown: Keep your questionnaire short

People often ask me: "How long can my questionnaire be?"

My answer is: "Short enough to encourage people to complete it; long enough to respect their efforts and obtain useful insight." But it also depends on the mode you are using.

As a starting point, I use the guidelines in Table G.1.

TABLE G.1 SUGGESTED MAXIMUM NUMBER OF QUESTIONS FOR DIFFERENT MODES

Mode	Maximum questions	Why this is the right length
Web invitation to web questionnaire	One question	Most people will refuse to answer more than one question.
Ambient	Ideally one question, but can support an extra question or two	These work best when they are no larger than a postcard. The text needs to be large enough to read easily, so you're very limited in the number of questions.
Kiosk	Mostly: one question Some designs can support up to about five questions	The "happy face" style of kiosk can only support one question. Some bespoke kiosks can support any length of questionnaire, but you can't expect people to stand and answer for more than a minute or two.
Email invitation to a web questionnaire	10 minutes maximum, for example: 10 closed questions and one open box	You are framing a more substantial piece of research. It's more of a conversation.
Paper	Ideally, keep within the 10 minutes maximum	In theory, a paper questionnaire can be any length you like. In practice, attention wanes.
Face-to-face or telephone interview	15 minutes maximum, mostly open questions	This ought to be a genuine conversation and open to whatever topics your respondent wants to raise.

Mode showdown: Get answers from the right people

In Chapter 2, we had a look at how to select the sample from your defined group, with three strategies:

- Catch people in the moment.
- Snowball up.
- Narrow down from a list.

If you've chosen "catch people in the moment," then the clear winner for your mode is face-to-face. As the interviewer, you'll be right there observing people and approaching them according to whatever sampling strategy you have decided upon. Of course, many of them will say "no," but it may be just as easy for them to say "yes" to a well-designed face-to-face approach.

The runners-up are ambient and kiosk. Both of them are available to people who want to respond "in the moment," just like the face-to-face approach, but response rates are likely to be much lower. Turning down a polite invitation from a real person takes some effort, whereas ignoring an ambient questionnaire or a kiosk takes almost no effort at all.

Without an interviewer, it's hard to know who is really answering, as I learned one day when I spotted a kiosk at the exit of a store. There were no other customers around, so I had a chat with the clerk at the desk next to it. She told me that, yes, they got lots of button presses: nearly all from bored children who were attracted by the fun faces and passed the time by tapping all of them. I've also seen a kiosk placed at the exit of a public restroom, which suggested to me that the only people who would answer were those with a lot more faith in the ability of others to wash their hands meticulously than I have.

Against that, a leader in the happy face kiosk market, HappyOrNot, claims that their response rates are far greater than is usually the case for ambient questionnaires, especially when installed in places with thousands of people who might want to express an opinion, such as a football stadium. And, indeed, a kiosk might be a way to let annoyed customers vent a little without confronting staff. ("Customer Satisfaction at the Push of the Button," *New Yorker*, 2018: www.newyorker.com/magazine/2018/02/05/customer-satisfaction-at-the-push-of-a-button)

And a final argument in favor of kiosks: they don't have to be the "happy face" type at all. I've seen visitors waiting in line to answer quite extensive questionnaires at several different types of museums.

If you've chosen "snowball up," then the clear winner as you start to build your list is the web questionnaire. The response rates on web questionnaires are generally terrible, but a web questionnaire is easy for people to share and forward to other people on social media.

All the other modes are much harder for people to share. Let's look at a story around face-to-face. Picture the scene: you're shopping in a mall, no urgency. An interviewer approaches you to do a questionnaire with an appropriate incentive—maybe a voucher for a coffee shop. You do the questionnaire, it's fine, and you'd like to recommend it to a friend. But the interviewer has moved on, and the friend isn't in the mall right now, so how do you do that?

If you've chosen "narrow down from a list," then the clear winners are phone interviews or a questionnaire on paper sent in the mail, as shown in Table G.2. Surprised? Because both of those are expensive options? I agree that it seems a bit strange, in these days of digital everything and expecting most people to have access to the web, to be recommending the apparently old-fashioned paper and phone. The reason: although response rates to mail surveys and to phone interviews are much lower now than was typical a decade or so ago, they are still much, much better than typical response rates on the other modes.

TABLE G.2 GETTING AN ANSWER FROM THE RIGHT PEOPLE

Strategy	Results
"catch people in the moment"	Winner: face-to-face
	Runners-up: ambient questionnaire, kiosk
	Loser: web invitation to web questionnaire
"snowball up"	Winner: web invitation to web questionnaire
	Losers: everything else
"narrow down from a list"	Winners: sent in the mail on paper and phone interviews
	Losers: everything else

Mode showdown: Cost of each response you can use

The final topic in our showdown is cost.

Stakeholders typically look at what they will have to spend on sending the invitation, and the different modes typically rank as shown in Table G.3:

TABLE G.3 HOW STAKEHOLDERS MIGHT RANK THE DIFFERENT MODES

Range of costs	Modes
High spend per invitation $$$$	Face-to-face
	Phone
	Paper
	Ambient
	Email invitation
Low spend per invitation $	Web invitation

If you look at the modes from the point of view of the people you want to answer, the ranking changes as in Table G.4. Many people are bombarded daily with opportunities to respond to surveys. The effort required to ignore a web or email invitation is low; the comparative rarity of other methods can make them seem intriguing and improve perceived reward.

TABLE G.4 POSSIBLE PERCEIVED EFFORT TO REWARD RATIO FOR DIFFERENT MODES

Effort to reward ratio	Mode
Poor effort to reward ratio	Web invitation
	Email invitation
	Ambient
	Paper
	Phone
Good effort to reward ratio	Face-to-face

Did you spot that the two lists are exactly opposite to each other?

One way to reconcile the different points of view is to calculate cost per response.

> The **cost per response** is the total cost of the invitations, reminders, and processing of all the responses divided by the number of responses.

There's an example of how it might work in Table G.5, based on these assumptions:

- The web invitations go to 250,000 people with no incentive, little follow-up work, and a fairly good response rate of 0.1% (good for web, that is).

- The paper invitations go to 500 people, with the cost of printing, packaging, and posting the invitation; a dollar bill in the envelope; more work on follow-up; and a reasonable response rate for paper of 50%.

TABLE G.5 AN EXAMPLE OF COSTS FOR WEB AND PAPER VERSIONS OF A SURVEY

	Web invitation to web questionnaire		Paper	
Preparation of invitation		$500		$500
Number of invitations	250,000		500	
Cost per invitation	0	$0	$2	$1000
Incentive	0	$0	$1	$500
Follow-up	0	$0	$1	$250
Response rate	0.1%		50.0%	
Number of responses	250		250	
Dealing with the responses		$1,000		$2,000
Total cost		$1,500		$4,250
Cost per response		$30		$17

In this example:

- Using paper is more work but goes to fewer people at just over half the cost per response of the web version.
- In actual dollars spent, the paper version costs nearly three times as much.
- To get 250 responses with the web invitation to web questionnaire version, we had to invite 250,000 people—possibly annoying a large number of them or reducing even further their likelihood to respond in the future.
- The paper version succeeded with 250 people and only failed for 250—not a big annoyance factor.

It's about asking stakeholders what they consider to be more important:

- Getting lots of good quality responses and bothering fewer people with the invitations
- Spending less money overall

And another way to work out the best mode? Iterate. Try the most convenient with the smallest number of invitations that will give you some results. Discuss the results with your stakeholders. Then decide whether to continue with that mode or try something else.

All the modes have strengths and weaknesses

I admit that my colleagues and clients can rarely be persuaded to change from their favorite mode: the emailed invitation to a web survey. But if your stakeholders are more open to different ideas, then maybe Table G.6, which compares the strengths and weaknesses, can help to persuade them.

TABLE G.6   COMPARING THE STRENGTHS AND WEAKNESSES OF MODES

Mode	Strengths	Weaknesses
Ambient	Timely: answers are based on recent, memorable experience	Response rate may be poor Many respondents see too many of these Must be very short
Email invitation to web questionnaire	Cheap, quick, and convenient You know who the recipients are Can be longer	Many of your recipients are probably already suffering from email overload Spam filters may catch your survey
Sent in the mail on paper	Fairly sure your survey will reach your audience; easy to enclose an incentive May be cost-effective when you calculate cost per respondent Can be longer	Unless heavily personalized, may be seen as junk mail Seen as high cost and old-fashioned by stakeholders
Face-to-face	Quite a rare method, so may get a decent response rate, particularly with a carefully chosen incentive and skilled interviewers Can be longer	May be hard to find your audience in a specific location High cost May be seen as old-fashioned by stakeholders Needs skilled interviewers
Phone	Enables you to create a good list to sample from and adjust as you go Can be longer	Intrusive for your audience and expensive for you Usually based on landline phones, so has coverage errors because many people are mobile-only now Needs skilled interviewers
Web invitation such as a pop-up or banner ad to web questionnaire	Immediate, quick, and cheap Seen as the default, possibly the only option by stakeholder	Response rates are terrible Has to compete with many other, usually bad, surveys; must be short

Some other modes to consider

If choosing between six modes isn't quite enough to think about, there are other modes available. For example, in the 2021 Census in the United Kingdom, each household received a mailed invitation with a code to access a web questionnaire. The invitation also offered the option to request a paper questionnaire through a website or by telephone, and individuals who did not want someone else to know their answers could request a private individual code.

And here are a couple of other ideas to think about.

With declining response rates to phone and web invitations, some organizations are returning to SMS (phone text message) questionnaires—an idea that was tried by market researchers once SMS became a widely used technology but got overtaken by web. When I first got one, as in Figure G.2, a couple of years ago, it was new to me, and I was happy to answer.

FIGURE G.2

The first question from a customer satisfaction questionnaire sent by SMS (phone text message).

> Text Message
> Mon 24 Sep, 18:49
>
> **Q1 of 4. Please rate your experience of the service provided by Ashton who handled the call, from 10 (excellent) to 0 (very poor)?**
>
> 10

Probably by the time you read this, the SMS questionnaire will have become so overused that its response rates will also be in decline.

Or can you think of something completely different? Tabetha Newman took on the challenge of finding an ambient method for a survey in Bristol, UK. She designed a fun "voting trolley," pictured in Figure G.3, where people answered by taking a ball and dropping it into the Yes or No trolley to answer the Most Crucial Question, very quickly and barely interrupting their walk. She had a longer paper questionnaire for anyone who wanted to answer supplementary questions.

COURTESY OF TABETHA NEWMAN, TIMMUS LTD

FIGURE G.3
Take a ball and drop it into the "Yes" or the "No" trolley.

I'll leave it to your imagination to come up with other interesting ways of getting your questions in front of the people you want to answer.

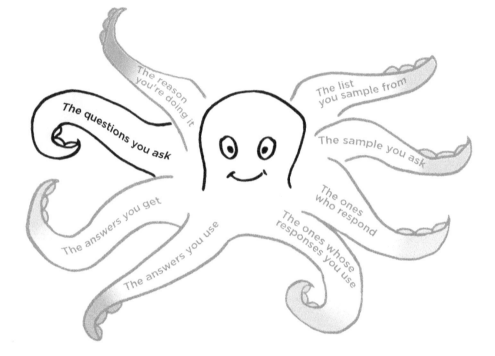

The reason you're doing it

The list you sample from

The questions you ask

The sample you ask

The answers you get

The ones who respond

The answers you use

The ones whose responses you use

CHAPTER 4

Questionnaire: Build and Test the Questionnaire

When you've worked out your questions, your next step is to turn them into a questionnaire.

We're still working on "the questions you ask" tentacle of the Octopus, and this chapter is mostly about the last of the four steps in answering a question, as in Figure 4.1, "Respond," the step where the people you're asking deliver an answer to you.

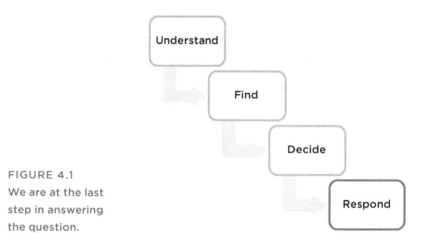

FIGURE 4.1
We are at the last
step in answering
the question.

What could possibly go wrong with your questionnaire?

If you've done the work so far conscientiously, with plenty of careful cognitive interviewing, then creating your questionnaire will be rather easy.

Dare I say that building a questionnaire can even be enjoyable? I love the somewhat mechanical work of copying those thoroughly tested questions into my choice of survey tool and checking that it all looks good and works.

Even more excitingly, this tentacle of our Survey Octopus ("the questions you ask") doesn't have any new error of its own.

But I have to admit that my library of screenshots has quite a few where something has gone wrong at the questionnaire stage. Here are a couple of my favorites in Figures 4.2 and 4.3.

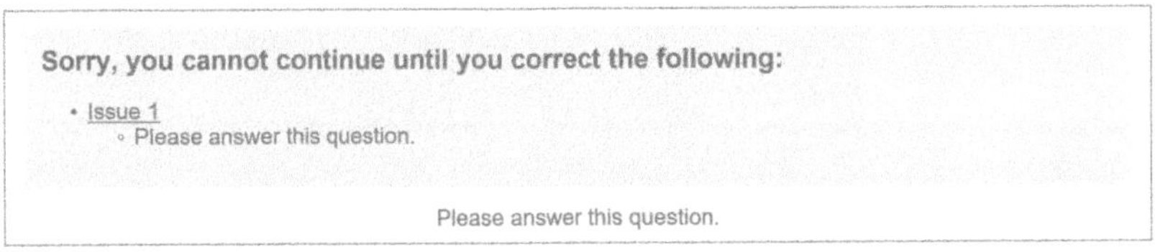

Sorry, you cannot continue until you correct the following:

• Issue 1
  ◦ Please answer this question.

Please answer this question.

FIGURE 4.2
Someone forgot to design their error messages.

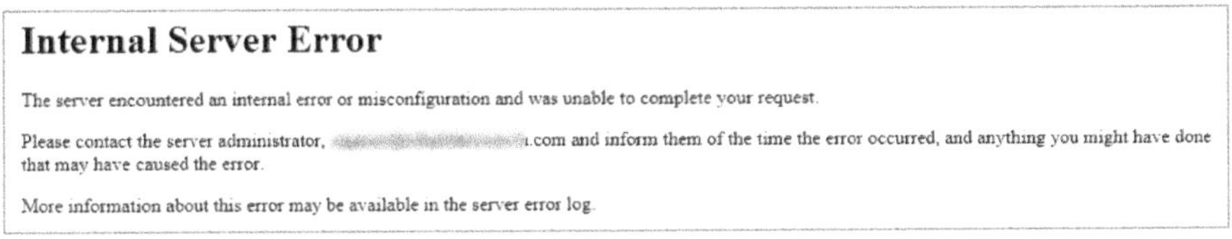

Internal Server Error

The server encountered an internal error or misconfiguration and was unable to complete your request.

Please contact the server administrator, ~~xxxxxxxxxxxxxxxxxx~~.com and inform them of the time the error occurred, and anything you might have done that may have caused the error.

More information about this error may be available in the server error log.

FIGURE 4.3
This questionnaire crashed.

But, of course, you'll test your questionnaire to make sure that it doesn't have any silly technical or build errors. So let's move on to creating it.

Good questions are easy to respond to

At this point, you have the words for the questions, but now you need to select ways for people to give you their answers. This section will mostly be about choosing response formats such as boxes to type into (for web and electronic questionnaires) or write into (for paper questionnaires), with some thoughts on images.

Use the simplest possible response format

I captured Figure 4.4 from a questionnaire sent out by a hotel chain, complete with their red and purple branding. It's got two questions: one closed and one open.

A **closed question** is one where the person must choose between the responses you offer.

An **open question** is one where the person can answer anything they like.

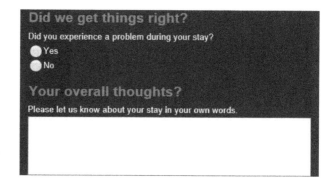

FIGURE 4.4
Two questions from a
questionnaire sent by
a hotel chain.

In this example, the hotel chain correctly matched the response formats to the questions. In electronic questionnaires, such as this one, there are two simple formats for closed questions:

- Radio buttons, where the person who answers can only choose one response

- Checkboxes, where the person who answers can choose one or more responses

(On a paper questionnaire, there's no way to enforce the difference between radio buttons and checkboxes, as the person can write what they like.)

And one format for open questions:

- An open box, sometimes known as a *text box* or *text area*, where the person who answers can type in whatever they like

There's a close relative of the radio button answer format: the rating format, where the person who answers has to choose from a set of responses that might range from "Strongly agree" to "Strongly disagree." These formats are often called *Likert response formats*, and they have a close relationship with Likert scales. Despite their familiarity, they are tricky, so I've put them in Spotlight H: "'On a Scale from 1 to 5' (Likert and Rating Scales)" after this chapter.

A quick aside that confused me when I first came across it: some market researchers, and some survey tools, still refer to radio buttons as *single punch* and checkboxes as *multi-punch*. This terminology came from the days long before computers when answers were recorded by punching holes in a paper card, as in Figure 4.5.

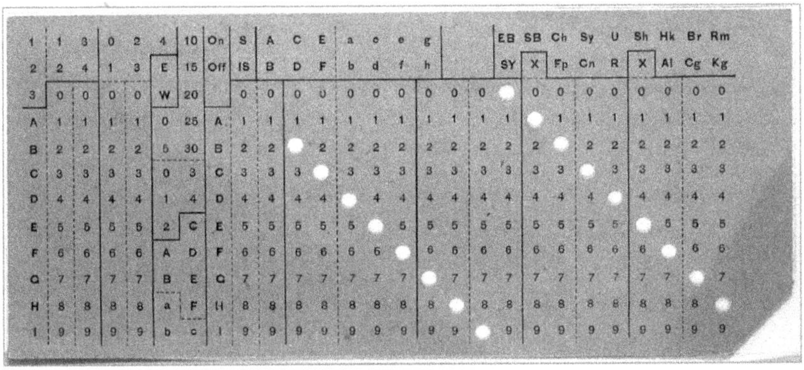

FIGURE 4.5

A punch card, used for recording answers for processing in Herman Hollerith's Electric Sorting and Tabulating Machine, ca. 1895.

Do not use drop-downs

For some types of interactions, I used to recommend drop-downs—also known as *select boxes*—and even coauthored a paper with Sarah Allen Miller called "Should I use a drop-down?" (Allen Miller and Jarrett, 2001)

It's not 2001 anymore, and these days the people who use the web come with a much richer variety of access needs and digital skills. After watching too many people struggle with the complexity of drop-downs, I have changed my recommendation to "Burn your select tags: No drop-downs." To find out more about this, watch Alice Bartlett's talk. (Bartlett, 2014)

What should you do instead? Four ideas, in increasing order of amount of work for you:

1. **Offer all the options as a set of radio buttons.**

   A long drop-down is really a set of radio-button options concealed behind a complex interaction. Yes, if you offer a long list of radio buttons, then the people who answer will have to scroll to find the one they need. But at least that scrolling action won't be hidden behind a click and a scrollbar that's different from the one for the rest of the page.

2. **Offer an open box instead and then clean the data.**

   One of the arguments in favor of drop-downs is: "We need to be sure to get accurate data." This argument equates "accurate" with "restricted to the set of options we thought of." By making the people who answer choose from *your* list, you're putting the work of mapping their answer to your list onto them—and risking that they will give up and drop out.

If you offer an open box, you take on the mapping work. If your list is a good one, then it will be easy, so why not? If your list isn't a good match for the real-world answers that people give you, then it will be harder. But you'll be iterating your survey anyway, so you'll have a chance to improve your list for the next time you do the survey.

3. **Offer fewer options.**

Run a pilot survey to find out which options are most popular using an open box. Typically, just a few options (sometimes only three or four) will be enough to cover 80% or more of the answers. Then run another pilot offering the most popular options, with an "other" option and a text box where everyone else can give their own answer.

4. **Consider an accessible autocomplete.**

The idea of "autocomplete" is that you start to type into a text box and suggestions appear below the box that you can choose instead of continuing to type. It's a standard feature on many search engines.

I've put it last on this list because autocompletes are really difficult for accessibility. It's not impossible to make one that works acceptably with a variety of access technologies and for the people who use them, but it's hard. I'm personally not at all sure that you can ever solve the problem for people who look at the keyboard as they type and then look at what they have typed as a separate matter, but I'm willing to believe it's possible, especially as the UK Government Digital Services offers an autocomplete that they have tested for accessibility in their web design system.

Given the poor accessibility of most survey tools, opting for an accessible autocomplete probably means you are opting to create your own survey tool, too.

Closed questions can work unexpectedly

Let's try a quick thought experiment, picking up on work by survey methodologists Norbert Schwarz, Hans-J. Hippler, Brigitte Deutsch, and Fritz Strack. (Schwarz, Hippler et al., 1985) They asked German citizens about how many hours each day they watched TV.

Half the people, chosen randomly, got a question with these answers:

- Up to ½h
- ½h to 1h
- 1h to 1½h
- 1½h to 2h
- 2h to 2½h
- More than 2½h

Try it for yourself—what did you pick?

My answer is 2h to 2½h, because I know that most days I enjoy watching TV from about 8 p.m. to 10 p.m.

And here are answers for the 68 people who got that question in Table 4.1. I've added two summary boxes for "Up to 2½ hrs" and "More than 2½ hrs" that we'll return to in a moment.

TABLE 4.1 LOW ANSWER CATEGORIES

Hours watching TV	Number of answers	Up to 2 ½ hrs	More than 2 ½ hrs
Up to ½h	5		
½h to 1h	12		
1h to 1½h	18	5 + 12 + 18 + 10 + 12 = 57	
1½h to 2h	10		
2h to 2½h	12		
More than 2½h	11		11
Total	68	57	11
	100%	84%	16%

Let's compare that with the rest of the group, who got a different set of responses:

- Up to 2½h
- 2½h to 3h
- 3h to 3½h
- 3½h to 4 h
- 4h to 4½h
- More than 4½h

Did you pick an answer before? If not, how about trying one now?

With a matched group, we ought to see approximately the same results in Table 4.2.

TABLE 4.2 HIGH ANSWER CATEGORIES

Hours watching TV	Number of answers	Up to 2 ½ hrs	More than 2 ½ hrs
Up to 2 ¹/₂h	40	40	
2 ¹/₂h to 3h	15		
3h to 3 ¹/₂h	5		
3 ¹/₂h to 4h	3		15+ 5+ 3 + 1 + 0 =34
4h to 4 ¹/₂h	1		
More than 4 ¹/₂h	0		
Total	64	40	34
	100%	63%	34%

But we don't see similar results. With the low answer categories in Table 4.1, we had 84% watching up to 2½ hrs of TV; with higher categories, that drops to 63%.

What lured those respondents into reporting higher rates of TV viewing when they saw higher categories?

We need to turn to the "Approximate Curve of Forgetting" that we met in Chapter 3, "Questions." Do you remember it? (I know, I'm asking if you remember the curve of forgetting—I couldn't resist, sorry.)

Watching TV is, for many of us, an unremarkable, repetitive event and therefore not something we are going to remember for long. So the thought process to create an answer might go something like this:

1. Look at the set of answers offered.

2. Assume that the answers cover the typical range.

3. Rate yourself as a less frequent viewer than average, average, or more frequent viewer than average, as in Figure 4.6.

4. Choose the answer that corresponds visually to your self-rating of behavior.

FIGURE 4.6
How many hours do you watch TV?

It looks like a range question, but it's a rating question. And it turns out, that's how a lot of people tackle questions like this. The experiment we've been looking at was from way back in 1985, but it's since been replicated several times—for example, with students reporting the hours that they study, or people reporting the number of times a week that they experience minor medical symptoms.

What to do about it? You have choices:

1. Use an open box instead, so you get an unprompted answer.
2. Do cognitive interviewing (as mentioned in Chapter 3) to find out what strategies people actually use for your particular question, and then choose response categories accordingly.

3. Find out what the true range of answers really is by some other method (we are back to "triangulation" again, which we met in Chapter 2, "Sample"), and make sure that the answer categories in your closed question do, in fact, reflect "about average" in the middle and the full range at the ends.

Design your open boxes carefully

I've just suggested to you that an open box might get better results than a range question. As with everything in questionnaire design, open boxes have their little ways, so let's look at them in more detail.

Open boxes can get surprising answers

It seemed quite counterintuitive to me that open questions can get more accurate answers than "choose an answer," so I was eager to try it. My first chance came when working on a survey of usability professionals about whether they wanted a certification scheme.

One of our Most Crucial Questions was: "What is the maximum that you would pay to be certified (in US$)?" In our first draft of the survey, we planned to offer these answers:

- Less than 100
- 100–299
- 300–499
- 500–1,000
- More than 1,000
- I wouldn't pay anything

Although those bands looked sensible to me, I persuaded my colleagues to try an open question instead.

Most people did reply with a number that would have fallen within those ranges, but we had a huge variety of other answers. The maximum we got was $20,000. As a bonus, we had other answers like "I would expect my employer to pay" or "2 cents." (My American colleagues explained to me that "2 cents" is an answer intended as an insult.)

These days, when I want a numeric answer to a question, I'll start with an open question for enough iterations of the questionnaire to feel sure that nearly all the people who will answer have a simple number as their response and that we have the full range of values. Then I'll consider whether people responding during the tests seem to find that typing their answer is too onerous, and if so, then I'll swap to ranges.

There's one small exception. If the question is about something that might identify the person who answered, such as their age, then I'd carefully assess whether I might be able to preserve their privacy better by sticking to a range. But even with age, I tend to lean toward an open box, as most people can type the age they want to tell me straight away, and it's slightly less effort for them than choosing a range.

Open boxes can save you from dropouts due to category errors

If the answer someone wants to give you doesn't match any of the options you've offered to them, then you've encountered a category error—one of the most common problems in questionnaires.

> A **category error** happens when the response options offered do not include any options that work for the person who is answering. A category error is a type of measurement error.

Category errors create unpleasant choices:

- Skip the question (which loses data).
- Answer incorrectly (even worse: you've now got a measurement error).
- Drop out of the questionnaire (worst of all: you've lost the opportunity to collect any more data from that person).

An open box avoids category errors by definition, but you can also save a closed question by providing an extra option within the responses that has a text box attached to it, like the question in Figure 4.7.

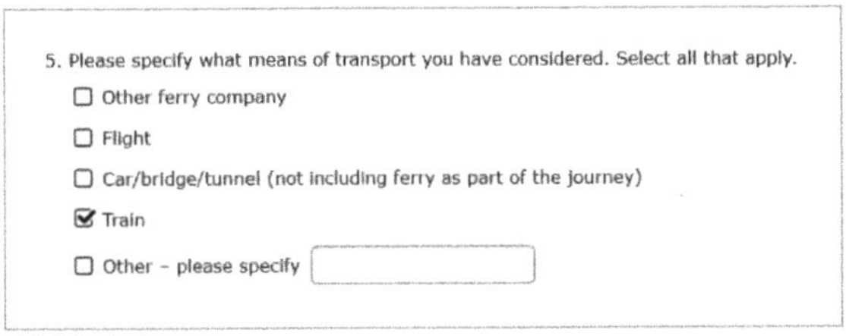

> 5. Please specify what means of transport you have considered. Select all that apply.
> ☐ Other ferry company
> ☐ Flight
> ☐ Car/bridge/tunnel (not including ferry as part of the journey)
> ☑ Train
> ☐ Other – please specify [ ]

FIGURE 4.7

A question from a ferry company, with space for other transport options, such as walking.

For convenience, I generally refer to this extra option as the "other" choice—but I don't always use the word "other" in the questionnaire, as in some sensitive contexts the people who answer could feel alienated by being described as "other." Here are some words to try:

- "Something else"
- "In your own words"
- "Your preferred answer"
- "Another answer"

If no one chooses your "other" option, you haven't lost anything (other than a few moments of programming).

Often, the responses to the "other" choice are some of the most interesting, because they challenge your assumptions about the people who answer.

If you're using an open box, get the size right

The size of the box that you offer for an open question suggests the length of the answer that you're expecting. In Figure 4.8 the box is small and looks like it's asking for a short answer. In Figure 4.9, a larger box looks like it's asking for a longer answer.

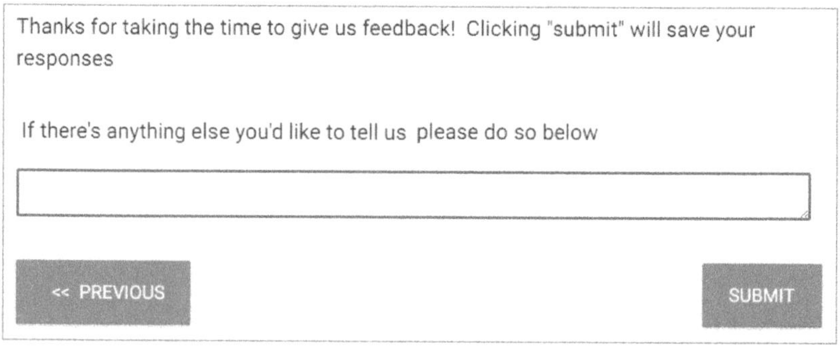

FIGURE 4.8
This questionnaire offers a small box for the answer, suggesting a short response.

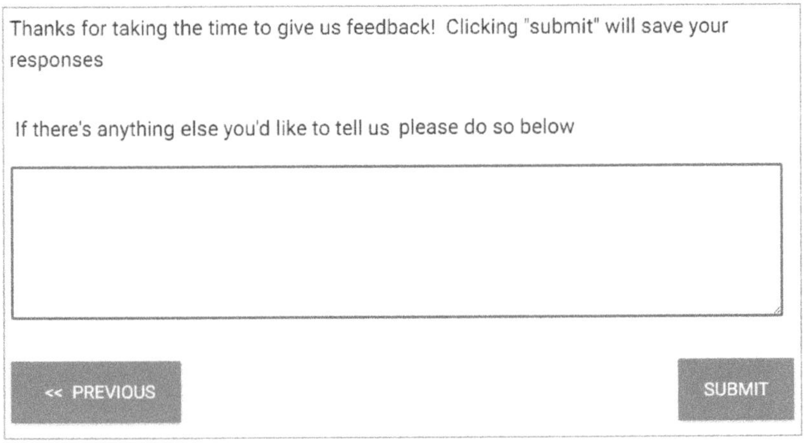

Thanks for taking the time to give us feedback! Clicking "submit" will save your responses

If there's anything else you'd like to tell us please do so below

<< PREVIOUS   SUBMIT

FIGURE 4.9
A larger box is looking for a longer answer.

Open boxes can be intimidating

But, as always with surveys, when you tug on one tentacle from the Survey Octopus in Figure 4.10 (this time, "the questions you ask"), you end up tangled in another tentacle (this time, "the ones who respond").

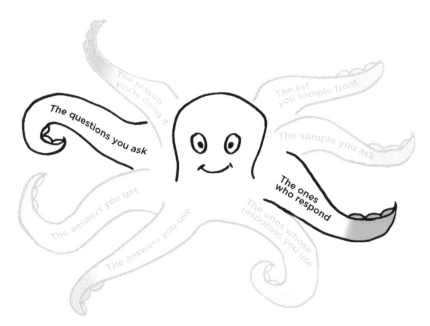

FIGURE 4.10
"The questions you ask" is opposite "The ones who respond."

An open question with a larger box means more perceived effort for the people who answer, so that may mean that you get fewer responses. It's a question of balance: longer, which usually means more interesting but fewer responses, or shorter and more responses? Only iteration will tell you which works for you.

Be careful even with the simplest answer formats

In Figure 4,11, there's an example using two of the simplest answer formats: an open box and a pair of radio buttons.

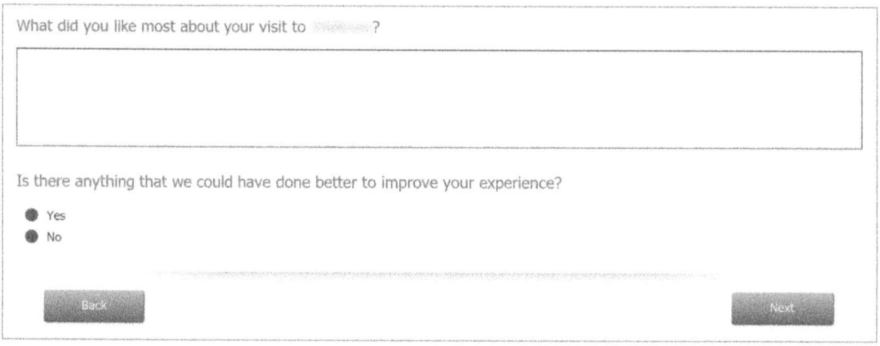

FIGURE 4.11

This screenshot includes the two simplest answer types: text box and choose an answer (and shows how even the simplest question types can be messed up).

Did you spot any of the problems with that screenshot?

The ones I noticed are:

- The first question assumes that there *was* something that I liked about my visit. What if I hated every single aspect of it?
- The second question is worded very awkwardly: "Is there anything we could have done better to improve your experience?" is a complex concept to think about. How about "What could we do better?"
- The two answer options are "yes" and "no." If my answer is "don't know" or "maybe," then there's nothing for me to choose.

- The questionnaire is using a custom style for the radio buttons. Although I haven't selected an answer yet, it's showing both answer options with solid dots, as you can see in the enlargement in Figure 4.12.

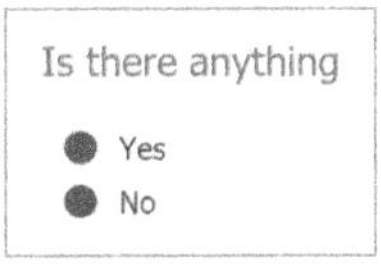

FIGURE 4.12
The two answer options have solid dots—breaking convention.

Choose the simplest possible styling for your questions

You want the people who answer to be focusing on thinking about their responses, not worrying about how to place their answer on your questionnaire. The simplest possible styling helps them to do that.

For example, with radio buttons: the simplest possible styling is to have an empty circle next to each option, as in Figure 4.13, with the selected circle getting a darker center when you select it, as in Figure 4.14.

FIGURE 4.13
Normal radio buttons have an empty circle next to the answer option before you choose an answer.

FIGURE 4.14
When you choose an answer ("partly"), the middle of the circle fills with a darker color.

If you're thinking, "Goodness, that's extremely obvious advice—why bother?", then I agree with you. Or, to be accurate, I did agree with you until I started browsing my library of screenshots of questionnaires. I started to notice all sorts of "stylish" variations—like the solid dots I mentioned previously.

Now, I'm guessing that you're quite a web-savvy person, and if you're not especially looking out for styling variations, then you'll probably barely notice them. If the person who answers doesn't notice, then no harm has been done (but no benefit either). If the person *does* notice, then at best that's a tiny distraction from focusing on answering the questions, but at worst they will stop in confusion. You may lose them, or they may answer inaccurately.

Do you think I'm exaggerating? On this question, possibly. But I've also had to help relatives through problems like this. I particularly recall a distressed family member who was stuck on an important form because they were unable to find a check mark anywhere on their computer, not knowing that a click into the box would solve it.

Despite this, survey tool creators seem to strive to do strange things with their interaction design. Here are two nonstandard interaction designs that I harvested from well-known survey tools. In Figure 4.15, the survey tool has styled radio buttons as square checkboxes labeled alphabetically.

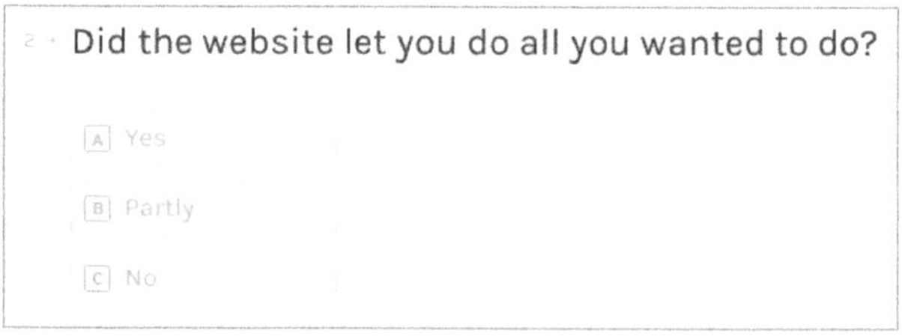

FIGURE 4.15
A survey tool styled radio buttons with checkboxes labeled alphabetically.

> 2 · Did the website let you do all you wanted to do?
>
> [A] Yes
>
> [B] Partly
>
> [C] No

In Figure 4.16, the survey tool has provided styled yes/no options as a continuous green strip, with "Yes" signaled by a check icon and "No" signaled by a "not allowed" icon.

15 This question has two answer options: Yes and No

✔ Yes   ⊘ No

FIGURE 4.16
A survey tool offered this strange arrangement for questions with Yes and No answers.

I haven't said which tools did these strange things, because by the time you read this, they are likely to change. I'm sure these peculiar interaction designs are both well intentioned:

- The labels A, B, C provide a quick keyboard shortcut (if you realized you can type A to select option A).
- The green "yes" and "no" create a change of scene and add some icons that might be fun in a repetitive questionnaire.

But both of them are unusual and potentially confusing. Why do that to the people who want to answer? Why create moments of hesitation? Instead, follow the advice in Table 4.3.

TABLE 4.3   THE ANSWERS THAT PEOPLE WANT TO GIVE GUIDE
            YOUR CHOICE OF RESPONSE SPACES

If your people want to give....	Then choose...
Exactly one answer and only one	Radio buttons
One or more from several choices	Checkboxes
Not sure, or anything else	Open box

Avoid fancy interaction devices

If you sign up to an internet survey panel, you'll find that you get offered all sorts of fancy question types:

- Sliders
- Maps
- Drag-and-drop
- And many more

These break up the monotony of long, tedious market research questionnaires and are popular with the people who join panels. So why keep away from them?

It's difficult to design a really easy interaction

These fancy question types have lots of details that are hard to get right. For example, one interaction designer said, "I've got a new slider, and people enjoy using it." So we get tempted to throw in a slider.

At a glance, the slider probably looks OK—but is it? Will it work equally well, no matter which device the person who answers chooses to use? What about no matter which browser they pick? What about if they choose to enlarge the text or to use a screen reader? And what if they happen never to have used a slider before—will they know how to use this one?

Even if a slider works reasonably well in theory, there can be subtle details that make it undesirable for answering survey questions. For example, the one in Figure 4.17 has two numbers (1 and 10) that are off the ends of the sliding scale. Can you select either of them or not? Does it start with the slider set at 1? At 5? If so, how do you distinguish an actual "1" or "5" response from a nonresponse? What about the problem that people might think of "5" as the midpoint, but it is not? (The midpoint is between 5 and 6.)

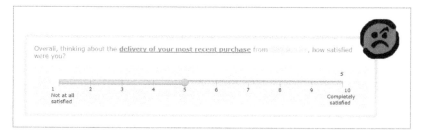

FIGURE 4.17

A questionnaire using a slider instead of radio buttons with some problematic details.

Fancy interaction devices are mostly created by survey tool makers to solve a problem you won't have: the challenge of long, tedious questionnaires. You're going to solve it by making short, interesting questionnaires.

Choose your images carefully

A decorative image can make your questionnaire more attractive. An informative image can help to convey a concept that is part of your question. But images can also sway answers. Let's have a look at them in a bit more detail.

Decoration can be informative or delightful

Your questionnaire is part of your organization's overall conversations with the people who answer. If your organization is a trusted brand, then showing that brand on your questionnaire can increase trust and therefore your response rate, such as the one from the UK Government Department for Digital, Culture, Media & Sport in Figure 4.18.

FIGURE 4.18
The UK Government Department for Digital, Culture, Media & Sport put its logo on each page of this questionnaire to show that it was sponsoring the survey.

If your typical brand styling is quirky, distinctive, or decorative, then consider whether you want to continue that into your questionnaire. Is this questionnaire going to look out of place if it is too neutral?

In 2016, Google and AIGA (The Professional Association for Design) partnered to run a survey as designcensus.org:

"The goal is to move beyond basic salary conversations and collect information that can be used to empower the design community to take charge of its professional development and achieve greater happiness through insight." (designcensus.org)

The questionnaire had a highly distinctive branding and interaction style, as in Figure 4.19.

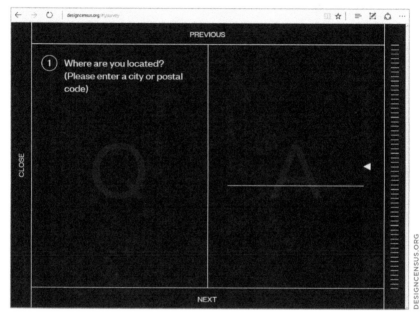

FIGURE 4.19
Unusual interaction design and branding from a questionnaire aimed at designers.

The questionnaire received over 9,500 responses. It's hard to say how representative these are, but you can explore most of the data yourself and decide: https://github.com/AIGAGitHub/DesignCensus2016

I first learned about it because the tweet in Figure 4.20 from @robweychert appeared in my timeline, with his response to a question in the survey: "54: Summarize the future of design in three words." He'd chosen the answer "get over yourself."

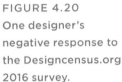

FIGURE 4.20
One designer's
negative response to
the Designcensus.org
2016 survey.

Although Designcensus.org clearly provoked some strong reactions in some respondents, when I looked at the dataset, I discovered:

- 9,596 responses
- 6,902 had answered question 54.
- 1,334 of those answers were a three-word phrase (like the "get," "over," "yourself" one we saw in Figure 4.20), rather than three separate words (for example, "useful," "practical," "valuable").
- Only 342 three-word phrases were somewhat negative (for example, "Struggle," "for," "pay").
- Only 25 of the negative three-word phrases, like the one in the tweet, were an opinion about the phrasing of question 54, about AIGA, or about the survey itself.

Nobody complained directly about the unusual interaction design and branding. That could be due to nonresponse error: maybe people who hated the branding gave up rather than waiting to the end to complain. But I'm inclined to believe that for this defined group of people answering these questions, the design succeeded in its aims. Certainly the next year's Design Census used the same design, and the published dataset has 13,159 responses.

If you can't be honest, at least be neutral

As always with surveys, it's not quite as simple as saying "always put your logo on your questionnaire." People may be willing to reveal things about themselves to a third party that they are not willing to tell your organization—or not in this context. Many organizations choose to get a market research business to do some of their research anonymously, especially when their brand is well known. "A motorcycle manufacturer sponsored this research" is likely to get different reactions than "This questionnaire comes from Harley-Davidson."

A team at Carnegie Mellon (John, Acquisti et al., 2011) ran an experiment that clearly demonstrated this effect. Their questionnaire asked people to disclose behaviors that were sensitive (for example, lying about income to a friend) or illegal (for example, trying cocaine). One-third of the people got a questionnaire with a "How bad are U?" logo and an informal font, as in Figure 4.21; one-third got a questionnaire styled with the Carnegie Mellon logo and a formal font, as in Figure 4.22; and the final third got a neutral questionnaire with no logo and a plain font.

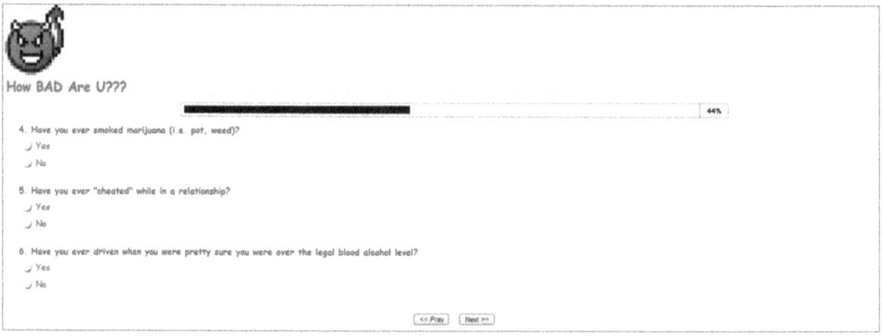

FIGURE 4.21
"How Bad are U???" styling on a questionnaire.

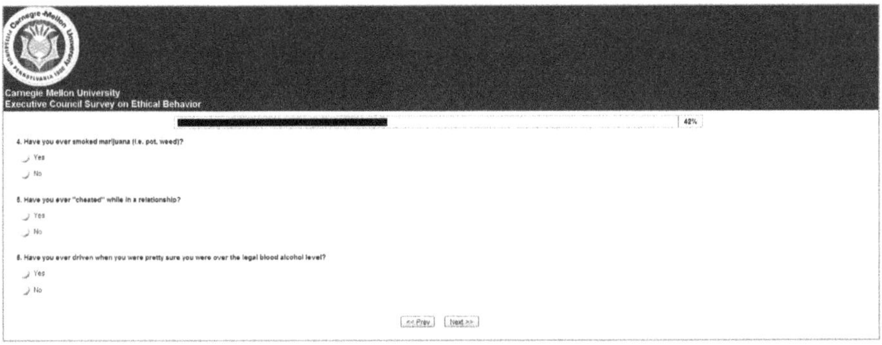

COURTESY OF LESLIE JOHN

FIGURE 4.22
Carnegie Mellon University styling on a questionnaire.

Although the people who answered perhaps should have been wary about disclosing personal information in the context of dodgy behaviors to a questionnaire with no safety or trust indicators, in fact, the "How Bad are U???" questionnaire elicited more dubious behaviors than the formal version.

Using dark patterns, like pretending to be a pop quiz, is fine for university researchers who have carefully considered the ethics of what they are doing and made sure that they destroyed the responses. It's absolutely not fine for your organization to pretend to be something that it's not—and it's illegal in some countries.

If your Most Crucial Question means that you need to ask questions on a topic, such as attitudes to bank brands, without revealing who you are ("Most Hated Bank"), then this is the time to bring in one of the market research organizations who will conduct your research appropriately under their neutral branding.

An image can change an answer

In another famous experiment, Mick Couper, Fred Conrad, and Roger Tourangeau (Couper, Conrad et al., 2007) used images of a healthy-looking woman jogging, or a woman in a hospital gown in a hospital bed in a questionnaire. Carefully matched samples of people rated their health; one group got a picture of a woman out running, and the other group got a picture of a woman in a hospital bed, as shown in Figure 4.23. The health status mysteriously improved when compared to a picture of a person in a hospital bed.

FIGURE 4.23

An image can change
an answer.

How would you rate your health?

Excellent
Very Good
Good
Fair
Poor

33% said
excellent or very
good

41% said
excellent or
very good

As the researchers put it in their discussion of images:

> "When shown a picture of a couple dining in a fine restaurant, respondents reported significantly fewer episodes (eating out in the past month) on average than when they were shown a high-frequency instance of the behavior (eating fast food in a car). Similarly, respondents exposed to a picture of grocery shopping reported more shopping trips in the past month than those exposed to a picture of clothes shopping." (Couper, Conrad et al., 2007)

Stereotypical images can be alienating

I've also seen far too many "clever" uses of images like the one in Figure 4.24. This highly stereotypical pair of images offers a choice between a person with short hair wearing a tie as "male" and a person with long hair and no tie as "female"—both with pale skin. I have a gender-fluid colleague who dresses exactly like the image on the left but identifies as neither male nor female, and another who dresses exactly like the image on the right and identifies as male. And what about those who wouldn't recognize their skin color in either image?

FIGURE 4.24

A question that asks you to choose
a stereotypical image.

As I wrote the previous paragraph, I wondered whether I was exaggerating the problem. The very same day, BBC news reported that Essex County Council, part of local government in the UK, had to apologize—and withdraw a questionnaire—after an attempt to use images went wrong. There's a screenshot in Figure 4.25.

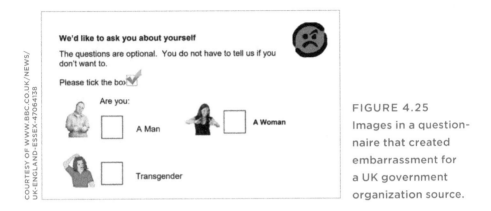

FIGURE 4.25 Images in a questionnaire that created embarrassment for a UK government organization source.

It was especially unfortunate for the Council as the image came from a version of the questionnaire designed specifically to help people with reading difficulties. The standard version in Figure 4.26 had a words-only version that is respectful of differences.

Q30. What is your gender?
- ○ Male
- ○ Female
- ○ Prefer not to say
- ○ Prefer to use my own term

Q31. Does your gender identity match your sex as registered at birth?
- ○ Yes
- ○ No
- ○ Prefer not to say

FIGURE 4.26 A words-only version of the question about gender.

If your question is about an image, use the image

If your survey is about people's feelings about an image, then of course include the image in the questionnaire. I answered a questionnaire for Cath Kidston, a brand famous for flowery prints, that included asking my opinion about several proposed options. As you can see, I particularly liked the one in Figure 4.27.

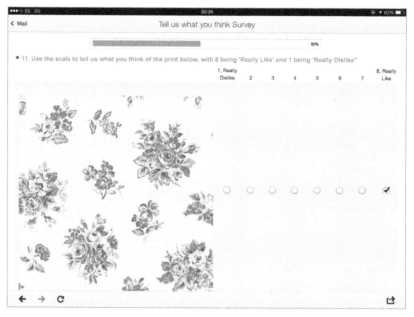

FIGURE 4.27

Showing an image is a good way to get a reaction to that image.

That print ("Highgate Rose") did go into production. About a year after I did the questionnaire, I spotted it on the teapot in Figure 4.28.

FIGURE 4.28

"Highgate Rose" teapot.

General rule: If the purpose of the survey is to get reactions to an image, then use the image. If you're considering using an image on a questionnaire for any other reason, then understand that the presence of the image will have an effect on the answers—possibly not the one you intended.

Consider the order of your questions

If you've managed to end up with a Light Touch Survey, then you don't need to worry too much about the order of the questions, as it will be obvious.

If your questionnaire edges toward the Big Honkin', then you'll probably have so many questions that they need some organization.

"Omnibus" questionnaires organize questions by origin

One method of organizing questions is the "omnibus." This is a sort of Big Honkin' Survey where different organizations provide questions for a single questionnaire so that the costs of fieldwork are spread out among them all.

The omnibus style is also used by operators of probability-based panels such as LISS (Longitudinal Internet studies for the Social Sciences) in the Netherlands. Participants in the panel get a questionnaire at intervals called *waves* by LISS. Social researchers can ask for their questions to be included in a single wave or multiple ones. In a typical wave, the people who answer will get about five different topics.

The range of topics is vast. I've seen everything from "Reasons to Snack" to "The Psychology of Vengeance," and it also gives researchers an opportunity to explore questions of current concern, such as topics related to Covid-19 in 2020, as in Figure 4.29.

202 Family Survey Dutch Population (FSDP)

203 How primary schools perform

206 Effects of the Outbreak of Covid-19

208 Victims in Modern Society

210 Questionnaire on the corona virus in the LISS panel

FIGURE 4.29
A few of the topics that appeared in the LISS panel questionnaires in 2020.

I'm not exactly recommending "topics in order of the organization that supplied them," but it shows that people who answer can be remarkably tolerant of strange jumps in topic.

Start with easy, unintrusive topics

A more conventional approach—and probably less disconcerting for the people who answer—starts the questionnaire with easy topics before moving onto the more detailed or more personal ones.

Don Dillman, an influential survey methodologist, tells the story of being given this list of questions, in this order, by a colleague who wanted his advice:

- What was your total family income in 2009?
- Do you like to play golf?
- What is your opinion on global warming?
- Are you married?
- Which political party does the best job of promoting economic growth?
- How many times have you gone bowling in the last year?
- What is your political party preference?
- Do you favor or oppose higher tax on fuel as a measure to reduce environmental pollution?
- What is your occupation?
- Please describe your favorite recreational activity.
- How old are you?
  —(Dillman, Smyth et al., 2009)

I felt that they worked better in three topics. (You may see them differently.)

Recreational activities:

- Do you like to play golf?
- How many times have you gone bowling in the last year?
- Please describe your favorite recreational activity.

Politics and climate:

- Which political party does the best job of promoting economic growth?
- What is your political party preference?

- What is your opinion on global warming?
- Do you favor or oppose higher tax on fuel as a measure to reduce environmental pollution?

Demographics:

- Are you married?
- How old are you?
- What is your occupation?
- What was your total family income in 2009?

If I couldn't persuade my colleague to split the topics into two or even three questionnaires, I'd probably start with the recreational activities as the least complex area, then onto the politics and climate topics, and finish with the most intrusive questions.

Try to start with interesting questions

My suggestion to put the representativeness questions at the end is opposite to many of the questionnaires that I see, which begin with "easy questions," such as age and location. But people are reluctant to part with personal information like this until they have built up some trust in your questionnaire—and, as I pointed out in Chapter 2, there are better questions for thinking about representativeness.

One obvious better option is to start with the Burning Issue. After all, that's what people most want to tell you, so that ought to get their attention.

There is a risk that they may drop out once they've gotten past the part that's most interesting to them, but I've been surprised by how often a sort of "question momentum" keeps them going: they've started, so they may as well finish.

Another option is to start with your Most Crucial Question, but think carefully about whether it might be seen as impertinent or intrusive on its own. I heard a striking example of this from Corinne Moy, market researcher, at a workshop she taught many years ago. A government client wanted to investigate the topic of whether people had unprotected sex on vacation, and they used telephone interviews for their questionnaire, as shown in Figure 4.30.

FIGURE 4.30
A question about sex might be startling at the beginning of a questionnaire.

In this example, Corinne and her team constructed a questionnaire that started with general questions about holidays and then moved toward the tricky question later on.

Does your Most Crucial Question take people by surprise, or do they like it because your questionnaire gets into the interesting topic really quickly?

I don't know, and neither will you until you test.

Do not screen people out

You may be a bit surprised to see that I recommended placing demographic questions at the end (if you have them at all).

In the days when it was all Big Honkin' Surveys, it was normal for interviewers to have quotas to fill, such as a specific number of women over 50, or residents of Kansas City, or recent purchasers of laundry detergent. The typical interview would start with some "screening" questions to determine which group the person who answered fell into, and if that quota was full, then they'd be "screened out," and that would be the end of the interview, as in Figure 4.31.

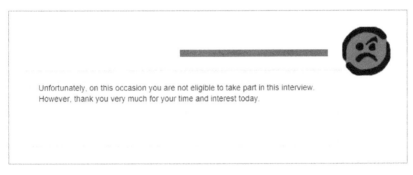

Unfortunately, on this occasion you are not eligible to take part in this interview. However, thank you very much for your time and interest today.

FIGURE 4.31
An unacceptable error message from a questionnaire with no incentive.

If you have opted for a hefty incentive (a topic we'll delve into in more detail in Chapter 5, "Fieldwork"), then you may need to limit the number of people who answer by group so that you don't use all your incentives on only part of the sample you are trying to reach.

But if you're asking people to answer purely for the pleasure of giving you their opinions, then there's little excuse for "screening them out." You may get too many answers from some types of people, but that's a great problem to have, and one that is easily solved when you clean the data (a topic we'll consider in Chapter 6, "Responses"). If you are concerned about luring people into the effort of providing answers that you may not use, then think of an easy-to-analyze question that provides them with something to answer without creating excessive work for you. Don't undermine their willingness to participate in future surveys by rejecting their answers to this questionnaire.

Finish the questionnaire with a thank-you

Always wrap up your questionnaire with thanks. On a paper questionnaire, a simple "thank you" at the end is sufficient.

If you've opted for anything electronic, then the person who has put effort into your questions needs to know that their answers have been transmitted to whatever computer will receive them, so provide a page with a reassuring message of some sort to tell them that it's been worthwhile.

You may choose to offer some sort of follow-up, such as contact details, the opportunity to register to receive the results, or something else that reflects what your organization is trying to do with the results of the survey.

If your organization sells something, it can be awfully tempting to offer an opportunity to purchase your products, such as sending them to your home page, but think carefully about whether this might contradict any previous messages about how you plan to use the answers. If it seems like you were simply trying to lure someone into buying, that's not a good look.

I don't know if I'm alone in this opinion, but I have a personal bugbear about organizations that end their "how did we do" questionnaire with an invitation to do the whole thing again on one of their review systems, such as one that sent me to Tripadvisor®, as shown in Figure 4.32.

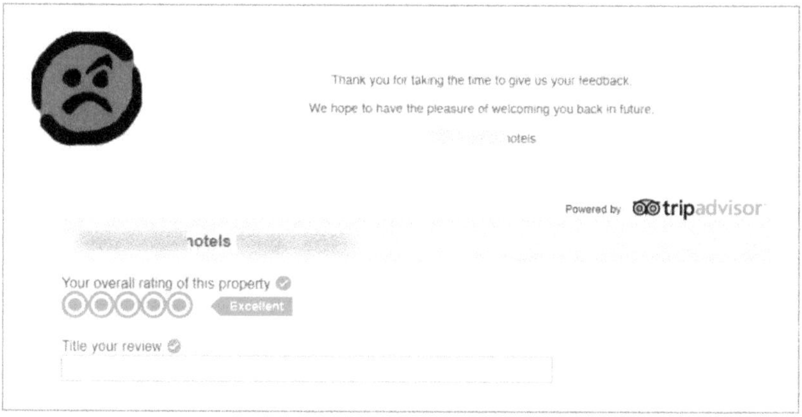

FIGURE 4.32

This questionnaire ended by sending me to Tripadvisor®.

Avoid introduction pages

If a thank-you page is essential, isn't an introduction page equally important—sort of "to match"?

No, not at all. I've spent hundreds, maybe thousands, of hours testing forms and questionnaires where I've watched participant after participant skip the introduction to get to the questions. I've seen the behavior so often that I'm far more surprised when someone actually stops to read the introduction.

If you do feel that your questionnaire needs some sort of introductory message, then it's better to include that on the page where the questions start. Most people won't read it, but it saves them the trouble of getting to another page.

If you absolutely must have an introduction page for reasons such as ethics board approval, corporate policy, or a stakeholder requirement, then keep it as short as you can, and expect to work hard on iterating it through your testing process.

Do not have "required questions"

There are no required questions in questionnaires. They are all optional, always.

Was that a bit brief?

Well, OK, in Figure 4.33 there is an example from a questionnaire about an event.

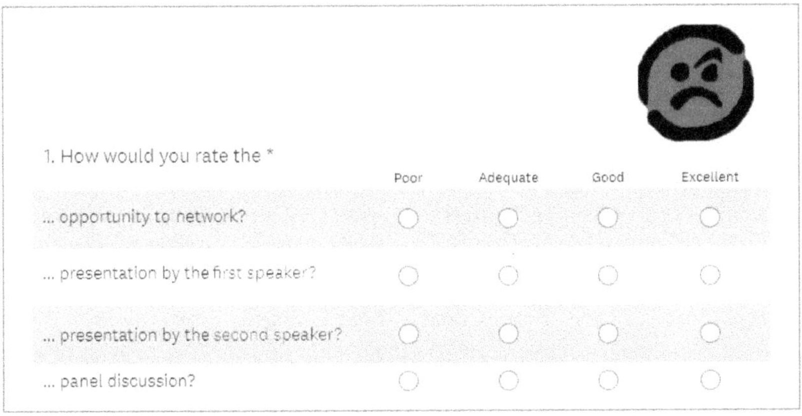

FIGURE 4.33
A question from a questionnaire after an event.

The thing that ruined the survey for me was that asterisk, which as a web-savvy sort of person, I noticed and interpreted as "you must answer this question." I had to leave before the panel discussion. How could I rate it? I was faced with the choice of providing false data for that part of the question or abandoning the survey, which meant that the organizers lost data.

If you are going to insist on required questions, then you need to be convinced that the value of that particular question is sufficiently high to justify:

- Losing some people who are trying to answer
- Getting some misleading data from others

You may be thinking: "Why not add a 'don't know' or 'not applicable' option and keep the question as required?" Obviously, that is a possibility. The difficulty there is that you're adding extra reading time and a bit of extra effort to the questionnaire. Maybe that extra effort is justified. Maybe it's that little bit extra that pushes some people who might otherwise answer into breaking off and you lose their responses. It's the Survey Octopus tentacle thing again: we're considering something in our Questions tentacle that may affect what happens in our Sample tentacle.

This is why it's so crucial to test your questions with people from your defined group. Testing is the way to find out whether the little details like "don't know" and "not applicable" are important. More importantly, testing is the way to make sure that people who answer will consider that each question is relevant and that they want to answer it so that when you're building your questionnaire, you don't need to tell them any question is "required."

If they do happen to miss a question, then don't nag at them. If taking part in your questionnaire is optional (I'm assuming you're not doing one of the few that's required by law), then each question is optional, too. It's acceptable to warn people, politely, if they skip a question and give them another opportunity to complete it. But if they don't want to answer, then accept their decision and let them move on to the next question.

Test your questionnaire

Remember back at the start of this chapter when I mentioned that the main thing that can go wrong with your questionnaire is forgetting to test it?

It's easy to believe that you've tested it yourself as you go backward and forward in your survey tool, getting it to work and checking that everything has been put into the right place. Sorry, that's *wrong*.

Questionnaires, like any document or piece of work that matters to you, somehow acquire typographic and other annoying errors that they hide from you while you're working on them. What you need is someone else to help you.

Test it to make sure it works at all

To test your questionnaire to make sure that it works at all ("mechanical testing"), enlist the help of an independent person with a picky mindset.

Get that person to try your questionnaire, both from the point of view of someone who is being as honest as possible and then trying every option to see if they can make it go wrong. A bit of testing would probably have unveiled the problem in Figure 4.34, where the questionnaire popped up in a tiny box.

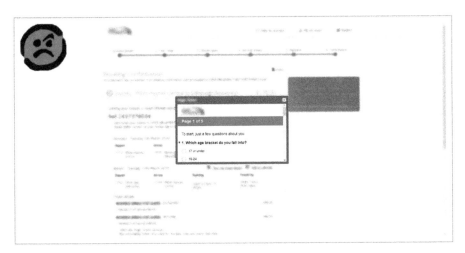

FIGURE 4.34

This questionnaire chose to pop up in a tiny box—possibly fine on a mobile, but not great on a desktop.

If you've opted for a web questionnaire, ask the person to use a selection of browsers.

Make sure that the browsers include the exact ones that your selected group of people are likely to use—especially whatever is the current default browser shipped by the biggest manufacturers of computers and mobile devices that are around.

I bought a cheap laptop purely for testing. I set it up by accepting every possible default option. I would never pick that combination of browser and search engine for myself, but some people don't know how to choose anything else.

As an example of the things that can go wrong, I made the mistake of testing a questionnaire aimed at people using Arabic in my English browser, as in Figure 4.35. I thought I had problems with English text turning up within the questionnaire, but in fact the Arabic version was fine.

FIGURE 4.35
On the left, Arabic questionnaire/English browser.
On the right, Arabic questionnaire/Arabic browser.

Consider another round of cognitive interviewing

At the end of Chapter 3, I recommended cognitive interviewing to check that your questions work well for the people you want to answer. If you've changed the wording of any of your questions while building the questionnaire, then it's a good idea to do another round of cognitive interviewing now.

Do a usability test—it's essential

In a cognitive interview, you ask the person who is answering to focus on the meaning of each question and their thought processes as they think of an answer.

In contrast, in a usability test, you get the person to try working through your questionnaire while you watch. You're focusing mostly on whether the questionnaire works mechanically as they answer it. Some people naturally think aloud as they go through, which is helpful because it will add to what you learned from previous cognitive interviewing. But if they forget—don't worry. Simply ask them at the end if there was anything they found difficult to answer, or unexpected, or in the wrong order.

A usability test of your questionnaire is one of the easiest (and most fun) types of testing you'll ever do. All you have to do is:

- Find someone who is willing to try to answer your questionnaire.
- Watch them as they work through the questionnaire, as in Figure 4.36. Don't rely on them telling you how it went, because they don't know the questionnaire as well as you do, and they may not realize that it didn't work as intended.
- As you watch, take notes about everything: what seemed to go easily, and what may have been a problem.
- At the end, ask them for their views on the questionnaire—take notes about that, too.
- Think about the notes and decide what to change.

FIGURE 4.36
Usability testing by watching someone try a questionnaire on their mobile phone.

Can you do better than getting one person to test your questionnaire for you? Of course you can!

Here are some extra ideas that will improve your testing:

- Get someone from your defined group of people—the actual people you want to respond to your questionnaire.
- Test with a few more people. If you've done usability testing already, you won't be surprised to know that usability testing experts usually recommend that you get three to five people (one at a time, not in a group) to test your questionnaire. After about

three people, you'll usually have a long list of changes that you want to make, and it's better to do some changes and then repeat the tests with some different people.

- Try including a few people with low literacy, or people who may not be not very good with computers, or perhaps people who have disabilities. It's easy to do and will save you from feeling terrible later if someone with a disability tries and fails to respond to your questionnaire.

Don't let these recommendations for extra ideas put you off. You'll learn a lot from getting anyone to test your questionnaire—well, anyone who hasn't been involved in making it.

If you're not familiar with usability testing and want to know more about it than I've written here, then Steve Krug's book *Rocket Surgery Made Easy: The Do-It-Yourself Guide to Finding and Fixing Usability Problems* is a good place to start.

If you are working on Big Honkin' Surveys and want a deep dive into usability testing from survey methodologists, then get *Usability Testing for Survey Research* by Emily Geisen and Jennifer Romano Bergstrom. They cover everything in detail, including topics like the difficulties that people have when trying to use a slider to provide their answer.

Take screenshots of your final questionnaire

Now that you have your questionnaire thoroughly tested, iterated, and tested again, you've got one last crucial task before you get it out to the people who will answer: take screenshots of each page.

This plea is particularly heartfelt. I often have to analyze data where I haven't been part of the questionnaire development. It's grim trying to guess what the question looked like for the person who answered from abbreviated questions in a data set. And if you ever lose access to the survey tool partway through a project, or the tool changes so that you can no longer re-run your particular survey, then you'll thank me for those screenshots.

Even if you've been responsible for the questionnaire throughout, it's possible that you may forget some detail or another before the results come in. You'll thank me for those screenshots.

At this point, you will know

This has been quite a long chapter because there is a lot to think about when making your questionnaire.

What you'll discover in practice is: most of what you know about your questionnaire is what you learn in usability testing.

If you reach this point and haven't done any usability testing, then:

1. Stop.
2. Go back.
3. Do some usability testing. You'll find that issues and improvements jump out at you immediately.
4. Make some changes and retest.

When you've made and tested those improvements to your questionnaire, you're ready to move on to getting that questionnaire out to the people you want to answer. And that's the topic of Chapter 5.

On the way to it, you'll find an optional diversion into the complicated world of Likert scales and response formats in Spotlight K.

"On a Scale from 1 to 5" (Likert and Rating Scales)

One of the most frequently asked questions in survey design is: "What's the best number of points in a Likert scale?"

In this Spotlight, I'm going to introduce you to Likert, the various components that make up one of his scales, and then how to make a Likert scale.

A Likert scale measures an attitude

Dr. Rensis Likert was a statistician. According to him, his name is pronounced LICK-ert not Like-ert. (Read the story on www.allaccess.com/forum/viewtopic.php?t=24251. It's fun.)

He wrote a famous paper: "A Technique for the Measurement of Attitudes." (Likert, 1932) His technique was to create a questionnaire that used a series of statements, such as 24 statements about "imperialism," to measure the respondent's attitude about something (in this case, imperialism). The output of a Likert scale is a single calculated score.

His paper has been so popular that his name is now associated with almost any question that asks users to select a response from a range of opinions.

Likert did not invent attitude scales

The Likert scale is a good example of Stigler's Law of Eponymy: "No scientific discovery is named after its discoverer." (Stigler, 1980) Likert was responding to previous ideas about constructing a series of statements to build a picture of an attitude. (Thurstone, 1928) (Allport and Hartman, 1925) Likert's version of the scale became famous because it is as solid on theory as earlier scales but is less work to construct and much easier to score.

But don't get the idea that a good Likert scale is easy to construct. The complexities are such that they continue to be one of the most researched topics in survey methodology.

A Likert scale has many components

Let's have a look at the components that make up a Likert scale. Our example is the System Usability Scale (SUS), a Likert scale devised by John Brooke in 1986 that continues to be the most popular questionnaire for measuring usability.

In Figure H.1, you can see the parts of a Likert scale. SUS has ten questions, each of which has a statement followed by five response points. Each question is a Likert item.

When you build a questionnaire with a Likert scale, you can choose to present each Likert item as a separate question, or you can combine them all into a grid, as in Figure H.1.

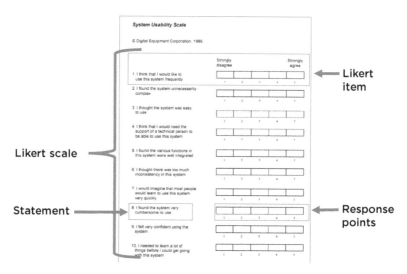

FIGURE H.1

The System Usability Scale is a Likert scale with 10 Likert items.

Many people use the term *Likert scale* for what is actually a *Likert item*, which is how we get the question, "How many points in a Likert scale?" Personally, I find that quite confusing, so I'm going to stick strictly to using the term *Likert scale* for the overall set of questions, and the term *Likert item* for the way a specific statement and its response points are put together.

Likert did not invent the Likert item

Likert used three styles of Likert items in his paper:

- A five-point one with answers from "Strongly Agree" to "Strongly Disagree," as in Figure H.2
- A three-point one with "yes," "no," as in Figure H.3
- A set of five longer statements that reflect opinions along a continuum, as in Figure H.4

24. Moving pictures showing military drill and naval manoeuvres should be exhibited to encourage patriotism.

| Strongly Approve (1) | Approve (2) | Undecided (3) | Disapprove (4) | Strongly Disapprove (5) |

FIGURE H.2

A Likert item with five response options.

1. Do you favor the early entrance of the United States into the League of Nations?

| YES (4) | ? (3) | NO (2) |

FIGURE H.3

A Likert item with three options: "YES," "?" and "NO."

15. Using the term "armaments" to mean equipment devised for war rather than for police purposes, our policy should be to favor:
   (a) absolute and immediate disarmament of all nations. (5)
   (b) rapid and drastic reduction of the armaments of all nations. (4)
   (c) slow but steady reduction of all armaments. (3)
   (d) maintenance for a long time of approximately the present military and naval strength of all the powers. (2)
   (e) our free military and naval expansion unembarrassed by agreements with other nations. (1)

FIGURE H.4

A Likert item with a set of statements.

Likert did not invent any of these response formats, and he did not express any preferences for one over the other in his 1932 paper, but his name has come to be associated with the five-point Likert item— and many variations of it.

We met another type of Likert item in Spotlight B, "The Net Promoter Score® and Correlation." The Net Promoter question is a Likert item with 11 points (responses 0 to 10), but the Net Promoter Score® is not a Likert scale because it only has one statement.

Likert items look easy but have lots of hidden complexity and are a popular topic for research. For example, I enjoyed a seminar that offered the results of three experiments on "don't know" options in response formats in web surveys, as in Figure H.5.

FIGURE H.5
A survey methodology seminar looking solely at "don't know" options in response formats.

17 October 2019 | City, University of London
How should we present 'don't know' options in web surveys?

City-ESS HQ-NatCen survey methodology seminar series

In this seminar we will explore whether and how to include a 'don't know' option, discussing a range of potential solutions and presenting the results of three experiments carried out by NatCen, Kantar and Ipsos.

One of the much-researched topics is indeed the number of response points. We'll return to the "correct" number later in this Spotlight.

Likert items often appear in grids

Because people who create questionnaires love their Likert items so much, and because it's hard work to bash a bunch of questions down to a single Most Crucial Question, it's also very common to see grids of statements—also known as *matrix questions*.

Unfortunately, many grids are full of problems that make them unpopular with people who answer. The grid can be hard to read, the questions are difficult to understand, finding an answer is too hard, they are not sure whether they want to give that answer, and there are problems like, "I'm not sure whether this point means good or bad." I've heard people say: "I always stop answering a questionnaire when I see a grid," and I've often seen a big spike in people abandoning a questionnaire at grid questions.

Let's have a detailed look at the sample grid in Figure H.6, which has seven Likert items.

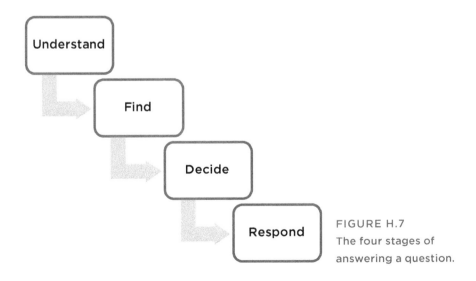

Please click below to indicate how you would rate the shop on each of the aspects shown. Click 'not applicable' if you feel unable to answer any on aspect shown.

	Very Poor	Poor	Good	Very Good	Excellent	Not applicable
Overall satisfaction with your visit	○	○	○	○	○	○
Overall service from the people serving you in the shop	○	○	○	○	○	○
Overall range of products & services	○	○	○	○	○	○
Overall value for money	○	○	○	○	○	○
Overall product quality	○	○	○	○	○	○
Overall product availability	○	○	○	○	○	○
Overall shop environment	○	○	○	○	○	○

FIGURE H.6
A set of Likert items arranged as a grid.

And here are some of the problems that I noticed with this grid, related to the four stages of answering a question, as in Figure H.7, that I talked about in Chapter 3.

Understand

Find

Decide

Respond

FIGURE H.7
The four stages of answering a question.

TABLE H.1 THINKING ABOUT THE STAGE OF ANSWERING
A GRID QUESTION

Stage of answering	Problems in this grid
Understand	The text is small. Some words might be unfamiliar, such as the phrase "aspects shown." There is an extra word ("on") in the phrase "to answer any on aspect shown."
Find	One statement is about "overall product availability": how does that relate to the actual experience of the product(s) they wanted to buy? And what about if they went to the shop for another reason, such as to return something?
Decide	Another statement is about "overall service from the people in the shop"—many of us know that clerks can be fired for poor ratings, so we may hesitate to give our true opinion.
Respond	There's the challenge of trying to remember the meaning of each radio button when you reach the bottom of the grid and the description at the top has scrolled off the page.

The "understand," "find," and "decide" problems here are all things that would equally apply to the questions considered individually, and you might reasonably argue that only the "respond" problem is specific to grids. But what I find in practice is that grids seem to bring out the worst in questionnaire design—they can be a dumping ground for too many questions that have not had enough attention.

You may argue "But not all grids! I've seen grids that are better than that." That's true. Alongside that, I've seen many, many grids that are at least as bad as my example, and some that are worse. I'm not saying that it's impossible to create a decent grid that people can answer, but it is definitely a challenge, so try to avoid them.

Some grids are not Likert scales

Sometimes, questionnaire designers happen to have several questions that seem to work nicely as Likert items, so they decide to organize them into a grid. The plan is to use the answers to each question separately to make different decisions. That's not a Likert scale; it's a set of questions arranged as a grid.

A Likert scale gives an overall score

Other times, the questions are sufficiently focused on a single specific attitude, and the answers can be combined to get an overall score for that attitude. This makes them into a Likert scale.

In my view, Likert's most important contribution from his famous paper was that he demonstrated that the simple method of getting a score by adding up all the answers to the individual response formats was as good as the more complex methods that his predecessors in scale development had proposed, such as getting a set of judges to assess each statement for its potential contribution to the overall scale.

Build a Likert scale in 13 tasks

Creating a Likert scale involves 13 tasks. I'll explain each one as we go. If you're not planning to create a whole scale but instead thinking only of one or two Likert items, then you can skip ahead to tasks 7 and 8.

Start your Likert scale with candidate statements

Task 1: Collect candidate statements, looking for between 50 and 100.

Likert recommended looking for any previous questionnaires on the topic to harvest their statements. He also mentioned reading newspapers and asking experts. If you recall Chapter 1, "Goals," you might also think of having some meetings with stakeholders. For maximum credit as a focused reader of this book, you'll think of interviewing some of the people you want to answer to discover their Burning Issues (in Chapter 2).

How many candidate statements do you need? Likert called for "a good number" but didn't say how many that is. I look for something in the range of 50 to 100, aiming for 10 or fewer statements in the final scale. (And if you can whittle them down to one Most Crucial Question, that's even better.)

At this point, don't worry about the precise wording of the statements. You'll sort that out in a later task.

Choose a single topic for your Likert scale

Task 2: Group your candidate statements into topics. Decide which topic you are exploring in this scale. Discard the statements for other topics, or save them to use for a different scale.

As you've collected the candidate statements, you'll have had one topic in mind, but what often happens is that although all the statements broadly fit the topic, there will be lots of variations within that—to the point where the topic expands from one to several.

A Likert scale is about measuring attitudes about *one* topic. In the end, all the statements must collect opinions on a single topic. If your statements range across several topics, then don't try to shove them all into a single scale.

Split up double-barreled statements

Task 3: Split any double-barreled or multi-barreled statements to make them into single-barreled statements—or throw them out.

Do you recall the "double-barreled" questions that we met in Chapter 3? It's a point that Likert mentions in his paper.

Many things have changed since 1932, but my library of recent screenshots has large quantities of double-barreled, or even more-barreled, Likert statements.

For example, the one in Figure H.8 includes this statement: "Thinking about when you set up, amended, or canceled a payment (direct debit or standing order)." It manages to squash six barrels into one statement; three tasks (set up/amend/cancel) relative to two different types of recurring payments (direct debit/standing order).

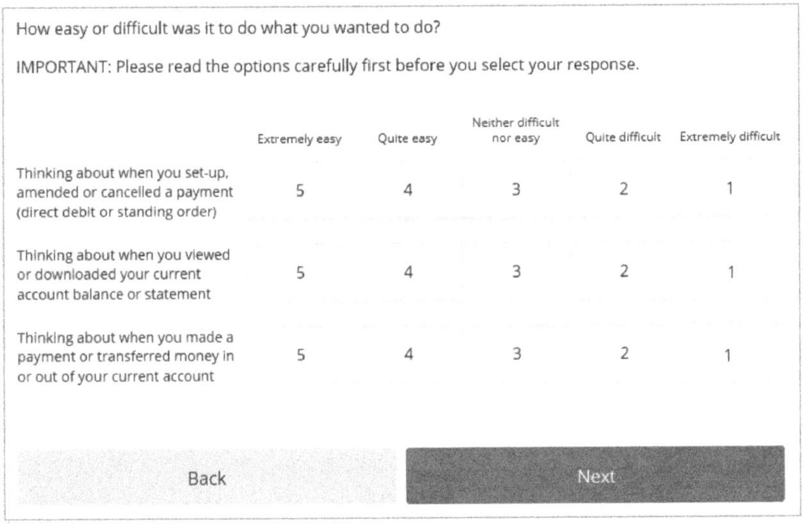

How easy or difficult was it to do what you wanted to do?

IMPORTANT: Please read the options carefully first before you select your response.

	Extremely easy	Quite easy	Neither difficult nor easy	Quite difficult	Extremely difficult
Thinking about when you set-up, amended or cancelled a payment (direct debit or standing order)	5	4	3	2	1
Thinking about when you viewed or downloaded your current account balance or statement	5	4	3	2	1
Thinking about when you made a payment or transferred money in or out of your current account	5	4	3	2	1

Back	Next

FIGURE H.8

A small Likert scale with multi-barreled statements.

Check that the statements are opinions

Task 4: Review your statements to check that they are opinions. Edit or discard any problematic ones.

A Likert scale is not a general knowledge quiz: you need statements of opinion to agree with or disagree with, not statements of fact.

Likert recommended writing statements with the word "should," as in

> "An American committing a crime in Shanghai should be tried by a Chinese judge."

I don't because the current usage of "should" is ambiguous. Have a look at this statement:

> "I should give up smoking."

In the case of the criminal American, do you agree with me that "should" means that we think the trial will be conducted by the Chinese judge, and we're commenting on whether or not we agree with that? And in the second case, have you, like me, heard a smoker say, "I should give up smoking" without any intention of doing so? "Should" is now a slippery word that can swap its meaning both according to the context and according to the views of the reader.

This is also a good time to check whether you are asking about predictions of future behavior. We met those back in Chapter 3, when discussing the problem that there is no curve of prediction. I can't stop you from including them, but I can point out that they are notoriously unreliable.

Test that the statements use familiar words in familiar ways

Task 5: Ask three to five people from your defined group to assess the statements for clarity. Either discard any unclear statements or reword them and test them again.

At this point, you've got a set of candidate statements of opinion about a single attitude, and your final editing step is to ensure that they make sense to people who will answer—especially using familiar words in familiar ways.

The best way to do this is to do some cognitive interviewing, which we met in Chapter 3. To recap: Find some people from your defined group. Get them to tell you what each candidate statement means in their own words and to tell you which statements are clear and which are not. If any statements with "should" survived from Task 4, pay particular attention to what people think "should" means in your context.

At this stage, they will probably also tell you whether they agree or disagree with each statement—that's also valuable data, as you want statements that reflect a range of opinions.

Another way to do this is to have a meeting with your stakeholders and try to guess whether the people in your defined group will understand the statements in the same way that you do. My experience is that this is possible but takes longer than asking some people in your defined group.

If you've been sufficiently ruthless in your "discard" policy, you'll have maybe half or fewer of your statements left. Decide now whether to try another round of editing and interviews, which will probably save you time overall, or to take the whole lot through to the next task.

Check that you have no more than 10 statements left

Task 6: If you have more than 10 statements left, discard some more.

You've done several rounds of editing now, and I hope you've discarded the majority of your "good number" of candidate statements. Ideally, at this point, you will have no more than 10 statements that you are sure that the people who answer will understand in the same way that you do.

If you still have more than 10 statements, take a good hard look at them and work out whether you can discard some of them.

Check that your statements are positive

Task 7: Look for statements that are negatively worded. Turn each one into a positive statement or discard it.

"Straight-lining" happens when the person who answers gets bored with the questionnaire and starts ticking the same answer for every statement. To avoid this, some market researchers tell us to write some statements positively, so that "Strongly agree" is good, and some negatively, so that "Strongly agree" is bad.

For example, one of the most popular Likert scales used by user experience professionals is the System Usability Scale (SUS), which starts with these two statements:

"I think that I would like to use this system frequently."

"I found the system unnecessarily complex." (Brooke, 1996)

When I've used SUS, I've found that people struggle with the "swapping in their heads" necessary for statement 2—and in general, negatively worded statements are harder to understand than their positive equivalents.

Choose the number of response points

Task 8: Choose the number of response points (5 is good).

As you've seen, Likert used 3-point and 5-point Likert items. NPS® uses an 11-point (0-10) format.

The flowchart in Figure H.9 is a summary of the method that I use to choose the number of points.

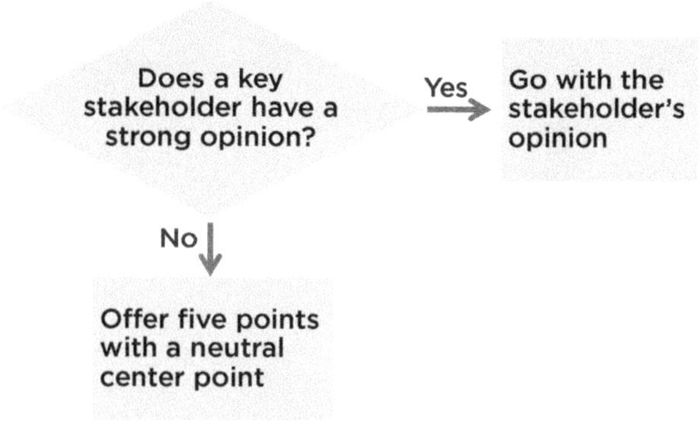

Does a key stakeholder have a strong opinion? → Yes → **Go with the stakeholder's opinion**

No ↓

Offer five points with a neutral center point

FIGURE H.9

A flowchart to decide on the number of response points.

And now, a bit of the theory behind the flowchart.

I've seen all sorts of discussion about any number of response points from 2 through to the theoretically infinite number of points in a line where the person answering can mark any point between two ends (a "visual analog scale").

In testing many questionnaires, I learned that the people who answer mostly care little about the number of response points that you offer—they are much more focused on the statements and their views on them. That's the rationale for the question in the flowchart about a key stakeholder's opinion: the choice of points in the response format is unlikely to affect the people who answer very much, so you may as well make the stakeholder happy.

If it's up to you to choose, then my next suggestion is to choose something with an odd number of points—5 is the most popular choice, but 3 and 7 also work. The odd number gives you a midpoint that works for people who answer who are genuinely neutral and for people who have answers that do not clearly map onto any of the specific answer options, such as:

- Don't know
- Sometimes one view, sometimes another
- Don't understand the question
- Not applicable
- Prefer not to answer
- It's not up to me to have an opinion on this topic (this last one may be uniquely British)

As with absolutely everything about Likert items, opinions differ. There is definitely a view that you can try to preserve the midpoint as a true neutral by adding a "don't know" or a "not applicable" option and making sure that the question is optional so that if someone prefers not to answer, then they can simply skip it. By all means, try whatever combination appeals to you; you will be testing your scale in task 12 and will find out then whether your preference works.

Not convinced by my assertion that the people who answer do not care greatly about the number of response points? Then have a look at the paper by a team at the Department of Dermatology at the University Hospital in Münster, Germany. (Phan, Blome et al., 2011) They needed to assess "pruritus intensity" (pain from itch, in every-day terms) and tested the three response formats in Figure H.10: a Visual Analog, one they called a *verbal rating scale* with 4 points, and a zero-to-10 format (11 points). They found that it didn't matter very much, although their (mostly elderly) patients found the unfamiliar Visual Analog harder to use.

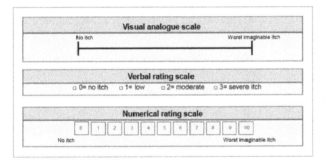

FIGURE H.10
Three response formats tested by (Phan, Blome et al., 2011).

If one citation isn't quite enough for you, then please feel welcome to engage with the literature. My recommended place to start is the chapter by Jon A. Krosnick and Stanley Presser. (Krosnick and Presser, 2009) They cite more than 80 papers on the topic of the design of Likert items.

Decide on your method of scoring for your Likert items

Task 9: Work out how you will score your Likert items. If you are planning to give your results to anyone else, check that they agree that your choice is appropriate.

When you've got your number of response points—I'm going to assume that you've picked 5—then it's time to sort out a method of scoring for them. Yes, you do have to do this in advance of creating the questionnaire; waiting until you have some responses is cheating. (And it provides lots of opportunities for heated discussions in meetings that you'd much rather avoid.)

Likert used two different methods for assigning scores within his items. Let's have a look at the 5-point format, as in Figure H.11.

---

24. Moving pictures showing military drill and naval manoeuvres should be exhibited to encourage patriotism.

| Strongly Approve (1) | Approve (2) | Undecided (3) | Disapprove (4) | Strongly Disapprove (5) |

FIGURE H.11

Statement 24 from Likert's scale about "Imperialism," with "Strongly Approve" scored as 1 through to "Strongly Disapprove" scored as 5.

An aside: I was challenged to rewrite that statement without using "Should.'" My version is:

> "Watching movies of military drill and naval maneuvers makes people feel more patriotic."

You may have a better one. That's all part of the fun of writing questions.

He showed that we can use a simple numeric method of scoring. For the 5-point items, he scored "Strongly Approve" as 1, "Approve" as 2, and so on through to "Strongly Disapprove" as 5. You will see that he put the score under each response, for the convenience of the person capturing the data from the paper questionnaires used in 1932.

He also explains in his paper why he chose to assign the values 4, 3, and 2 to his 3-point items, as in Figure H.12.

FIGURE H.12

A Likert item with three options: "YES," "?" and "NO."

1. Do you favor the early entrance of the United States into the League of Nations?

| YES (4) | ? (3) | NO (2) |

If you ended up with some negative statements, despite everything that I said in task 7, then you need to swap the scoring around. If we have another look at the first two statements in the System Usability Scale (SUS):

1. "I think that I would like to use this system frequently."

2. "I found the system unnecessarily complex." (Brooke, 1996)

For statement 1, "Strongly agree" gets a score of 5, "Agree" scores 4, "Neutral" scores 3, "Disagree" scores 2, and "Strongly disagree" scores 1.

But for statement 2, "Strongly agree" gets a score of 1, "Agree" scores 2, "Neutral" stays the same at 3, "Disagree" scores 4, and "Strongly disagree" scores 5.

There are many other ways of scoring a response format. Here are some other popular scoring methods:

Top box:	Strongly approve	1
	Approve	1
	Undecided	0
	Disapprove	0
	Strongly disapprove	0

Widely used in market research, on the basis that there's often little difference between levels of approval, and some people simply don't like to pick the "strongly approve" option.

Percentage:	Use these weightings:	
	Strongly approve	100%
	Approve	75%
	Undecided	50%
	Disapprove	25%
	Strongly disapprove	0%

Similar to Likert's method, but some prefer it on the basis that it starts at 0.

NPS®:	(Requires a scale from 0 to 10)
	Count scores of 9 or 10 as "Promoters"
	Count scores of 0 to 6 as "Detractors"

Overall score is the percentage of promoters minus the percentage of detractors.

(We met this in Spotlight B.)

You can find academic papers to defend any of these scoring methods, including NPS®, and many others. I'll throw in one more that is my personal favorite:

Raw: Report the numbers of people who chose each option, or (equivalently) report the percentage of all the people who answer who chose each option. Do not attempt to aggregate the responses into a score. I have to admit that although I use this method all the time when reporting on questions presented as Likert items, I'm not able to use it in Likert scales because the whole point of a Likert scale is to aggregate the responses into a score.

I was searching for an academically respectable method myself a few years ago. I was fortunate to have an invitation to the Internet Survey Methodology workshop in Bolzano, Italy—luckily for me, coinciding with Bolzano's famous annual Christmas market as in Figure H.14. The workshop was conveniently full of top survey experts, so I asked them.

FIGURE H.13

A perk of attending a workshop in Bolzano, Italy was browsing the Christmas market for goodies such as marzipan fruits.

Broadly speaking, the message from the experts was (I paraphrase): "It doesn't much matter. Pick one and stick to it." They also pointed out that any rating question is hard work for the people who answer, which we'll return to in a moment.

If you do not happen to have a survey methodology workshop scheduled at the right time for your survey, here are a few ways of getting agreement on your scoring method:

1. Go with the HiPPO (highest paid person's opinion).

2. Find a statistician. Do what they say.

3. Read a selection from the literature on Likert scales and statistics, make up your own mind, and write a paper defending that choice.

4. The approach that I use the most, a workshop with stakeholders:

   - Give them the data in the slide in Figure H.14.

   - Get each person to calculate the answer on their own, quietly. (I've had at least seven different answers in various workshops.)

   - Everyone then reveals their score and calculation method.

   - Discuss which one is best.

A 'Like / Dislike' question got these responses

Strongly dislike	2
Dislike	6
Neither dislike nor like	14
Like	31
Strongly like	13
Total responses	**66**

Please work out:
the percentage of respondents who 'like'

FIGURE H.14

Some example data and the instruction for a workshop rating response calculation.

Decide how to create the score for your Likert scale

Task 10: Decide how to calculate the overall score for your Likert scale from the scores for the individual items.

Now that you have the individual item scores, it is time to work out how to combine them into a single overall score for the scales.

Likert described a variety of statistical methods for how to do this, especially because he was responding to previous ideas. He demonstrated that the simple method of adding up all the individual scores was just as good as two previous, and more complicated, approaches. For example, one of the earlier methods, created by L.L. Thurstone (Thurstone, 1928), involved getting judges to assess how much each individual item ought to contribute to the overall score.

Looking again at SUS, the System Usability Scale, it has 10 statements overall. After swapping around the scores for all the negatively worded statements, we end up with 10 statements, each of which can have a score from 1 to 5. If we just add up all the numbers, the worst score is 10 and the best is 50. But stakeholders like scores that go from 0 to 100, so the final step is to subtract 10 from the total and then multiply by 2.5.

Think about whether a rating response is appropriate

Task 11: Try turning each statement into a direct question. Decide whether to ask it as a direct question, turn it back into a statement, or discard it.

Task 1 was to check whether a Likert Scale is appropriate. Now let's check to see whether a rating response of any kind is appropriate for your statements.

At that workshop in Bolzano, I was reminded that rating questions are quite hard work for the person answering, who has to:

- Understand the statement to determine what they are being asked about.
- Find their own opinion, typically by creating an answer.
- Decide how their answer compares with the statement.
- Respond by translating that comparison into a response value.
- Check that they have the response value the right way round: "Was 1 good or bad? I forget."

- Finish that question by choosing the appropriate response on the questionnaire and then do that again for all the other statements.

At the workshop, I asked one of the professors what he would do with the statements that I was struggling with. He said firmly, "I'd turn them into direct questions."

Let's try that with "The ease of registering for an account on xxx website," which I took from Figure H.15 with 5 responses about satisfaction plus "N/'A," which I took to mean "not applicable."

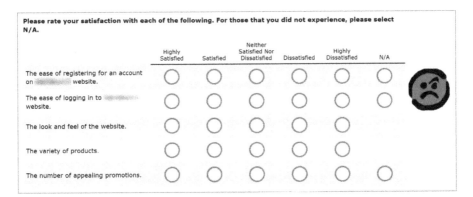

Please rate your satisfaction with each of the following. For those that you did not experience, please select N/A.

	Highly Satisfied	Satisfied	Neither Satisfied Nor Dissatisfied	Dissatisfied	Highly Dissatisfied	N/A
The ease of registering for an account on ____ website.	○	○	○	○	○	○
The ease of logging in to ____ website.	○	○	○	○	○	○
The look and feel of the website.	○	○	○	○	○	
The variety of products.	○	○	○	○	○	
The number of appealing promotions.	○	○	○	○	○	○

FIGURE H.15
Some statements from a Likert scale about satisfaction with a website.

Here's my suggestion for an equivalent direct question:

Did you register for an account on our website?

( ) Yes, and it was easy

( ) Yes, but it was difficult

( ) No

( ) Don't remember/prefer not to say

When you have them all as direct questions, you can offer response options that are tailored to the exact question, rather than generic ones that try to match all the questions.

Test your Likert scale

You are now ready for the most important of all the tasks. On no account can you skip this one:

Task 12: Test your scale with people from your specified group. Then go back and try again based on what you find in testing.

No excuses.

You can also look out for whether people are getting bored by too many positive statements—and if so, decide whether to reduce the number of statements or turn some of them back into negative wording.

Run the statistics on your Likert scale

Task 13: If you are going to use this scale more than once, then get at least 100 people from your defined group to answer your scale and run statistical tests to make sure that the scale has test/retest reliability.

At this point, you have a series of statements that you know your defined group of people can understand and answer. You also know that your scale works for your Most Crucial Question and reflects the Burning Issues. You are on the way to making sure that your scale is valid.

If you only want to use your scale once, then think about whether or not the answers you receive will help you make the decision. If they will, then you're done.

If you want to use the scale repeatedly, most likely for a series of comparative surveys, then it's time to look at the "test/retest reliability," also known as *reproducibility.*

> **Test/retest reliability** says that if a person completes the same scale on two different occasions, with no other changes in between, then the result is the same.

For example, suppose that your Likert scale aims to measure whether or not people like your website. If you get a group of people to answer it in the morning and then again in the afternoon (with no changes to your website in between), then you'd like it to give you the same result each time.

If a Likert scale is reliable, you can use it with confidence to measure over time, because you'll know that the changes in scores come from actual changes in attitude, not from variability in the answering process itself.

To ensure that you have test/retest reliability, you need to get at least 100 people from your defined group to answer your scale and then run these tests:

- **Factor analysis:** This statistical process helps you work out whether your scale is genuinely about different aspects of the same thing or is hiding two or three separate topics.

- **Cronbach's alpha:** This process tells you whether the items within your scale point in the same general direction or not. If all the items are positively worded, then you'd expect that someone answering who has an eventual overall positive score would mostly give positive answers on the items. A high Cronbach's alpha confirms that fact.

UCLA has an introduction to factor analysis: https://stats.idre.ucla.edu/spss/seminars/introduction-to-factor-analysis/a-practical-introduction-to-factor-analysis/ and also one for Cronbach's alpha: https://stats.idre.ucla.edu/spss/faq/what-does-cronbachs-alpha-mean/.

Congratulations—you have a Likert scale

You have seen that building a good Likert scale is rather a major effort, and even creating a good single question with a Likert item has its challenges.

Do you think I'm exaggerating these tasks somewhat? I can assure you that I'm not. For example, look at the paper by Jill Dawson, Ray Fitzpatrick, David Murray, and Andrew Carr, which describes the development of the "Oxford Hip" (Dawson, Fitzpatrick et al., 1996)—a questionnaire that my orthopedic surgeon asks me to complete every five years to assess how I'm getting on with my hip replacement. It's a Likert scale and includes items about everyday life, such as walking and getting dressed, as shown in Figure H.16.

Perhaps it's not surprising that a typical medical questionnaire goes through all those steps.

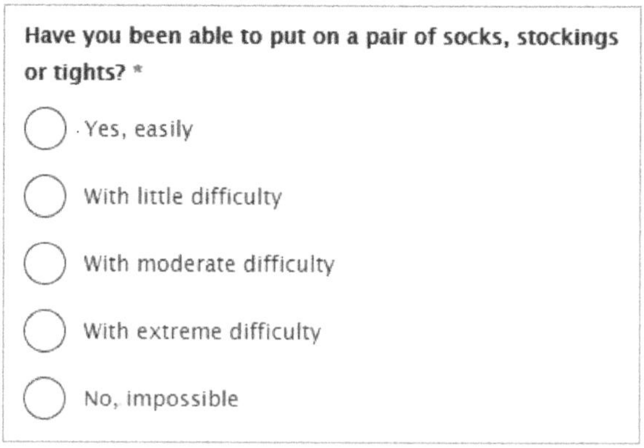

FIGURE H.16
A question from
the Oxford Hip
medical assessment
questionnaire.

Have you been able to put on a pair of socks, stockings or tights? *

- ◯ ·Yes, easily
- ◯ With little difficulty
- ◯ With moderate difficulty
- ◯ With extreme difficulty
- ◯ No, impossible

Maybe it's a bit more surprising that when John Brooke developed the System Usability Scale (SUS) that I mentioned earlier, he used a process really rather similar to the one I've described, as he explains in his paper. (Brooke, 1996)

Obviously, I can't force you to do all 13 tasks. All I can do is to explain that if you want valid and reliable data from your Likert scale, then that's the sort of effort you need to put in.

A final word: avoid ranking questions

As part of this Spotlight, we looked at the effort required when someone has to assess their opinion and use it to answer a question in a Likert item.

There's a similar type of question that you may meet: the ranking question, which asks people to put a number of options in order of their preference, such as the example in Figure H.17.

Ranking questions are even more difficult for people to answer than rating questions. The processes include:

- Looking down a list to assess the items
- Comparing each one to all the others to determine how to order them
- Adjusting the list, often using an unfamiliar interaction
- Reviewing the list, often to satisfy a validation that insists that all the items are ranked, whether the person has a view on them or not

Please answer this question by dragging and dropping your choices to the box on the right.

Q1   Which of the following describes why you are a member of BCS, The Chartered Institute for IT? *(Please select up to three and rank in order, starting with your main motivation)*

For professional recognition
To get career advice and inspiration
To access CPD and personal development tools
To help me learn and progress in my field
For networking and knowledge sharing opportunities
For opportunities to be involved and share my expertise
To access thought leadership, industry or policy updates and best practice
To support the purpose of 'making IT good for society'

Progress ▨▨

← Back   ⟲ Reset   💾 Save   Next →

FIGURE H.17
Ranking question from a professional association.

When I got the example question in Figure H8.17, I was a bit stumped, as I wasn't interested in any of the professional association's content—but couldn't see exactly how to tell them that.

Ranking questions also poses some challenges for scoring. The statistical tests for ranking are different from the ones for rating. Also, you don't know how different any two items on the list are. The items ranked 1 and 2 could be really similar, or they could be very different.

If you are thinking about ranking, consider using ratings instead and then look at the average ratings. The task of rating the items will be easier for the people who answer, and you will still get an overall order for the items at the end. You will also know how different the items are by comparing their average ratings.

However, if it is definitely essential to get the people who answer to provide a ranking (for example, if you want them to give their priorities), then be sure to test your questions even more carefully than usual and make sure that you decide on a scoring method that is acceptable before you get the results.

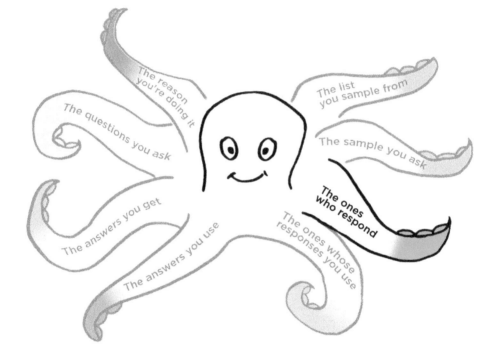

The reason you're doing it

The questions you ask

The list you sample from

The sample you ask

The ones who respond

The answers you get

The answers you use

The ones whose responses you use

Fieldwork: Get People to Respond

At this point, you have a questionnaire. In this chapter, we'll go through a few steps to prepare it for launching, and then at last it's time for the fieldwork. This is the exciting phase when you get it out to the people you want to answer, watch their responses as they come in, and start to enjoy the results from your hard work so far.

Decide on your invitation, thank-you, and follow-up

The invitation is the thing that introduces your questionnaire, describes the reward people will get for answering (which doesn't have to be financial), and explains or links to your privacy policy. For an email invitation to a web questionnaire, it will be a separate matter and needs as much attention as the questionnaire itself. For other types of questionnaires, you may be ahead of me and have already designed your invitation as part of the questionnaire.

It's also worth giving some attention to the thank-you, nearly always the last item in your questionnaire, and to decide whether or not to offer any follow-up.

Choose a reward appropriate to your survey

Back in Chapter 2, "Sample," we looked at why people choose to respond to surveys. A quick reminder: Giving an incentive can help to encourage response, but only if the *perceived* reward is in balance with the *perceived* effort.

The best incentives are guaranteed and immediate. For example, the San Francisco travel authority offered a free ride on their famous cable cars as an incentive to fill out a tourism survey—right at the place that sells cable car tickets and other souvenirs like the little ornament in Figure 5.1. I happily joined the line for the opportunity to do that questionnaire.

If the "reward" that you're offering is a feeling of being helpful ("help us by sharing your opinions"), then make sure that at least one (optional) question is an open question with space for any opinion, not just a long series of opportunities to rate their agreement with your opinions.

If people are answering because they are interested in your topic, then an appropriate reward can be the opportunity to get a copy of your report. Sometimes, even offering a link to the results of a previous survey can be enough to improve response, as the Australian Bureau of Statistics found in an experiment on an official survey of financial businesses. (Burnside, Bishop et al., 2005)

FIGURE 5.1
My cable car souvenir from San Francisco.

You'll know whether you've chosen the right rewards when you examine your response rate. That's one of the many reasons why you'll do a pilot test: to check that the reward is pitched correctly.

Some respondents don't want anonymity

Have you heard about Henrietta Lacks, shown in Figure 5.2?

FIGURE 5.2
An imagined portrait of Henrietta Lacks, created in 2017 by Kadir Nelson to commemorate her contribution to science.

She died from cancer at age 31 in 1951, but her cells (the "HeLa" strain) turned out to be exceptionally suitable for medical research. They were used for decades without any acknowledgement of her contribution or telling her family anything about it.

Her story raises challenging ethical questions about consent, anonymity, and confidentiality. We must be careful about our choices around anonymity and confidentiality, as discussed in Spotlight E, "Privacy":

> **Anonymity:** You will not be identified as the individual who gave those responses.

> **Confidentiality:** Your responses will only be seen by whoever you agree may see them.

We also need to think hard about whether any of the people who answer might welcome the opportunity to be acknowledged for their contributions. For example, I worked on a survey of students for a UK university. From previous research, we knew that most of the students loved the university. When we offered the students choices about anonymity and confidentiality, less than a third opted to remain both confidential and anonymous (see Table 5.1).

TABLE 5.1   PERCENTAGES OF UNIVERSITY STUDENTS WHO CHOSE DIFFERENT LEVELS OF CONFIDENTIALITY AND ANONYMITY

Effect	Choice we offered	%
Neither confidential nor anonymous	"I am happy to be quoted, and please mention my name."	26%
Not confidential but anonymous	"I am happy to be quoted, but make sure any quotation is used anonymously."	42%
Confidential and anonymous	Neither of the above	31%

Let's contrast a similar job for the tax authority: the taxpayers were extremely reluctant to take part at all until they were reassured that their responses would be completely anonymous and confidential.

Decide whether to offer any follow-up

Some people want a personal response, and therefore refuse to be anonymous. They may have been unable to find any other way to raise an issue and see this as an opportunity to get help, or they may just want to vent in a personal way.

Even when you specifically tell people that you do not want them to give any personal details and that you will treat all contributions as anonymous and confidential, they may go right ahead and put personal details in there.

You have some choices here:

- Redact the personal details from your dataset and do nothing else. This solves the anonymity problem, but may risk upsetting the person who provided the details.
- Extract the personal details from the dataset and put them into your usual process for dealing with contacts. This ought to help the person who provided the details, but risks giving you a headache when you consider the implications for your privacy policies and assurance of confidentiality.
- Do something else that you or your organization considers to be more appropriate.

Decide whether to send any reminders

Reminders can increase your response rate.

The usual best practice in a Big Honkin' Survey is:

- Offer a reminder after a suitable interval, usually a week or two.
- Provide the second attempt in a different mode, so if the original invitation were to a web survey, then the reminder would be something else, such as a paper questionnaire (assuming that you have their mailing details).
- Try again after another suitable interval, ideally in a different mode again—such as a postcard offering to send out another paper questionnaire.

Does this work for a Light Touch Survey? I don't think so. It seems to be overkill. Accept that some people won't answer and move on.

Make it easy to get the questionnaire back

If you're doing a web survey, check that the links work and that when the person finishes answering, the data from the questionnaire arrives at wherever it ought to be.

If you're doing an email survey, make sure that the email address works and that there is plenty of space in the inbox it's being returned to. Avoid fancy artwork or images that will fill your users' mailboxes and your own.

If you're using a mail survey, include a postage-paid addressed envelope and also put the address at the end of the questionnaire in case the envelope gets mislaid.

If you're doing an ambient survey, include an address at the end of the questionnaire (and maybe a web link, too). Also, think about whether you could offer prepaid postage. Some people will take it away with them to complete later. Not many, but you can hope.

If you're doing a face-to-face survey, make sure that you've thought about who types in the answers and how to store the paper responses.

Create a good invitation

Your invitation is as important as your questionnaire. It's time to go back once again to the trust/effort/reward triangle that you met in Chapter 2.

Make sure that your invitation looks trustworthy

The survey invitation in Figure 5.3 is one of my favorites. When I show it to participants in workshops, they nearly all condemn it as spam: it seems to be a combination of cheesy clip art and illegible text that influences the vote. (It's not spam—it's a genuine invitation from a local government department near me.)

FIGURE 5.3

Invitation to a survey about Luton as a place for businesses.

Make sure that you test your invitation without images. Figure 5.4 is one that I got from the printer manufacturer Epson.

FIGURE 5.4
Invitation to a survey about an Epson printer with no images.

If I hadn't been collecting surveys for this book, that massive blank "no image" would have made me delete the email straight away. As it was, I clicked for the images and then laughed out loud at the result in Figure 5.5. This didn't look anything like a business that valued genuine feedback; it looked like a business that was urging me to give it a five-star review.

I lost all trust in the survey and declined to answer. Even more amusingly, when I replaced the printer a few years later I got exactly the same invitation, with the only changes being the precise model name and the photograph of the newer printer.

To create trust:

- Say who you are.
- Say why you've contacted this person specifically.
- Include your contact information to show that a real person who can be contacted is behind the survey.

FIGURE 5.5
Invitation to a survey about an Epson printer with images.

To increase perceived reward:

- Explain the purpose of the survey.
- Explain why this person's responses will help that purpose.
- If there is an incentive, offer it.

To help the person estimate the effort:

- Outline the topics of the survey.
- Say what the closing date is for the survey.

- Do *not* say how long it will take (unless you have tested the heck out of it and are extremely sure that you know the answer).
- Say how many questions there are (if possible—in a Big Honkin' Survey with lots of skip patterns, this may be tricky).

Some mistakes to avoid:

- A closing date before the invitation date
- A link to the questionnaire that doesn't work
- Personalized invitations from a patchy database, so some of them say "Dear #namehere" or "Hi Mrs!"
- Relying on images that do not display with images turned off when displayed as plain text

Keep the invitation short

I've taken over 200 words to tell you what to include in your invitation. And now the bad news: that's definitely the maximum you can have for your invitation. Even shorter is better.

I've included the example survey invitation from Trello (a task management application) in Figure 5.6.

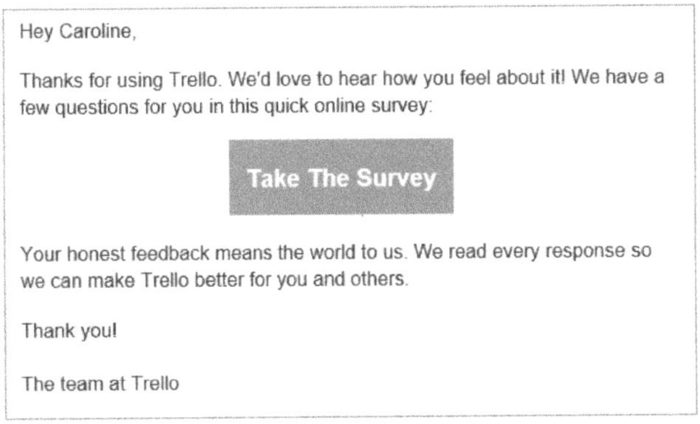

Hey Caroline,

Thanks for using Trello. We'd love to hear how you feel about it! We have a few questions for you in this quick online survey:

Take The Survey

Your honest feedback means the world to us. We read every response so we can make Trello better for you and others.

Thank you!

The team at Trello

FIGURE 5.6
This survey invitation from Trello worked for me—57 words.

This invitation worked for me in 57 words:

- It says that they are Trello.
- They've contacted me because I've used Trello.

To increase perceived reward:

- They want to make Trello better.
- They read every response (valuable to me as a survey specialist, because I'm aware that many organizations don't bother).
- There was no financial incentive, but there was a feel-good factor that was OK with me.

To help the person estimate the effort:

- It's about my use of Trello.
- (They skipped the closing date—oh well.)
- They say a "few questions" and "quick"—could be better, but they've done enough with the rest of the invitation that I'm going to overlook the vagueness here.

Write a "thank-you page" for politeness

Overall, I think your invitation is as important as your questionnaire because if the invitation does not work, then the questionnaire definitely will not work.

A pleasant "thank-you page" tops it off with good feelings, as shown in Figure 5.7. This is also the place to reinforce any offer of follow-up that you made within the questionnaire—or, if you definitely decided to keep all responses completely anonymous and confidential, to put appropriate contact details so that if the person who answers definitely wants some follow-up, then they can contact you.

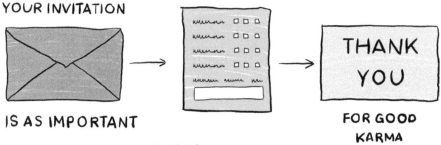

YOUR INVITATION

IS AS IMPORTANT

AS YOUR QUESTIONNAIRE

THANK YOU

FOR GOOD KARMA

FIGURE 5.7

Your invitation is as important as your questionnaire; a good "thank-you page" creates good karma.

Carefully pick the moment to offer the invitation

If you've ever failed to find the information you needed on a website, only to have a customer satisfaction box pop up on your screen, you'll understand how infuriating a badly timed survey can be.

Or as user researcher Hal Shubin tells it: "One memorable respondent swore at me for wasting his time. If he wasn't interested enough to stay and look around the site, he wasn't going to fill out even a one-question survey."

Think about the overall experience that you want customers to have, and the point in that experience that might be a polite and appropriate moment to invite their feedback.

And remember that chances are you'll only have their attention for a moment. If you only want to ask one question, don't ask "Will you answer our survey?" Instead, ask an actual question that will give you useful data, such as your Most Crucial Question or one that works as an appropriate preparation for it.

Do a pilot test

When you first get your questionnaire to the people you want to answer, you will inevitably find out some things that you will need to change immediately, which is why it's essential to run a pilot test with a smaller group than your eventual main survey.

I usually do a pilot test with about 10% of my sample—enough to get a feel for what is happening. But if I have to pull the survey early to fix problems, then I haven't embarrassed myself in front of the entire sample. Usually, the pilot does go well enough that I can include the results from the pilot test in the eventual report.

If it's an electronic survey—web or email—and I haven't previously had time to get the questionnaire tested by people using a range of assistive technology or people with disabilities that are not helped by assistive technology, then the pilot is the last, and maybe the most important, opportunity to make sure that you're not excluding anyone.

Typical things to look for in your pilot test include:

- Invitation is going to the wrong people.
- Invitation doesn't display correctly.
- Link to the questionnaire doesn't work.

- Responses do not arrive where expected.
- Links out to Help or Contact do not work.
- Response rate is greatly different than expected.

If you're doing a Big Honkin' Survey, then Canadian Viewpoint, a leading provider of fieldwork, publishes a great checklist for you: "9 Essential Checks for a Pilot Test" https://canview.com/2018/03/9-essential-checks-questionnaire-pilot-test.

If you've managed to stick to a Light Touch Survey, you still definitely need to do a pilot test—and (bonus) it will be quicker.

Start to do data cleaning and analysis on the pilot test responses

As the responses arrive during your pilot, look at them straight away to make sure that you can deliver the results you need. Try cleaning the data that you get in the pilot right away and coding any open answers (both discussed in Chapter 6, "Responses").

Create draft deliverables from your pilot

What do your stakeholders want from your survey, and in what format?

Way back in Chapter 1, "Goals," I mentioned trying to create a presentation before you even go ahead with doing the survey. If you didn't manage to do that before, start now.

Some stakeholders like plain numbers; others prefer graphs. Some love a few crisp slides with a snappy fact on each one; others want the whole story in every excruciating detail. There's more about this in Chapter 7, "Reports."

When you pull together your draft presentation or report from those few answers, you'll quickly find out whether you did, in fact, ask the questions that give you the answers you need.

Don't skip your pilot test and do iterate

I wish I could show you my extensive collection of screenshots of questionnaires from highly reputable organizations, often created by respected market researchers, that have obvious errors in them that would have been easily caught by a pilot. Wrong links, bad error messages, branching that doesn't work. Even entire surveys sent out at the wrong time.

Please don't skip your pilot test. Make it as close as you possibly can to the main survey. Compromise only on one thing: the number of people you ask. You'll thank me—really you will.

And don't be afraid to iterate. Typographic errors will jump out at you. You may have forgotten to ask the Most Crucial Question. It's much better to fix these problems and then to rerun your pilot on another 10% of the sample than to waste the valuable opportunity created by a main survey.

Launch your fieldwork and look after it

Hooray! You've done everything you can to make sure that your fieldwork goes smoothly. After all that effort, you may think now is a good time to get a well-deserved break—perhaps head off for a quick vacation as in Figure 5.8.

FIGURE 5.8
Fieldwork isn't the best time to leave on vacation.

Umm, no. No matter how carefully you did your pilot test and all the other preparation work, you do need to be around to check on what's happening in fieldwork, and maybe to make some urgent decisions.

For example, if you have chosen to get your sample through "snowball up" recruiting, then be especially watchful. If response rates suddenly jump up, that might be excellent news because it's grabbed people's attention. Or it might be an example of the Justin Bieber-North Korea problem that we met back in Chapter 2: naughty people, or worse, may have decided to hijack it for reasons you never expected.

Keep checking your responses throughout fieldwork

As your responses come in, read them as often as you can—as in Figure 5.9—to make sure that there are no nasty surprises.

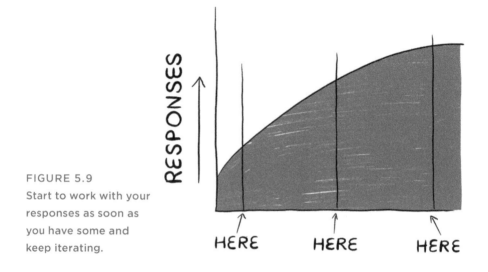

One tactic that has worked for me is to do a complete analysis and report on the first 100 responses:

- I can get a sense of whether I am on course to create the report that my stakeholders need.
- I have a record of any statistical tests and exactly the way that I did them. These details can be really hard to remember in detail when it's time to do the full analysis.
- I can estimate how long the full analysis will take me.

Don't be afraid to end fieldwork early

If all goes well and the stakeholders can make their decision based on 100 responses, why not stop there? It's cheaper and easier for everyone.

It's OK to end fieldwork early for other reasons, too. If something goes wrong or a big event happens entirely out of your control, then don't be afraid to stop the survey early. It's better to end quickly and regroup than to waste the time of the people you want to answer—and your time as well.

If you've offered follow-up, do it promptly

If you have an incentive that depends upon successful completion of the survey, make sure that you deliver the incentives rapidly. People do talk to each other, and news of delayed incentives can reflect badly on your organization.

Also, if you've offered any other type of follow-up, then keep on top of it and also do that promptly.

What could possibly go wrong with fieldwork?

When I think about things that can go wrong in fieldwork, I'm tempted to list only one thing: failing to do a pilot test.

When I was reading books about survey methodology, again and again I'd find authors emphasising the importance of that pilot test. And every time I've skimped my pilot test (or been forced to skip it altogether by clients who wouldn't listen to me), I've greatly regretted it.

Once you've got past your pilot test and into the full fieldwork stage, these are the main things to look out for:

- Response goes viral (in a bad way)
- Not keeping an eye on the responses
- Waiting too long to pull the survey
- Failing to get the incentives out promptly
- Not doing the planned follow-up for people who request it.

At this point, you will know

At this point, you have responses. It's the most exciting part of the whole survey process.

Double the response rate

Tabetha Newman runs Timmus Limited, a research business based in the UK. She assesses the impact of strategic change within an organization or benchmarks between organizations.

We learned about Tabetha's "voting trolleys" in Chapter 3, "Questions." She's posing with one of the trolleys in Figure C3.1.

FIGURE C3.1
Tabetha Newman with a voting trolley.

She told me about a survey where she doubled the response rate—but without changing the questionnaire. I was intrigued.

Q. Could you tell us a bit more about using online surveys to measure strategic change?

If an organization plans to implement new policies or practices, it's a good idea to measure attitudes before and after to quantify and describe the impact. This is where comparative surveys can help.

Q. Why did you get called in on this project?

It was a bit unusual for me. Typically, I get involved in designing and running both the before-and-after surveys. If you have a consistent design, then you can compare and contrast before and after.

On this project, the client did a standardized survey as part of a national benchmarking process every two years. The previous two surveys had a response rate of around 25%, which was disappointing. I was employed to manage the survey during fieldwork and write the report. But I was not allowed to change the questionnaire itself. This was a shame, as it had 18 pages of complicated questions.

Q. So what attracted you to this work, given that your hands were tied when it came to the questionnaire?

I'm a behavioral ecologist and statistician, and I could see the potential to demonstrate that the invitation and fieldwork are as important as the survey itself. I thought that some behavioral ecology ideas (sometimes called nudge ideas) could increase the response rate, with the ultimate aim of making valid and reliable generalizations about that population of people as a whole.

Q. So what did you do?

I focused my attention on everything that surrounds the questionnaire: the email invitation, the introductory page, the reminder email, the thank-you page, and the method of contacting participants.

I found out about the changes that had been done in response to the previous survey so that I could tell people about them. If people feel that they can genuinely influence what happens, then they are more likely to participate—otherwise, it feels like a waste of their time.

It's all about thinking: "What's the reward for my respondents? Why would they bother? How can I reduce their effort as much as possible? How can I get them talking positively about this survey?" People are influenced by others working around them.

There is always the worry that the people who choose to answer are not representative—for example, they might be particularly happy or unhappy, which galvanizes them to complete the questionnaire. So I also ran a random subsample ahead of the main fieldwork, to find out whether their opinions, representing 5% of the population, matched the opinions of those in the eventual main survey. It was extra effort: selecting people, contacting them ahead of the main fieldwork, and offering incentives to ensure that all of them replied. Luckily, my client was fantastically supportive and was keen to discover what would happen.

continues

Q. What were the main changes that you made?

First, I identified the most senior staff member who was relevant to the topic. He agreed to put his name on the email invitations, reminders, and thank-you. This made outgoing emails more personal.

I got permission to track who had completed the questionnaire so that I didn't bother them again when they had done it. I used the Online Surveys tool, which allowed me to personalize the emails with participants' names.

In the invitation email, I listed the positive changes that came about thanks to the people who participated in previous surveys.

Choosing my moment for the survey invitation was crucial—the best time of day tends to be late morning (after urgent emails are answered) and avoiding Mondays and Fridays. I opted for a Thursday 10:30 a.m. invitation time, because I knew all staff took a tea break at 11 a.m., which might give them time to complete the survey.

I wrote everything using persuasive language that asked people to join in with their colleagues—"social pressure." I updated the reminder emails with information about the live survey ("50% of staff have already sent us their opinions—please join them and help to influence...") to add to the social pressure. They also received a carefully worded thank-you email once they had participated.

I kept the fieldwork short, so people felt compelled to answer sooner rather than leave the invite in their inbox.

All communications materials were short and written to interest the people we wanted to answer—not tell them what the client wanted them to know!

Q. And what results did you get?

The response was amazing. We had a 49% response rate, almost double what we had previously. The random subsample approach also worked: 79% of that subsample answered the questionnaire, and their answers were not statistically different from the wider response. The client ended up with a reliable data set and actionable metrics that they could use to influence future strategic planning.

Those results are great, aren't they? Thanks very much.

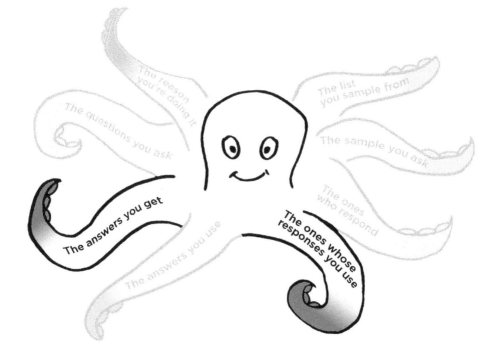

The reason
you're doing it

The list
you sample from

The questions you ask

The sample you ask

The ones
who respond

The answers you get

The ones whose
responses you use

The answers you use

Responses: Turn Data into Answers

W e've reached the exciting point when people have answered our questions, and it's time to make decisions about which of those answers we can use.

This involves:

- Cleaning your data
- Deciding whose answers you will use
- Getting to know your numeric data
- Looking for themes in your open answers, also known as *coding*

In this chapter, I'm going to distinguish between an answer, a person's response, and a data set.

An **answer** is one individual's answer to a specific question.

A **person's response** is all the answers from one individual.

A **data set** is all the responses from all the people who answered.

If you've been following along with the Survey Octopus, then in this chapter we'll be tackling two tentacles. In Figure 6.1, you'll see that on the right, you can think about "the ones whose answers you use"—this is where you decide whether to include or exclude a person's response from the data set. On the left, you think about "the answers you get"—this is where you decide what to do with the answers to specific questions.

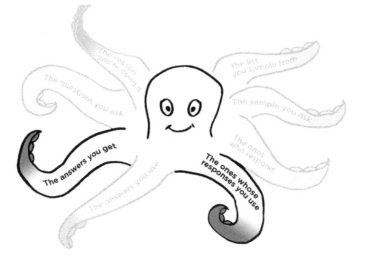

FIGURE 6.1

This chapter is about "the ones whose responses you use" and "the answers you get."

Clean your data

Responses never arrive clean and tidy. There are always some issues that you'll have to sort out in the data cleaning stage, as in Figure 6.2.

If you've opted for a paper questionnaire, you'll have to type the answers into a spreadsheet or other database, or arrange for someone else to do it. Whoever does the typing, it's well worth getting someone who didn't do the typing to check that each person's response has been typed in accurately, as some typing mistakes are inevitable, and we all vary in our ability to read other people's handwriting.

Let's have a look at the things you need to do for any survey:

FIGURE 6.2
Like a kitchen floor, survey responses benefit from a good cleaning.

- Check that the data set has exported properly.
- Set up a log page and start your backups.
- Consider what you need to redact or delete.
- Consider how you plan to use your columns.
- Check that the data set has exported properly

When I get a data set to analyze, my first steps are:

- Get it into a spreadsheet and have a look at it. Has it exported correctly from wherever it was captured? Have any of the answers to open questions been truncated?
- Check that I have the right data set: the column headings match the current version of the questionnaire.
- Check that I have the correct number of responses in the spreadsheet: one row of data for each person's response.

Yes, I have had examples of the wrong data set, especially when a survey tool is being shared across several teams.

Set up a log page and start your backups

A log page is a place to keep notes on what you do during your data cleaning and analysis. I like to set up my log page as a separate worksheet in the same spreadsheet as the data and to date-stamp each entry—or timestamp if things get hectic.

TIP HOW TO TIMESTAMP

In Excel and in Google Sheets, there are shortcuts for inserting the time or the date:

On a Microsoft PC:

- Insert date: CTRL (press the CTRL and semi-colon keys at the same time)
- Insert time: CTRL (press the CTRL, SHIFT, and semi-colon keys at the same time)

On a Mac: It's similar but with CMD instead of CTRL

Excel picks up the current time zone from your computer; in Sheets, you have to set it up for each spreadsheet.

Although spreadsheets these days claim to keep backups for you, my experience is that their version control isn't great. I highly recommend creating a backup and naming it clearly before you do any major change to the data set, and frequently for minor changes. I've been saved many times by a backup I've taken before some change unexpectedly went wrong.

Just between you and me (don't tell my clients), I'm always under the illusion that this time, cleaning and analysis will be so quick that I don't need a log. Invariably, something comes up, and I have to have a break. When I return, I recognize that I need to re-create the notes that I had previously neglected, as in Figure 6.3 (complete with typical hasty misspellings and quirky punctuation), and I once more chastise myself because it's harder to do after the break. After that, I'm pretty careful.

	A	B	C
1	Date	Observation/note/activity	Relevant worksheet
2	22-Jul	Remembered to set up a log page for this dataset; catching up with some things I've alredy done	
3	22-Jul	Data sent by client around two weeks ago. Redacted personal data.	Private data
4	22-Jul	Set up a 'Columns' sheet that describes the columns currently in use	Columns
5	22-Jul	Renamed several columns to shorter names for analysis purposes	Columns
6	22-Jul	Set up a 'Pivot' sheet to hold all the pivot data	Pivot
7	22-Jul	calculated time to complete in minutes	Time to complete
8	22-Jul	set up a column that topped out time to complete at 'over 1hr'	Columns
9	22-Jul	found a couple of entries that had unrealistic time to complete	
10	22-Jul	changed the IP address column to exclude those unrealistic entries	Columns/use of 'exclude' in former IP address column
11	22-Jul	Added in client's research questions	Research questions

FIGURE 6.3

The first entries in a log worksheet. I started this after about two elapsed weeks, three hours work so far in total.

Consider what you need to redact or delete

Here are things that I look for during the cleaning process:

1. Are there any repeated or implausible responses?
2. Is the time to complete outside a reasonable range?
3. Do I need to redact any personal data?
4. Are there any curse words or racist language?
5. Are there any systemic errors in capturing characters other than the standard 0 to 9 and a to z?
6. Is there anything else odd that's specific to this survey?

Look for any repeated or implausible responses

Some survey tools automatically refuse repeated responses from the same person; others allow them, on the basis that some people (such as my own parents) have a single shared computer for the household.

Either way, glitches can occur, and it's worth looking for any rows that are completely identical. There may be genuinely two different people whose answers are all the same—especially if you've taken the Light Touch Survey idea to heart and only have a small number of questions.

More often, they are simply a repeat where someone has accidentally (happens quite often) or deliberately (not unknown) sent in more than one answer. Do you remember the Justin Bieber fanzine survey that we met in Chapter 2, "Sample"?

Look at the start time and the time to complete

Many survey tools tell you the start time for each person's response. If the start time is before the questionnaire opened for real people to answer, then that usually means that you still have some made-up responses left over from testing.

You may also get some start times that tell you someone answered after the questionnaire was meant to be closed—a late response. I usually delete test entries but allow late responses.

Sometimes, the survey tool reports the time it took the person to complete their response, but more often you have to work it out by subtracting the start time from the time of submission.

Has someone taken a ridiculously short time? That might be what market researchers call a "speeder"—someone who was only interested in the incentive and did not actually consider the questions.

Has someone taken a ridiculously long time? Read their response to see if it makes sense. They may have had to break off for a meeting or errand. Consider excluding very long times from "average time to complete" or report the median times instead.

Look for personal data and decide whether to redact it

If you have done your work on privacy appropriately, the decisions about personal data will be easy because you'll have worked out how to handle personal data long ago.

But I often get survey data sets to analyze with lots of personal data in them, where no one seems to have considered privacy or whether I'm allowed to see the personal data. I handle this by redacting all the personal data I can find and then destroying any copies of the data set that had personal data in them. I've put some things to try into Table 6.1.

Look for	Try this
Email address	Change to "email provided."
Address details	Shorten to less identifiable data, such as city, state, province, or even country.
	Watch out for lone respondents from small towns, less-populated states such as Alaska, or people who come from countries where only a few people answered.
	You could preserve anonymity by using a single larger group for people from several smaller areas.
ISP address	Check that the ISP addresses are unique and then delete all of them.
Hidden details in open answers	Even when you ask people not to put personal details in their answers, some of them will.
	Read every answer and redact the personal details.
	(I assume you have already dealt with any personal follow-up in your Fieldwork phase.)
Job titles	A job title plus organization may be enough to identify an individual, and sometimes the job title alone may be enough.
	For example, if you have the job title "Forms and survey specialist" in your answers, it's rather likely to be me.

Look for swear words or curse words

Some people may choose to express strong feelings by using equally strong language, as in Figure 6.4. In some organizations, you may find it difficult to share or use this data set because of policies around using inappropriate language at work.

FIGURE 6.4
Sometimes, people choose strong language for their answers.

Sad to say, sometimes, someone answering may use language that is racist or otherwise deeply offensive to you or other team members. Be aware that the data cleaning process itself may be stressful for you and any others on your team.

I usually redact offensive words by inserting asterisks after the first letter, so that the word becomes f***, n*****, or whatever. My view is that this preserves the sentiment—however unpleasant—without continuing the abuse or creating corporate hassle. You may prefer some other strategy.

I'm always a bit surprised when someone's response is not only full of offensive language but also has contact details and clearly expects someone in the organization to follow up. If you have a follow-up process, make sure that whoever is dealing with it is warned about the redacted language.

Correct any systemic errors in capturing characters other than the standard 0 to 9 and a to z

Tools have different ideas about how to capture and display characters, such as curly quote marks and accented letters, like the ones in Figure 6.5.

I make sure I've got a copy of the original data backed up (yes, I am going to keep repeating this), and then do a ruthless global replace on errors like these.

FIGURE 6.5
On the left, the character as typed. On the right, what the spreadsheet displayed.

Look for things to check that are specific to this survey

Everything I've mentioned so far in data checking applies to most surveys, but in nearly every survey there are some topic-specific things that you can check.

For example, in a survey for a fashion website, we got about 20 respondents who estimated amazingly high fashion budgets—$20,000 or more a month. When I inspected their other answers, they'd put rubbish in all the open questions. I excluded their data. But there were some genuine answers around $10,000/month.

Consider how you plan to use the columns

These days, many survey tools helpfully export the full text of the question as the column header. This is great if no one remembered to take screenshots of the final questionnaire, but a little awkward if the questions are long ones. For example, a questionnaire included two long questions that both started "If you attended a conference about…". No problem with the questions, but inconvenient as a column heading for analysis.

I usually rename the columns for analysis purposes to names about 10 characters long—retaining the original question in my notes so that when I create my report, I can include the exact wording that was in the questionnaire rather than any abbreviation.

Case study: cleaning data

I got a data set for analysis for a Big Honkin' Survey where I hadn't been involved in creating the questionnaire. Table 6.2 shows some of the problems I had to solve on a data set with over 10,000 responses.

TABLE 6.2 A SELECTION OF PROBLEMS WITH A BIG HONKIN' SURVEY

Problem	Decision to make
Two mostly similar questionnaires went to slightly different groups of respondents.	Whether to analyze the two sets of data separately or to try to reconcile columns to create one larger set?
The questionnaire asked about 10 features of the product in random order, but because of a programming error, it asked about one of the features twice. Some people answered inconsistently, as in Figure 6.6.	Which answer to accept, or whether to accept neither?
One question offered an "other" box, but the place for the "other" answer was too short.	How to interpret the truncated answers?
When the matched data came back, every response that did not match was deleted.	Accept losing those responses, or do several hours of work to find and reinstate the missing responses?

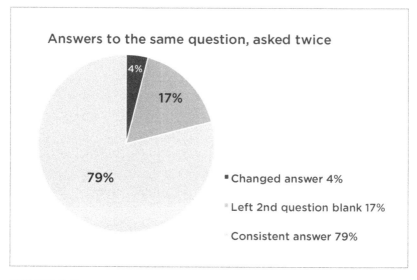

Answers to the same question, asked twice

4%

17%

79%

■ Changed answer 4%

▪ Left 2nd question blank 17%

Consistent answer 79%

FIGURE 6.6

People do not always answer the same question the same way.

I've included this case study for three reasons:

- To reassure you that decisions like this are likely to be needed on any sizeable data set.
- To warn you that data cleaning takes time and requires thought.
- To remind you that planning your analysis before you run the survey (and testing it during the pilot) can help save time and resources during analysis.

Mostly, working on the analysis of data sets with over 10,000 entries has convinced me that it's worth trying really hard to convince clients and colleagues to keep the sample size as small as possible.

Decide whose responses you will use

When you've got a data set that is appropriately cleaned (and backed up—did I mention backups? OK, I know I did, but it really is important), you'll typically have a spreadsheet where each row contains a single person's response. Within that, the person may have decided *not* to answer one or more of your questions. This is called *missing data*.

It's time to make decisions about whether to include or exclude each person's response.

Decide what to do about missing data

For a Light Touch Survey, you don't need to worry too much about missing data. You'll be doing another survey soon, so if a person's response is incomplete, it's fine to exclude it from your data set.

If you're doing a Big Honkin' Survey, missing data will be one of the biggest challenges. I'm always extra glad when I've analyzed my data set as it arrives in small batches, so that I've got a policy for missing data and agreed on it with my stakeholders. Table 6.3 shows some strategies for dealing with missing data.

TABLE 6.3 STRATEGIES FOR DEALING WITH MISSING DATA

Strategy	Notes
Remove the person's response from the data set.	Is the simplest method. Loses data.
Remove only the problematic answer for that person, but keep the rest of their response.	Preserves as much of the response as possible. Means that there are different sample sizes for each question. Can cause problems for statistical techniques that need entries for every data item. Can be confusing in the reports.
"Impute" the missing values using statistics. (Explanation coming up.)	Preserves as much of each person's response as possible and means that the sample size is the same for every question. Is statistically more complex. Can be hard to explain to stakeholders.
Design a better survey in the next iteration	Doesn't help right now with this data set.

Impute means "replace with an estimate"

Let's say that you want to know the mean of something in your data set—for example, the number of purchases last month by the people who answered, but Person A skipped the "age" question.

If you remove Person A's entire response from the data set because of the missing age, it's as if they never took the survey, and you lose any variability from Person A.

For example, maybe Person A is younger than most but is an unusually keen purchaser. You'll have lost that extra variability.

To impute means to replace a missing answer with an estimate based on the rest of the data set.

Chances are that Person A's age is probably fairly close to the average, but you may be able to get a more accurate estimate by finding another respondent in the data set with similar responses.

To impute age, you could

- Use the mode age (the most common one).
- Use the mean age (the arithmetic average).
- Use a random age selected from all the other responses.
- Compare the problematic response with those from all the other people who answered. Find another person's response that matches the problematic one as closely as possible, and then use the age of the matched response.

Any of these will give a small reduction in variability on age, but will preserve the rest of Person A's response so that you can analyze it with the whole data set.

Have I tried imputation myself? No! But I'd be remiss if I didn't mention it.

If you do decide to try it:

- Create a new column that includes all the imputed values.
- Do every analysis with and without the imputed values, to find out what the difference is.
- Try to find someone who knows how to do this to help you.

Think about representativeness

Back in Chapter 2, I explained that the representativeness of people who answer is more important than the number of people who answer. I hope you decided to include a question or two that you could use to assess whether you get the representative sample you aimed for.

Well, here we are, and now it's time to check those questions.

Here's an example from a survey of people doing research. The client had two representativeness questions:

- Job title
- The types of research-related activities that they did

By comparing the answers to those questions, I could see that the client had a good response from people doing user experience (UX) research, but only a few responses from academics or people doing market research. Their main focus was UX research so that was OK, but what was the best way to report on the other respondents?

In this example, I suggested to the client that we exclude the few responses from people other than UX researchers. Given the original goals of the survey, they accepted that.

Decide whether to "weight"

If their goal had been different—perhaps to compare opinions from UX researchers and market researchers—I might have opted to "weight" the responses: People in the underrepresented group get a higher weight, and those in overrepresented groups get a lower one.

> To **weight** a survey means to assign a multiplication factor to each response in proportion to its representativeness.

If you are working with Big Honkin' Surveys and want to know more about weighting, try www.cessda.eu/Training/Training-Resources/Library/Data-Management-Expert-Guide/3.-Process/Weights-of-survey-data.

I work mostly on Light Touch Surveys where it's better to iterate than to try more complex statistical processes such as weighting. Weighting can help a bit, but sometimes iteration helps even more.

For example, for that survey of researchers, the client decided they had enough data at the time, but I'm sure that a few changes to the sampling method and the survey invitation would have helped us to reach more academics and market researchers on the next survey.

Adjustment error comes from decisions about who to include

The decisions about how to assess representativeness and whether to weight, and if so, what multiplication factor to use, are not easy, and they get an error all to themselves:

> **Adjustment error** happens when you make less-than-perfect choices about whose answers to include and how to weight them.

In Figure 6.7, you can see how adjustment error fits into the Survey Octopus between "The ones who respond" and "The ones whose responses you use."

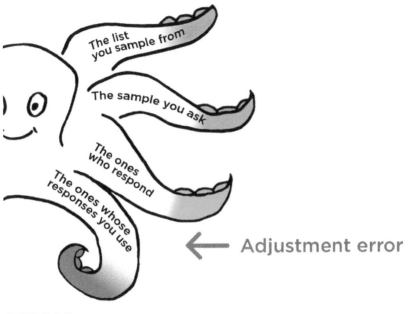

The list you sample from

The sample you ask

The ones who respond

The ones whose responses you use

← Adjustment error

FIGURE 6.7

Adjustment error happens when you make decisions about whose answers you use.

In the sorts of surveys that I do, adjustment error isn't one that I worry about all that much. I've always found that it's OK to go for the simplest options (delete entries with missing data, skip the weighting). But I had to include the more complex options for completeness.

Get to know your numeric data

Right at the start of this journey into surveys, we had a look at "the number"—the result of the survey, known to survey methodologists as the *survey statistic*.

Now that you have a nicely cleaned data set, it's time to think about making use of the answers. We'll look first at the numeric data, and then we'll tackle looking for themes in your open answers.

Get to know your data using descriptive statistics

Almost every survey I've worked on has at least one question that gives a numeric answer. I start by thinking about some descriptive statistics. The ones that I use the most often are the simplest.

n is the number of entries in the data set.

The **minimum** (min) is the smallest value for a specific answer.

The **maximum** (max) is the largest value for a specific answer.

The **range** is the maximum minus the minimum.

The **mode** is the value of the most frequent answer.

The **median** is the middle value. (Arrange all the answers from smallest to largest, and the median is the value of the one in the middle.)

The **mean** is the arithmetic average of the answers. (Add them all together and divide by n.)

Min and *max* are particularly useful for checking whether your data are plausible. Could anyone really have an answer this big? Or this small?

Range is convenient for comparing two data sets or as an abbreviation for talking about both maximum and minimum at the same time.

Mode is often useful for making decisions: for example, a good experience for the most frequent type of customer.

Here's an example from a data set about a conference. The organizers wanted to know whether to include a souvenir from their city in the conference swag bags. I took a quick look at the data, in this case, the city of each participant—sketched in Figure 6.8 and with the data in Table 6.4.

The mode? People from the conference city! The idea of a souvenir lost its luster. Instead, the organizers pleased the mode by opting for donations to charities based in their city that also had activities across their whole country, which was fine by the attendees from the two other cities. The few attendees from other countries could buy their own souvenirs!

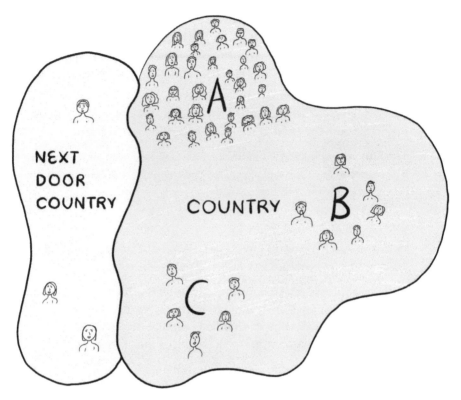

FIGURE 6.8
Locations of people attending a conference.

TABLE 6.4 LOCATIONS OF PEOPLE ATTENDING A CONFERENCE

Conference city A	59	(mode)
City B	12	
City C	5	
Next door country	3	
(other)	1	
(no answer)	15	

You won't hear much about modes in statistics textbooks or college courses. That's because despite the usefulness of modes for practical decisions, they don't have the convenient mathematical properties that make them useful for statistical significance.

Median (the middle value) can be handy because medians are not affected by a few very large or very small values—but like modes, they don't come with many helpful mathematical properties.

Mean (the average) is the one that gets the most attention from statisticians because of something called the *Central Limit Theorem,* which is the basis of many statistical tests.

A mean is sensitive to outliers

Unfortunately, means do have quite a big problem: they are easily distorted by an outlandishly extreme value.

Outlandishly extreme? There's a popular statistical story: "Bill Gates walks into a bar, and on average everyone in the bar becomes a millionaire." Bill Gate's wealth is so great that if you add it into any calculation of mean wealth, it will send that mean soaring.

If you design for a mean, you may design for something that's not very relevant to most people.

Some statistics tell us about how spread out the data is

Mean, median, and mode are all "measures of central tendency"—they tell you what's happening in the middle of your data. Our next measures are about how spread out it is.

A **variance** is a measurement of how spread out the values are compared to the mean. The sample variance is calculated by subtracting the mean from each value, squaring each result, adding all the results together, and dividing the result by the number of values minus 1.

For example, if I ask someone a question about age, I might get a mean of 57 years. The calculated variance might be 16, and it's expressed as "years squared." Comparing squares is tricky, so people generally use standard deviation instead:

The **standard deviation (s.d.)** is the square root of the variance.

Taking the square root brings us back to plain age, so for my age example I'd now have mean 57 years, standard deviation 4 years.

You may have met the normal distribution before: it's that bell-shaped curve that crops up in many types of measurement. The standard deviation tells us whether the curve is rather narrow, like the one on the top in Figure 6.9, or spread out, like the one below.

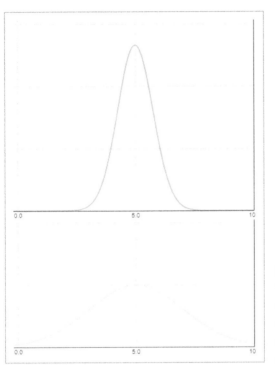

FIGURE 6.9
The normal distribution at the top has a smaller standard deviation than the one below.

Get to know your data using charts

As well as working out the descriptive statistics for your numeric data, it's a good idea to put it into a chart to see whether it does have the shape of a normal distribution or of something else. This sort of investigation was pioneered by John Tukey, whose book *Exploratory Data Analysis* included all sorts of inventive ways you can make charts with only a pen and pencil. (Tukey, 1977)

To see why, have a look at Anscombe's Quartet (Anscombe, 1973) in Figure 6.10. Anscombe created four data sets that share the same descriptive statistics, as in Table 6.5, but have different patterns when looked at as charts.

TABLE 6.5 DESCRIPTIVE STATISTICS FOR ANSCOMBE'S QUARTET

Descriptive statistics	Value
Mean of x	9
Standard deviation of x	3.32
Mean of y	7.50
Standard deviation of y	2.03
Correlation between x and y	0.816

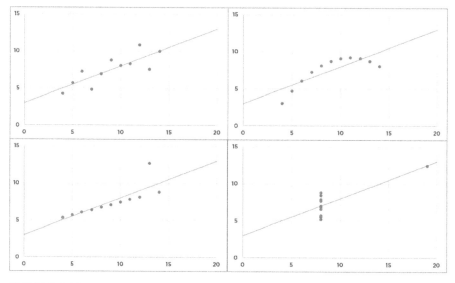

FIGURE 6.10

Anscombe's Quartet: Four data sets that have the same trend and descriptive data.

The two lower charts both have outliers.

An **outlier** is a data point that seems noticeably different from the rest of the data.

Outliers are always worthy of investigation, to think about whether they are genuine but unusual (possible), or whether they reflect some mistake in the data collection and cleaning (sadly, more likely).

More recently, Alberto Cairo constructed his Datasaurus. The two data sets in Figure 6.11 share the same descriptive statistics, but the joke is obvious in the charts.

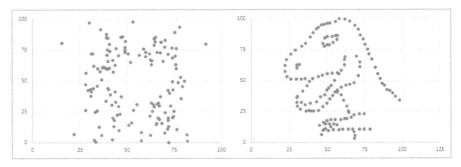

FIGURE 6.11
Cairo's scattered data set on the left and the Datasaurus on the right share the same descriptive statistics.

I hope I have convinced you that it's worth putting your data into a chart—and if you personally find charts tricky to read (and many people do), then I recommend finding someone who is more comfortable with them to help you.

There are no rules for data exploration using charts. Here are some things I do a lot:

- Throw the data for one answer into a few different charts. Are there any patterns that jump out?
- Compare the data for a couple of answers with each other, usually using x/y plots like the Datasaurus. Does anything look odd, or are there any patterns?

I haven't yet found any dinosaurs, but I've definitely identified outliers and found plenty of ideas for analysis.

At this stage, don't worry whether a chart doesn't work or if the color choices are horrible. Play around and see what looks interesting. For example, Figure 6.12 has two charts from a question in a data set that I analyzed. "No preference" seemed rather large to me and jumped out as an anomaly when I looked at the bar chart. The default colors on the tree map happened to emphasize that the "Large" choice was the least appealing, so that gave me the idea of checking back to the client's goals to see whether "Large" had any particular importance for them.

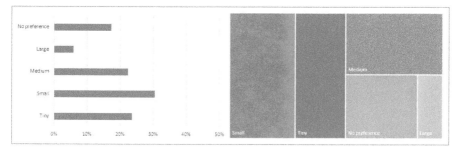

FIGURE 6.12

Two charts from a question about "preferred size": bar chart and tree map.

You may also have spotted that my judgment was affected by a chance color choice from my chart software. That's the negative side of human perception: we are evolved to find patterns, including ones that aren't really there. That's why we need to check back to goals and compare them with descriptive statistics.

Get to know your data using comparisons

If you managed to get your questionnaire down to the minimum of a Most Crucial Question and a representativeness question, now is a good time to compare them.

Your survey tool may offer some "cross tabulations" (crosstabs) that compare two questions with each other. Excel and Google Sheets both call crosstabs *Pivot Tables.*

My tips:

- Have all the data in one worksheet, with only the column titles in the first row and the data in columns below.
- Sometimes, pivot tables inexplicably don't work. Try a different combination of rows and columns, because they sometimes suddenly spring to life.
- When the pivot table yields something useful, I take a snapshot of what it came up with by copying the values from the table into a separate worksheet. I find this easier than re-creating the table from my notes the next time that I need it.

Here's an example from exploring the 2019 AIGA design census data (designcensus.org/). The questionnaire had two questions I wanted to explore (the wording is a little odd):

- "I've worked in design for:"
- "My age is:"

I put those two questions in as row and column respectively, as shown in Figure 6.13. I chose "I've worked in design for:" as the value to count.

The table I got was far wider than I can show here. When I looked at it, I was surprised that it started ages 0, 1, 5, 14, and 16 as the first five columns, as in Figure 6.14. I also noticed that one person was only 5 years but claimed 20 years in design, and another was 14 years old and also had 20 years design experience. I decided to exclude people with ages under 16 years.

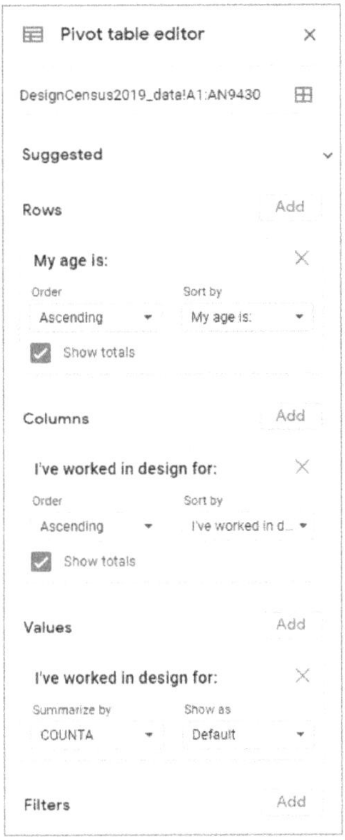

FIGURE 6.13

The Pivot table editor in Google Sheets was set up to compare age and years in design.

I've worked in de	0	1	5	14	16
1 - 4 years	2				
10 - 14 years	3				
15 - 20 years	2	1			
20+ years	9		1	1	
5 - 9 years	1				
Less than 1 year	1				1
Grand Total	18	1	1	1	1

FIGURE 6.14

The resulting pivot table allowed me to think about representativeness.

A quick swap of rows and columns gave me a Table 6.6 that was handy for thinking about representativeness, so I copied that to a new sheet and excluded people who claimed to be under 16 or over 100. I also put the data into bands so that I could check more easily whether people had a length of experience in design that was plausible for their age. I've replaced percentages under 1% with "-" to make the table easier to read.

TABLE 6.6 COMPARING THE AGE OF DESIGNERS WITH THEIR TIME WORKING IN DESIGN

Age	Number	"I've worked in design for:" (% of all responses)					
		< 1 year	1 - 4 years	5 - 9 years	10 - 14 years	15 - 20 years	20+ years
16-19	44	-	-	-	-	-	-
20-29	3999	3%	23%	15%	1%	-	-
30-39	3146	-	3%	12%	13%	4%	-
40-49	1273	-	-	1%	2%	5%	5%
50-59	658	-	-	-	-	1%	6%
60-69	244	-	-	-	-	-	2%
70-79	38	-	-	-	-	-	-

My interpretation of this table is that people in their 20s who have worked in design for 1-4 years are easily the largest group of respondents, but the survey did receive quite a substantial response from older designers—who tend to have more experience.

Then I had a look at the chart for age on its own, in Figure 6.15, to make sure there wasn't anything strange hiding in the data.

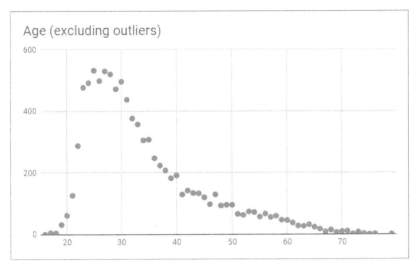

Age (excluding outliers)

FIGURE 6.15
The age profile of people who answered the Design Census 2019.

Look for themes in your open answers: Coding

Back in Chapter 4, "Questionnaire," we met the punch cards that were invented by Hollerith in the 1880s to hold the census data for processing. The job of transferring answers from the paper question-naires to the cards, illustrated in Figure 6.16, was called *coding*—a term that eventually transferred to the use of punch cards to program computers and then to programming itself.

FIGURE 6.16
Coding using a Hollerith machine.

In those days, interviewers, called *enumerators* for a census, traveled to ask the questions in face-to-face interviews. The interviewers had a set of instructions—usually called a *codebook*—to tell them what to write for each question on the paper record of the interview, for example:

"Column 9. Whether single, married, widowed, or divorced. Write "S" for single or unmarried persons, "M" for married, "Wd" for widowed (man or woman), and "D" for divorced."

1900 decennial survey: www.census.gov/programs-surveys/decennial-census/technical-documentation/questionnaires/1900/1900-instructions.html

You'll need to code your open answers for analysis

If you've chosen paper questionnaires or face-to-face interviews, then you'll find that coding the answers is a lot quicker than typing in the full actual words. This example is from a codebook from 2015:

(Are/Is) (name/you) now married, widowed, divorced, separated, or never married?

1 Married - Spouse PRESENT

2 Married - Spouse ABSENT

3 Widowed

4 Divorced

5 Separated

6 Never married

www2.census.gov/programs-surveys/cps/methodology/intman/CPS_Manual_April2015.pdf

One definite advantage of web and electronic survey tools is that they code the answers to closed questions for us. This example is from a survey of user research professionals. We asked the question:

"Do you use Picture-in-Picture Video when you do usability tests?

( ) Always

( ) Most of the time

( ) Occasionally

( ) Never

( ) Other (please specify)"

And Table 6.7 has a snippet from the spreadsheet of answers from respondents 28 through 32.

TABLE 6.7 A FEW OF THE ANSWERS TO A SURVEY QUESTION ABOUT USING PICTURE-IN-PICTURE VIDEO

Respondent	Do you use Picture-in-Picture video when you do usability tests?	PIPP Other (please specify)
28	Always	
29	Most of the time	
30	Other (please specify)	I would if I had the capabilities.
31	Most of the time	
32	Never	

The second column shows how the survey tool we used provided results to a radio button question. The 30th person to respond chose Other and added "I would if I had the capabilities."

So 4 of these 5 entries were already coded for me, and I had a little bit of work to do on entries in the PIPP Other column.

Prepare for coding by thinking about tentacles

"Prepare for coding" is about having a look back at the tentacles of the Survey Octopus to remind me what I'm looking for. I've compared the tentacles and activity in Table 6.8.

TABLE 6.8 ACTIVITIES TO PREPARE FOR CODING

Tentacle	What I'm trying to do	Activity
The questions you ask (Questions)	Check whether there are too many "other" answers, which may mean that you have a problem with the question.	Read the answers, think, maybe iterate the questionnaire.
The people who answer (Sample)	Work out whether people are choosing "other" because they are not in the defined group.	Read the answers, think, maybe revisit sampling decisions.
The reason I'm doing it (Goals)	Find a way to use the open answers to help make a decision.	Do coding with the goals firmly in mind.

An example of preparing for coding

Let's have another look at that Picture-in-Picture example.

The advantage of using Picture-in-Picture video in a usability test is that the researcher, and probably also stakeholders, can see the participant's face alongside the screen the participant is looking at, which helps them to understand the participant's remarks and actions. The disadvantages are that some participants may feel awkward about being on a video, the recording is identifiable personal data which creates obvious privacy challenges, and it means using extra technology.

We only wanted answers from user experience professionals with some experience of the issues and the technology. The question "Do you use Picture-in-Picture Video when you do usability tests?" was one of the ones that we used for representativeness.

Only 9 of our respondents answered "other" to this question. Table 6.9 has the additional information exactly as they gave it to us.

TABLE 6.9 VERBATIM RESPONSES TO PIPP (OTHER)

Respondent	PIPP (Other)
30	I would if I had the capabilities.
43	I only do UserTesting.com studies, without PPiP, and I don't do other types of moderated studies.
76	I used to - when I started but now most of my studies are unmoderated and don't have this
93	We use 2 screens for face + screen
109	When participant is in person, yes, always
117	When possible - nature of work doesn't always allow
136	When requested by clients (usually never with healthcare)
176	I record the user expresions using Lookback connected to Marvel
198	I haven't due to technology restrictions

This time, as I read the answers, I decided that everyone did indeed have some experience with the ideas and the technology, so they were part of the defined group of people I was looking for.

Because this question was about representativeness, not goals, my decision was to leave these answers as they were in the "other" category and not to do any more coding work on them.

Some open answers only need a little organizing

The answers we just looked at were relatively lengthy comments. Sometimes, the open answers are much shorter, and only need a little bit of organizing.

Here's a case study: A questionnaire aimed mostly at people who live in the UK provided an extra option with the question:

And what country outside the UK do you live in?

Most of the answers were simple to organize into consistent country names. For example Table 6.10 has some examples that I coded easily as Argentina.

TABLE 6.10   EXAMPLES OF ANSWERS THAT WERE CODED EASILY

Before coding	After coding
ARGENTINA right now	Argentina
Argentina.	Argentina
Argentine	Argentina

Some of the examples in Table 6.11 posed slightly more challenges.

TABLE 6.11   EXAMPLES OF ANSWERS THAT POSED MINOR PROBLEMS

Before coding	Problem	After coding
Canada, Germany, and Spain	Which country to choose?	More than one country
Canada, originally from the UK	Is it OK to ignore the extra comment?	Canada
Catalonia	Some people consider Catalonia to be a separate country. Others consider that it is part of Spain.	Spain

And a few answers, for example those in Table 6.12, suggested that people had chosen to write about something completely different.

TABLE 6.12 EXAMPLES OF ANSWERS THAT HAVE NOTHING TO DO WITH A COUNTRY

Before coding	After coding
Visa for me to live with my family in Manchester	Not a country
i need to travel to UK, definitely , on the next, Give me a total support.	Not a country
HUMBLY REQUEST BEFORE THE RESPECTABLE MR (continues as a long request)	Not a country

Overall, we started with just over 2,000 total answers to the question, with 362 different ones. It took about an hour to:

- Code all the easy variations to consistent country names.
- Decide what to do with about 100 answers that were more problematic.

We ended up with 162 different countries, plus "UK" and "not a country."

Choose a strategy for coding longer comments

My experience is that some types of question—such as the "other" options we've just been looking at—get rather short answers that are quite quick to code, but a general open box question, such as "any comments?" can get much longer answers, especially when longer answers are encouraged by giving people a fairly big box to type into. Some people provide detailed essays, which is lovely, but means a lot more work to do.

Table 6.13 has the coding methods that I use most often.

TABLE 6.13 A SELECTION OF CODING METHODS

Method	What you do	Good for
Light touch coding	Send all the comments to the stakeholders.	Stakeholders who are really interested in the survey and want to make the effort of reading them
Adjectival coding	Choose an adjective that sums up the response.	Revealing overall levels of "for" and "against" sentiment
Descriptive coding	Summarize the basic topic of the comment in a word or short phrase.	Exploring or being open to new ideas
Task area coding	Allocate each comment to the part of the organization that is responsible for that type of work.	Making sure that follow-up happens promptly
In vivo coding	Choose small chunks of the respondents' own words that are representative of the overall response.	Helping your stakeholders understand how people think about the topic and the words they use
Provisional coding	Set up a predetermined start list of codes before releasing the survey.	Supporting or disproving an existing idea or suggestion

For more details, and lots more methods, have a look at *The Coding Manual for Qualitative Researchers* by Johnny Saldaña. (Saldaña, 2013)

How I use a spreadsheet for coding

I'm often doing my coding on my own, and here's what I do when I need to do something more intensive than light touch coding.

The terms "first phase coding" and "second phase coding" come from the qualitative researchers, because at this point we are doing qualitative analysis.

First phase coding

1. Create a column for uncoded answers. Copy the answers to be coded into it. Keep the original data column untouched in case of queries later.

2. Sort the spreadsheet to put uncoded answers into alphabetical order.

3. Read the uncoded answers to get some ideas for codes.

4. Create columns for two or three of the codes that jump out. I usually start with "don't know" and "not applicable" as my first two codes, to help me get going.

5. If an uncoded answer matches a code, then I move it into the column for that code. If an answer matches two or more codes, I split it up into the relevant bits. If only part of the answer matches a code, I move that part into the column for the code and leave the rest uncoded. This means that the uncoded column is gradually emptying.

6. Repeat the process from step 2 until there are few enough remaining unprocessed answers to keep them as "other" and stop.

I find it quicker overall to deal with no more than three codes in each pass and to repeat the sorting, rather than to have lots of codes available.

There are many other ways to do this. For example, you might decide to sort the spreadsheet some other way, or place a check mark in the column for a code rather than moving the uncoded answer into it, or work with more codes at once, or find some other variation that you prefer. It's mostly a question of trying what works for you on a sample of your data and then iterating.

Second phase coding

When I've got everything into an initial set of codes, I look at them critically with my original research goals in mind. Have these codes helped me to get to the number that will create a decision? Do they need to be grouped further, summarized, or divided?

Typically, the second phase coding can take as long as the first phase because it takes time to think critically about whether the codes are useful and to adjust them.

Decide whether to smooth open answers

In the PIPP example, you may have noticed that we had one response with a small spelling mistake which I chose to ignore:

176 I record the user expresions using Lookback connected to Marvel

In larger data sets, it's inevitable that a few people will make typing errors when answering open questions. Here's an example from a previous AIGA Design Census, this time in 2017, http://designcensus2017.aiga.org/ that included one question with an open answer:

35 -Right now, I can't stop listening to:

Quite a few designers mentioned a design podcast, "99% invisible with Roman Mars." Here is a selection of some of the misspellings:

99 present invisible

99% Invicible

99%indivisible.

Personally, I'd ignore the errors, code all of them as "99% Invisible," and report them as such. On the other hand, here are three of the answers that started with "Christmas Music."

Christmas Music Not by choice

Christmas Music. It's November, ya know.

Christmas music. I'm sorry; I know it's not even Thanksgiving yet!

If I wanted to count genres of listening material, I'd probably smooth them all to "Christmas Music." But if I wanted to do "In vivo" coding where the actual words of the person who answers are important, then I'd definitely preserve the exact punctuation and spelling.

It's especially important to think respectfully about answers from people who may come from a different culture, speak a variety of English that is different from your own, or may have struggled with technology or through a disability to give you their answers. Ask yourself:

"Am I representing the people who have answered accurately, respecting the effort they have made?"

Test your coding: involving the team

If you're working as part of a team, it's tempting to leave the coding to one person, but then you will have focused all the knowledge of the responses in one person.

To split the work up effectively:

- Give each person a few responses—maybe a dozen each.
- If they are new to coding, give them a bit of training on how to do it.
- Everyone codes their responses.
- You all compare your work so far.

- You decide together on a common set of codes. (This is the fun bit.)
- Each of you codes another dozen to confirm whether you can stick to the codes.
- You all reconcile any remaining differences about coding.
- You all split the remaining responses across the team and code them.

It means that the coding gets done a lot faster, far more people in the team really get to know the data, and quite likely they'll agree with your advice to survey a smaller sample next time.

If you want to get really fancy, you can look for inter-rater reliability:

> **Inter-rater reliability** happens when every member of a coding team codes each response in the same way.

If you have a one-off survey with a relatively small data set, then it's possible to get everyone to code the same set of responses—then check how much they agree with each other.

With a large data set or a more frequent process, you'll probably prefer to split it all up. One way is to allocate randomly so that each item gets looked at by two people, but everyone gets a different batch—then look at any discrepancies. Or pick whatever seems sensible to you.

Consider CAQDAS for a large, continuing data set

If you often do surveys that get lengthy answers to open boxes, then you may want to investigate the group of tools that are collectively known by the acronym CAQDAS (*Computer Assisted Qualitative Data Analysis Software*).

CAQDAS tools offer a variety of ways of doing more complex coding than the spreadsheet methods I've talked about.

I tried dabbling with a couple of the tools a few years ago, but I found that the brutal learning curves at that time defeated me. It's always been more cost-effective for me on any particular project to use an ordinary spreadsheet, and I don't repeat the same analysis often enough to justify the effort of learning a CAQDAS tool.

But maybe the tools are easier these days, or you'll need them more often than I do, or you'll find that things like multi-user analysis are sufficiently important to you to make it worthwhile to learn to use a CAQDAS tool.

The CAQDAS project at the University of Surrey, UK, has a description of what to look for in your CAQDAS tool and reviews on the major tools: www.surrey.ac.uk/computer-assisted-qualitative-data-analysis/support/choosing.

Try sentiment analysis but be skeptical

If your goals are about finding out whether the people who answer are positive or negative about something, then you can try putting the comments through one of the many "sentiment analysis" tools. There are plenty of them at all price points, starting with free. Some of them focus on social media comments, but others will accept any text you put into them.

I haven't tried any paid-for services. The results from a couple of free services were disappointing. They gave me an overall score, but I got a better idea of the sentiments from reading the comments.

If you have access to a sentiment analysis tool, then you may as well give it a try, but make sure that you read the comments yourself, too.

Try a word cloud but be skeptical

The simplest way to visualize a set of comments is to throw them into a tool that creates a word cloud (also known as a *tag cloud*). These tools come and go, so possibly the only time-consuming part is to find one that still works: search for *tag cloud generator* or *word cloud*.

I located a cloud generator and tried the answers to: "35—Right now, I can't stop listening to:" from the AIGA data set I was looking at earlier. I got the cloud in Figure 6.17.

FIGURE 6.17

A word cloud for things that designers were listening to in 2017.

Total time: 10 minutes. Is it worth it? My experience is: usually, no. But sometimes if I've done some adjectival coding first, then it can be handy to have some contrasting word clouds—perhaps with "positive" and "negative."

What could possibly go wrong with responses?

When you're dealing with responses, you've got two tentacles to think about, in Figure 6.18: "The ones whose answers you use" (right) and "The answers you get" (left).

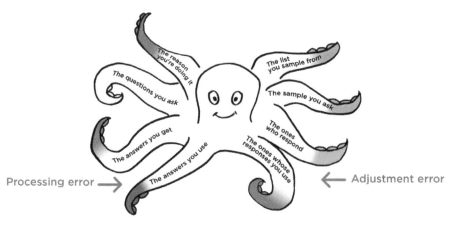

Processing error →

← Adjustment error

FIGURE 6.18
Response is a two-tentacle chapter with two errors.

Problem: Adjustment error

Toward the start of this chapter, we spent quite a lot of time thinking about whether to include or exclude each individual person's response and how to weight them. These decisions can end up making quite a lot of difference to the overall result of the survey, so they get an error of their own.

> **Adjustment error** happens when you make less-than-perfect choices about whose responses to include and how to weight them.

Adjustment error is a major concern for survey methodologists working on surveys of national importance, such as a Decennial Census, but most of us don't need to worry too much about it.

Problem: Processing error

The matching tentacle on the left-hand side of the Survey Octopus is "The answers you get." This is about looking at the answer to an individual question.

Once upon a time, this tentacle was rather a major obstacle, because there were so many opportunities for errors to creep in during the laborious process of turning written answers into something that was suitable for analysis—mostly, a lot of tedious typing.

If you've chosen an electronic mode, then the people who answer have most likely done the typing for you, but surprise! As you found out when cleaning the data, they, too, make typing errors, plus they may misunderstand the question and do all the other fun things that we had to deal with when data cleaning.

Also, remember me begging you to keep a log and do frequent backups? As I mentioned, the error that haunts me the most is messing up the spreadsheet so that I lose hours of work.

And finally, the decisions about what to do about outliers, and how to code any non-numeric answers, can also have their issues. So that gives us our processing error.

> **Processing error** covers all the mistakes that you make when cleaning the data and calculating the final results, other than the ones included in adjustment error.

At this point, you will know

Your survey process is almost over. You've tackled all but one tentacle of the Survey Octopus, and you've done your best to keep on top of all those different types of errors.

You've got a good quality data set and clear goals that say why you collected it. And you've got some numbers, whether directly from the survey or by creating some crosstabs.

There's only one thing left to tackle: turning those numbers into decision. That's what we'll do in the next chapter, "Reports."

Meanwhile, there's Spotlight, I which focuses on creating good charts.

A Good Chart Is Easy to Read and Honest

In the previous chapter, we had a look at using charts to get to know your data. Those charts are for you. If they don't mean anything to anyone else, that's OK.

This Spotlight is about charts that you use for communicating data.

Here's my list of the attributes for a good chart:

- Honest
- Easy to read, including for people with low vision or who see colors differently
- Correctly labeled
- Has a clear message
- Works for the people who will read it

And also, do not forget:

- It has an alternative presentation in numbers for people who find charts difficult to read, or who use assistive technologies that don't work with charts.

Let's take a look at a couple of bad charts and think about how to turn them into decent ones.

Don't use 3D charts

Avoid all 3D charts. They distort the data and add unnecessary visual noise.

Here's a rotten example chart from data about job titles at a UX conference. I wanted to show the proportions of people with a job title that included "UX designer" who also described themselves as "senior designer" or "manager." In the 3D pie chart in Figure I.1, the slices at the back look smaller than they actually are, so they give the impression that those two slices are roughly equal and add up to just over a quarter of all the designers.

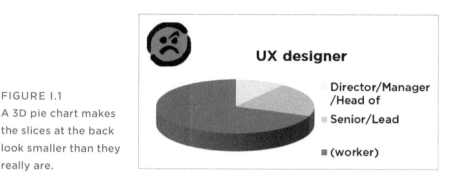

FIGURE I.1
A 3D pie chart makes the slices at the back look smaller than they really are.

The rule of avoiding 3D charts applies to bar, column, and area charts as well. I can just about accept a 3D chart when you are trying to show data on three axes, but even then the chart can be difficult to interpret.

The 2D chart in Figure I.2, with exactly the same data, reveals that there were roughly twice as many senior UX designers as managers, together adding up to just under a third of UX designers.

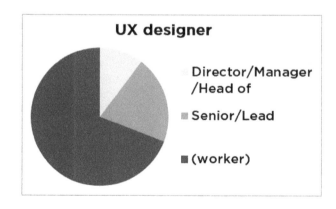

FIGURE I.2
A 2D pie chart makes it easier to see the proportions better.

If I add labels to the chart as in Figure I.3, does that make it better again? Or does it add visual noise? The choice depends on whether I think the people I'm making the chart for will want the precision of the extra numbers.

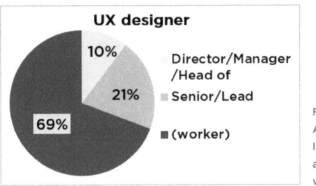

FIGURE I.3

A 2D pie chart with labels adds precision at the expense of visual noise.

And, of course, let's include that extra Table I.1 for people who find charts difficult to read.

TABLE I.1 PROPORTIONS OF PEOPLE WITH THE TITLE "UX DESIGNER"

Director/Manager/Head of	10%
Senior/Lead	21%
(worker)	69%

A simple pie chart is sometimes OK

I went with a 2D pie chart because I had a small number of slices and wanted a simple comparison.

Unfortunately, it's easy to mess up pie charts. If you don't want to appear on the many blogs devoted to pie charts that fail, follow these rules:

- Have a maximum of six slices within the pie.
- Make sure that the slices are clearly different from each other (no similar categories).

- Slices must work for people who have specific problems with color vision, or who are viewing the chart in black and white.
- And, because it bears repeating, no 3D.

If you have lots of smaller categories, you might try rolling them up into an "everything else" slice to keep under the "maximum of six slices" rule, but I'd consider reaching for a different chart first.

Avoid fancy charts

Most spreadsheet programs offer some charts that may be fun to explore, but may not work for the people who will eventually read the chart.

- For example, with my job titles data set, I tried a "concentric donut chart" in Figure I.4. If you work with concentric donut charts every day, this one may tell you something. All it does for me is confuse me.

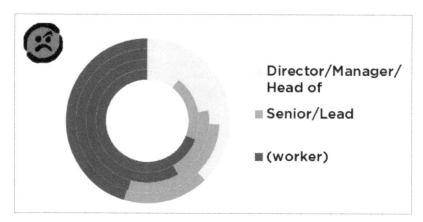

Director/Manager/
Head of

■ Senior/Lead

■ (worker)

FIGURE I.4
A concentric donut chart did nothing for me.

I mostly use two types of column chart

Personally, I find that I nearly always reach for two types of column chart: the side-by-side and the staked percentage.

For example, in Figure I.5, I'm trying to show a 3 by 4 comparison—three levels of job title within four work areas. I've presented them as side-by-side columns.

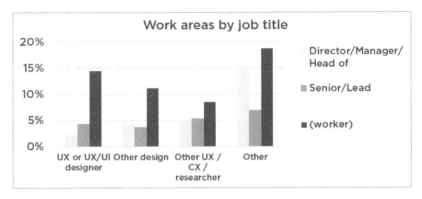

FIGURE I.5
A side-by-side column chart.

When I look at this chart, I notice that people at the "Director" level are much more numerous in the "Other" work area, and there are almost none of them in the "UX or UX/UI designer" work area. You may see something different or nothing at all.

The stacked percentage column chart may be a bit less familiar. It compares the percentages of something within a category—in this case, the proportions for my four job titles as in Figure I.6.

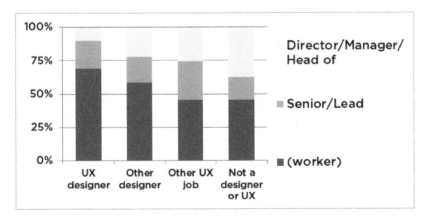

FIGURE I.6
A stacked percentage chart makes it easier to compare across different types.

Bar charts are flipped column charts

In the column charts you just looked at, you may have noticed that it can be horrible trying to read labels that are stacked under the columns.

The bar chart is a close relative of the column chart, swapping the vertical columns for horizontal bars. This gives more horizontal space for the label, as in Figure I.7.

Bar and column charts are equally useful. I have a very slight preference for column charts because it's a tiny bit easier for stakeholders to read "up" as "more."

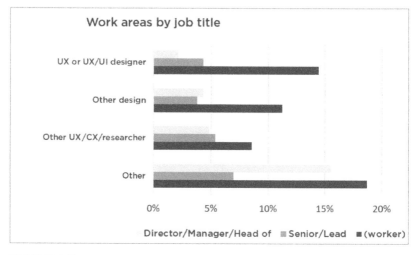

FIGURE I.7

A bar chart can work better when the labels for categories are longer.

Focus on the message in the data

When experimenting with charts, I find that it's easy to get pulled into trying to show what the data says, and it's easy to forget that my aim is to help my stakeholders make their decisions.

For this data set, my stakeholders were the organizers and speakers at a UX conference. I thought a bit harder about what they were interested in and what I'd learned from the data. They were planning the next year's conference, and mostly wanted to know:

- What level of UX knowledge can we expect in the audience?
- Are people in the audience more likely to be doing the work or managing it?

My closest approximation for "level of UX knowledge" was to assume that if people had "UX" in their job title, they'd know something about UX. It's not ideal, but sometimes we have to work with the data we have and then iterate our surveys.

So I went for a simpler classification: all the job titles with a UX theme in one category and everything else in another.

My final chart in Figure I.8 shows that roughly a third of the conference attendees have a UX job title, but if they do have a UX job title they are more likely to be doing the work than managing it. After all those explorations of different chart types, I've come back to a variation on the column.

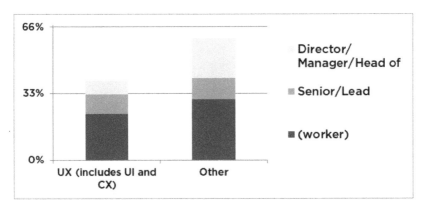

FIGURE I.8

A column chart shows that around a third of attendees have a UX/UI/CX job title.

281

And finally, of course, here is Table I.2 for anyone who doesn't like charts for whatever reason.

TABLE I.2 COMPARISON OF WORK AREAS AND JOB LEVELS

% of total attendance	UX (includes UI and CX)	Other
(worker)	23%	30%
Senior/Lead	10%	11%
Director/ Manager/ Head of	7%	20%

Remove visual clutter from charts

Depending on the spreadsheet/charting program you use, you'll find that you get varying amounts of visual clutter in their default options. Figure I.9 shows what the previous chart looked like with Excel defaults.

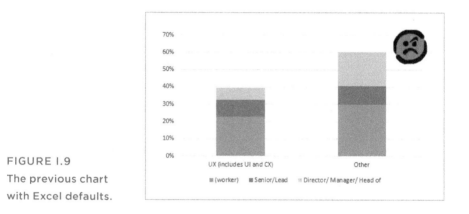

FIGURE I.9
The previous chart with Excel defaults.

You may prefer it, but I decided to:

- Change the vertical scale. The default runs from 0% to 70%, but I opted for 33% and 66% instead to make it clearer that one column is just over one-third of the data, and the other is nearly two-thirds.

- Increased the font sizes, a lot.

- Moved the legend away from the column labels.
- Changed the color scheme so that it works in monochrome for people viewing this book on noncolored devices or who do not see all the colors.

For other charts, you might also want to consider:

- Reducing the number of decimal points (don't claim precision that your data won't support).

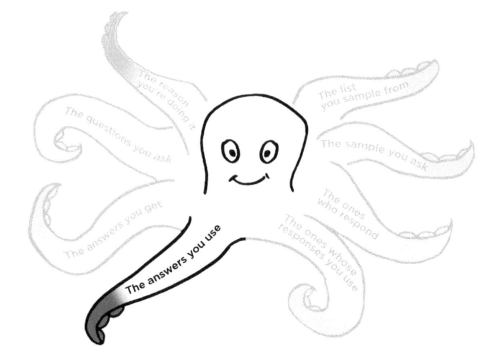

The reason
you're doing it

The list
you sample from

The questions you ask

The sample you ask

The answers you get

The ones
who respond

The answers you use

The ones whose
responses you use

Reports: Show the Results to Decision-Makers

You've done all the hard work to make sure that you have turned your responses into solid data.

If you are the person doing everything, including making the final decision on what actions to take based on what the survey told you, you may be finished.

If you are doing the survey for others to make the decision—or the decision is up to you, but you have to convince other people that you made the right one—then you almost certainly have to report or present what you learned through the survey. That's what we'll look at in this chapter.

Our main tentacles in this chapter are the answers that you'll use and the reasons why you're doing the survey (from way back in Chapter 1, "Goals").

Think about what you learned, numerically

Let's think about numbers a bit more, and this time from the point of view of turning them into decisions. In Chapter 1, you also thought a bit about the type of number you wanted—such as whether it might be purely a number, a range, a mean, median, or a mode.

When the number that you report is entirely about the data in the survey responses, it's called a *descriptive statistic*.

> A **descriptive statistic** is a statement about the data in the survey responses.

If you asked everyone and everyone replied, then there's an exact match between the data you got and the defined group of people, so there's nothing to make any inferences about. However, in real life, it's highly unusual to get that exact match, so let's assume that you have to think about inferential statistics.

> An **inferential statistic** is a statement about the defined group of people based on the data from the survey responses.

Inferential statistics don't have to be complicated. One of my favorites is the percentage. Here's a typical descriptive statistic:

> 54 out of 78 people who answered prefer XYZ.

If I change that to:

> 69% of people who answered prefer XYZ,

then it's still a descriptive statistic. But when it becomes:

69% prefer XYZ,

it's become an inferential statistic, because I've stepped away from describing my sample to making a claim about (we hope) my defined group of people or (if I don't provide a context) even people in general.

My claim is an exact one, which may be overoptimistic based on my sample size. If I'm reasonably sure that I've dealt with the issues in my Survey Octopus appropriately and used a sampling method that gave me a random sample, then I can produce an inferential statistic with a confidence interval (usually at 95%):

69% ± 0.1% prefer XYZ.

I might also choose to focus on the minority, carefully flipping the question to preserve the wording as asked (the confidence interval stays the same):

31% ± 0.1% do not prefer XYZ.

Which approach is right for your report and your decision? I don't know, but I'm sure you'll know because you've done your work in the "Goals" chapter correctly(see Chapter 1). Focus on that, and you'll be fine.

Consider the strength of views as well as the direction

Back in Chapter 2, "Sample," you thought about what might happen to the zone of response if people with strong feelings happened to be more likely to respond, as in Figure 7.1.

Now you need to think hard about modes and means. If you look at that sketch, you'll see that the mean reaction is right in the middle—with two roughly equal peaks at the extreme somewhat balancing each other out. The sketch has two possibilities for mode: one at "hate it" and another at "love it."

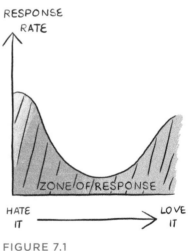

FIGURE 7.1
This zone of response might happen when people with strong feelings are more likely to respond.

As you look at your data, consider whether you need a split report:

> A **split report** reflects the views of one or more strong minorities, as well as the overall majority.

I had a striking example of the need for the split report when doing a survey for a professional organization about whether to offer a certification scheme. The majority was clearly, but not passionately, "go ahead," but the minority objectors were strongly opposed.

Avoid cherry-picking the open answers

Many of us are more comfortable with qualitative research than surveys. In qualitative research, the stories from small numbers of respondents are the essence of what we do. And it's true that a vivid comment can really perk up your report or presentation.

That means that when you come to selecting the insights from your survey data—and especially, when you've put a lot of effort into coding the answers when dealing with responses—you can fall into the trap of *cherry-picking*.

> **Cherry picking** is reporting a small number of comments instead of focusing on the overall responses including numeric ones.

So look at the numbers. Most respondents just answer the questions; they don't write essays for you.

In Chapter 6, "Responses," I explained how I tackled the coding for a question about PIPP in a survey of user researchers. We had:

- 9 people who chose the answer "other" with open text.
- 191 people who chose a frequency option ranging from "always" to "never."

We decided that with a big majority going for a frequency option, and with sensible reasons why a smaller proportion chose "other," we could safely continue with our analysis using the 191 responses.

Decide what news to deliver and when

If you were successful in limiting yourself to a Light Touch Survey, you'll only have asked the Most Crucial question and a minimal number of representative questions, so you can tell everyone everything about your findings.

If you ended up with something that was more like a Big Honkin' Survey, then you'll have done a lot of hard work to get to this point, and it's tempting to want to tell everyone everything about your findings—as in Figure 7.2. Don't do it.

FIGURE 7.2
Is it really essential to include everything in your report?

Let's go right back to your goals. What are the most important insights you want stakeholders to take away from your survey? Keeping your report focused—and that usually means *short*—will help them to make the decisions that were your aim all along.

Other things to consider:

- **It's never a good idea to surprise people with bad news.** Assuming that you began your analysis as soon as responses started to come in, you may want to alert stakeholders to some of the headlines early on.

- **Stay on top of your survey timeline.** It's possible to spend so long on cleaning the data set of responses and producing a beautiful presentation that you miss the moment when a decision was made.

- **It's OK to have some gaps in the results**—"more work needed"—rather than holding up delivery.

Here's an example of how to deal with "not enough data." Nick Cochrane of Zebra People (a UK recruiter) and I had this problem when we were working together on a survey. Nick's aim was to create a report for his clients on freelance rates compared to permanent salaries across the range of vacancies that Zebra People focus on.

We had a great response rate in general, with solid data for nearly all of the 200 categories that Nick wanted to report on, but we had some gaps where we only had a few responses within a category. We decided that turning the numbers into a mean or median would be unreliable with such a small sample.

Instead, we decided to acknowledge the problem in the report—there's an example in Figure 7.3—and we used it to create an opportunity to talk directly with the people the report was aimed at: employers looking to fill jobs and people looking to change jobs.

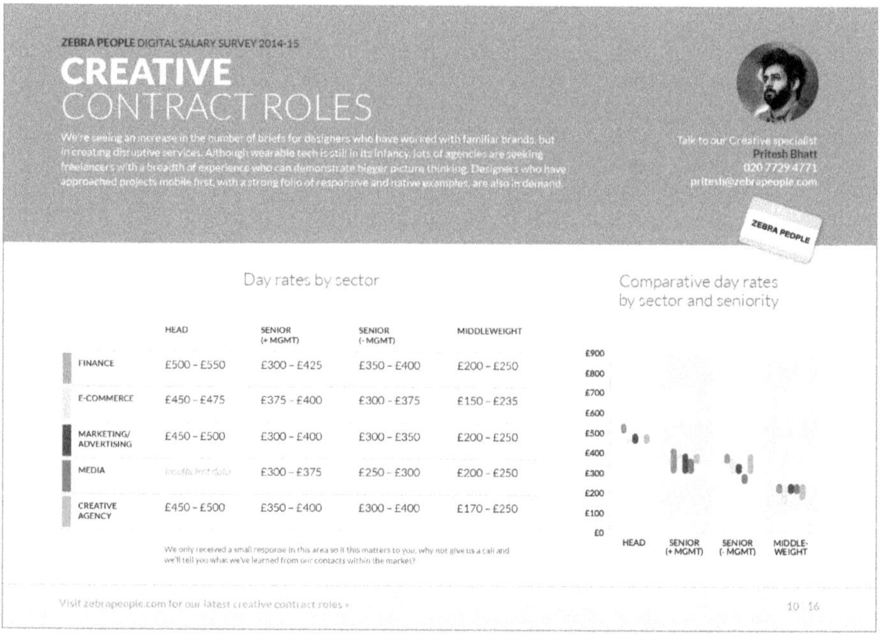

FIGURE 7.3

Zebra people: report on salaries of project management jobs by sector.

Decide what format to use for delivery

Most of us reach instinctively for our preferred word processor or presentation design program when we're thinking about delivering the results from a piece of research.

Before you dive directly into that report or presentation, here are a few other ideas, as shown in Table 7.1.

TABLE 7.1 SOME OTHER IDEAS FOR REPORTING RESULTS

Idea	Notes	Good for
"This week's results"	A very short announcement: you could have an email list, an Intranet page, or a channel on your organization's messaging service.	Frequent iterative Light Touch Surveys
A poster	Focus on having the number as your key result. Keep other text to a minimum. Use large print throughout so that people can read your poster easily from a distance.	Academic audiences or getting insights out to a large organization
An infographic	As with a poster, be highly selective about the detail you include—it's not a report. There's an example in Figure 7.4.	A summary of a few key numbers related to each other
A sticker or T-shirt	Made famous in the UK when the designer Katharine Hamnett wore a T-shirt saying "58% don't want Pershing" when she met then Prime Minister Margaret Thatcher in 1984.	A single number with a very brief phrase, communicating the answer to one Most Crucial Question in an eye-catching way

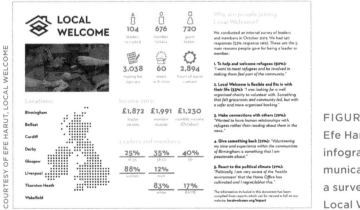

FIGURE 7.4
Efe Harut created this infographic to communicate the results of a survey for UK charity Local Welcome.

Present slides in assertion/evidence format

I'm going to focus on results delivered in slides for a moment.

One of the things I see far too often is slides structured like Figure 7.5 with a topic—just a noun—and then subtopics—often little more than nouns and a few adjectives. This was (as far as I recall) the default offered by Microsoft PowerPoint when it launched in 1990, and it has remained weirdly popular.

FIGURE 7.5
Topic/subtopic slide and an example.

Don't do that.

Do this instead: assertion/evidence format. (Garner, Alley et al., 2009)

> Assertion/evidence format has the main point of every slide in a full sentence, supported by optional further detail or evidence.

The assertion/evidence format, shown in Figure 7.6, forces you to think about, and express, the main point of every slide (the "assertion") in a sentence. In my example, I added a sentence to emphasize the main point of the slide. The "evidence" below can be bullet points like the example, or something else such as an image, table, chart, or even a video.

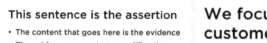

FIGURE 7.6
Assertion/evidence slide layout and an example with a sentence and supporting bullets.

If you can't create a single sentence that works for your slide, then you've got two options:

- Split the slide up into single points that each have a summary assertion.
- Drop the slide altogether.

When you have all your slides in assertion/evidence format, you can use a great tip that I got from Aga Bojko, author of *Eye Tracking the User Experience: A Practical Guide to Research*. (Bojko, 2013)

> "Create a document that has the headers of all your slides. Check that it tells the story of the presentation."

The assertion/evidence format also means that:

- Someone who wasn't at your presentation will see all the major points when they review the slides later.
- If you can't present the slides yourself because of a last-minute emergency or technological problems, then someone else can present for you and be confident that they have covered all the major points.
- Even if someone can't see or understand a chart or other image, they won't miss the point of the slide because that point is right there in the assertion.

I used topic/subtopic format for a long time before I discovered assertion/evidence format, so it took me a while to get used to writing the assertion sentence for every slide, but now I wouldn't do presentations any other way.

Write documents in assertion/evidence format

After I became an enthusiast for the assertion/evidence format in slides, it gradually dawned on me that I could write documents, especially reports, in a similar way.

Have you noticed that most of the headings in this book are complete sentences? Take a look at the table of contents, and you'll see that the key points are laid out there.

I admit that it does take practice, and if your organization has a specific report style, then it may take a bit of a fight to get them to accept headings as full sentences. I've tried sneaking full sentences in as all the lower-level headings to get colleagues familiar with the idea.

Choose "inverted pyramid" for most presentations

For overall flow of your presentation, here are three typical styles to get you started (see Table 7.2):

- Inverted pyramid
- Methodology first
- Presentation Zen

Inverted pyramid is the journalistic style that starts with the most important message and then supports it with extra detail. Inverted pyramid also adapts well to placing extra detail in an appendix. It's also known as an *executive summary*.

Methodology first is the traditional style of many scientific papers. They start with what they did and proceed to what they found. This process invites criticism of your methodology, but it can also build confidence that your findings are based on good process.

Presentation Zen is a term coined by presentation designer Garr Reynolds. (Reynolds, 2012) The style has a series of compelling images, possibly accompanied by a few words, to provide an engaging background to a powerful speech. The slides do not stand alone without the speaker, so if you opt for this style, then make sure that you record your talk and provide a transcript of your speech for anyone who might need it and couldn't be there at the time.

TABLE 7.2 FOR AND AGAINST EACH PRESENTATION STYLE

Style	For	Against
Inverted pyramid	Gives greatest attention to the most important message	If the results are surprising, it may lay you open to challenges of the method.
Methodology first	Builds confidence in methodology	Busy readers may be too bored by the method to get to the results.
Presentation Zen	Great support for delivering a compelling message	It's not much use to anyone who wasn't at the presentation.

There are many ways of showing the same results

Here's how the same data might look, depending on your survey goals. It's adapted from a question I saw in a real survey, but I made up the data.

1. Show them the data

The format, as in Figure 7.7, has the question at the top, with the actual data displayed in a table and with no further interpretation.

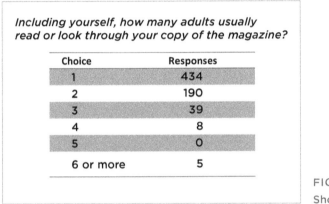

Including yourself, how many adults usually read or look through your copy of the magazine?

Choice	Responses
1	434
2	190
3	39
4	8
5	0
6 or more	5

FIGURE 7.7
Show them the data.

Best for:
- People who want to see all the data
- A quick reference to look up later
- A record of the exact question asked
- Sharing results from a relatively simple question

2. Put data in assertion-evidence format

As you've seen, I'm keen on the assertion-evidence format with a single sentence that has the main point of the slide and supporting evidence.

Let's say that the decision-makers are mostly interested in whether people share their magazine or not. In Figure 7.8, I've converted the data into respondents who don't share (adult views the magazine) and respondents who do share, and then converted the raw data to a percentage.

About a third of our 676 respondents share their magazine	
Adults	
Don't share	65%
Shares with 1 other	28%
Shares with 2 others	6%
Shares with 3 others	1%
Shares with 4 others	-
Shares with 5 or more	less than 1%

FIGURE 7.8
Assertion/evidence
format for the data.

Best for:

- People who want to see the main interpretation, as well as the supporting data

3. Focus on the main message

The version in Figure 7.9 combines all the smaller categories of data into one. I've now got three categories, which is within my personal maximum of six for a pie chart.

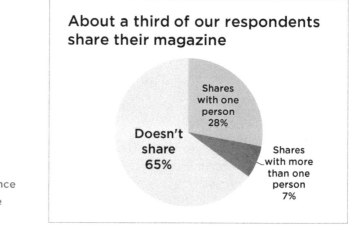

FIGURE 7.9
Assertion/evidence
format with a pie
chart.

Best for:

- Stakeholders in a hurry who like a little bit of data

4. Compare before and after an event

Those three versions are just about all I could do with the data from a single question.

Let's say I've been working for a client who had a campaign called *Share the fun*, and I used a survey before and after the campaign to assess the impact.

In Figure 7.10, I've changed the assertion to match the goals of the survey and ditched the pie charts because it's hard to compare two pie charts.

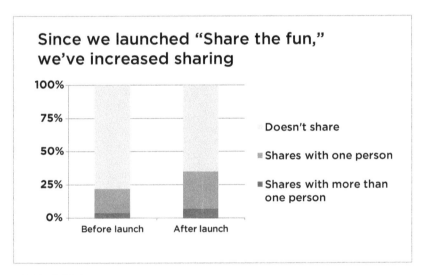

FIGURE 7.10
Assertion/evidence with comparative bar chart.

Best for:

- Comparing before-and-after data

5. Compare results within the survey

Another type of survey might look at which age groups are most likely to share their magazine. Instead of comparing before-and-after across a campaign, this survey asks two questions: the one you've already seen, plus age.

The decision to be made based on this survey is: "Should the client aim their campaign about sharing at a particular age group?"

This time, in Figure 7.11, I've done a comparison by age.

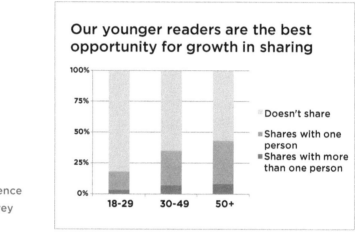

FIGURE 7.11
Assertion/evidence and within-survey bar chart.

Best for:

- Pinpointing the basis for a decision
- Stakeholders who like to see the numbers behind the recommendations

6. Draw out a key point with a compelling image

Sometimes, you want to focus your stakeholders on the decision. You've got the solid data from your survey, and you can make it available if they want it.

This version backs up the key assertion with a memorable image that is relevant to the assertion.

The difficulty here is in picking the image. It has to be strong, accurate, and relatable. The image that I've used in Figure 7.12 may say "young person who is enjoying reading a magazine" to your stakeholders, or it may say "this organization is focusing too much on men."

COURTESY OF TAMBA BUDIARSANA WWW.PEXELS.COM/
PHOTO/MAN-SITTING-ON-CHAIR-READING-BOOK-4070924/

FIGURE 7.12
Assertion with a
compelling image.

Best for:

- Face-to-face presentations when you'll provide backup data separately

You can do the same things with reports

You may decide to report your results in several formats.

For example, ARK is a research institute in Northern Ireland. Since 2008, they have done an annual survey with P7 children—equivalent to U.S. grade 5, when the children are about 10 to 11 years old. In 2018, they had questions on learning languages other than English or Irish, including this one:

LANGLRN: Which language(s) do you learn?

The abbreviated question name LANGLRN is there so that you can download the raw data www.ark.ac.uk/klt/datasets/.

You can also see the data for each question on the web. There's an example in Figure 7.13.

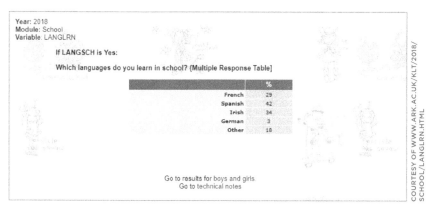

FIGURE 7.13
Summary table for the LANGLRN question in 2018.

Or you might enjoy the same data presented in the summary of results for the children themselves, in Figure 7.14.

FIGURE 7.14
The LANGLRN question for children.

The best insights come from using surveys alongside other methods

Way, way back in the "Goals" chapter, I talked about the matrix for choosing the right method in Figure 7.15.

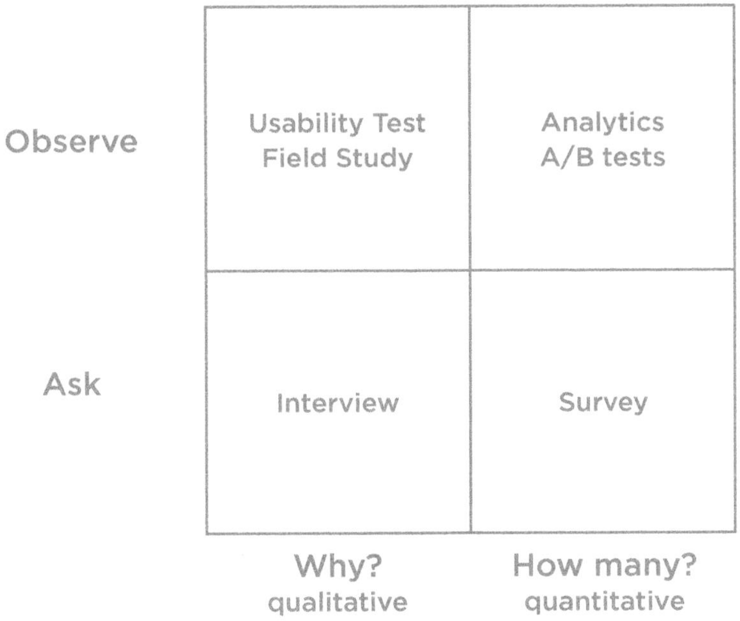

	Why? qualitative	How many? quantitative
Observe	Usability Test Field Study	Analytics A/B tests
Ask	Interview	Survey

FIGURE 7.15
A matrix for choosing the right method.

We've come a long way, and done at least two of the methods during the process of doing this survey:

- Interviewing people in your defined group to find out what their Burning Topic might be
- Usability testing the questionnaire

Now is the time for a quick reminder: the best insights happen when you use a survey alongside other methods. So have a look around for any other results you might have.

For example, if you've been asking about whether people find your website useful, then do you have any analytics that you can compare to see which areas of the site are actually in use?

If you've been asking customers why they decided to sign up, can you have a look at your conversion rates? As you can see in Figure 7.16, a survey is one of a range of tools in our user experience box, alongside many other things including usability tests and interviews.

FIGURE 7.16
A survey is just another tool in the box.

I mentioned a Local Welcome infographic earlier. Let's have another look at it, in Figure 7.17, to see how the designer Efe Harut used a variety of sources. On the left, you'll see a photograph of people taking part in a charity activity and a map of activity locations. In the middle at the top, there is some triangulation with key facts about activities taken from other data held by the charity. In the middle lower down, there are some numbers from representativeness questions on the survey—also cross-checked with other data. And finally on the right, there are answers to the Most Crucial Question, with carefully selected "in vivo" quotations to illustrate typical comments.

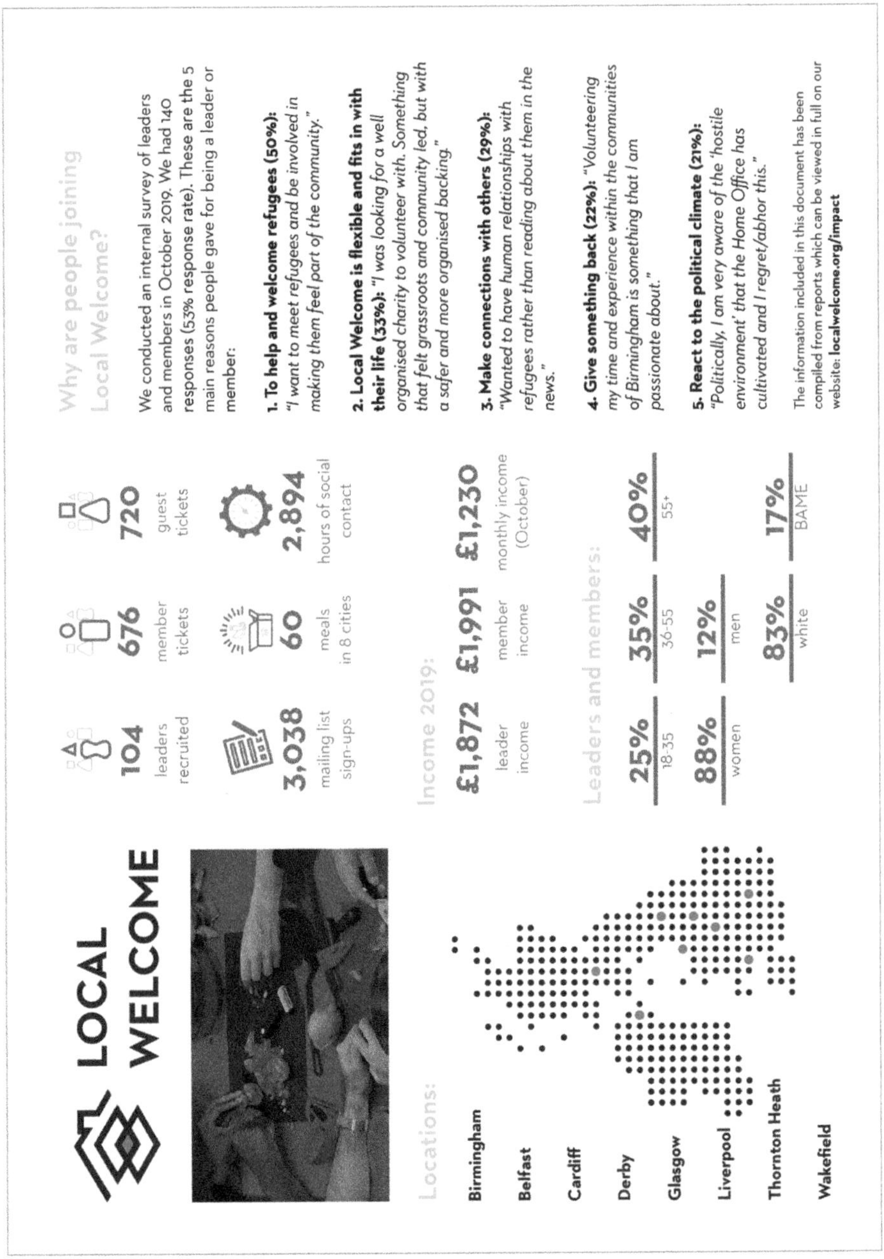

LOCAL WELCOME

Locations:

Birmingham

Belfast

Cardiff

Derby

Glasgow

Liverpool

Thornton Heath

Wakefield

104 leaders recruited

676 member tickets

720 guest tickets

3,038 mailing list sign-ups

60 meals in 8 cities

2,894 hours of social contact

Income 2019:

£1,872 leader income

£1,991 member income

£1,230 monthly income (October)

Leaders and members:

25% 18-35

35% 36-55

40% 55+

88% women

12% men

83% white

17% BAME

Why are people joining Local Welcome?

We conducted an internal survey of leaders and members in October 2019. We had 140 responses (53% response rate). These are the 5 main reasons people gave for being a leader or member:

1. To help and welcome refugees (50%): "I want to meet refugees and be involved in making them feel part of the community."

2. Local Welcome is flexible and fits in with their life (33%): "I was looking for a well organised charity to volunteer with. Something that felt grassroots and community led, but with a safer and more organised backing."

3. Make connections with others (29%): "Wanted to have human relationships with refugees rather than reading about them in the news."

4. Give something back (22%): "Volunteering my time and experience within the communities of Birmingham is something that I am passionate about."

5. React to the political climate (21%): "Politically, I am very aware of the 'hostile environment' that the Home Office has cultivated and I regret/abhor this."

The information included in this document has been compiled from reports which can be viewed in full on our website: **localwelcome.org/impact**

FIGURE 7.17
Local Welcome infographic.

What could possibly go wrong with reports?

When I first introduced you to the Survey Octopus almost at the start of this book, I described it as representing the choices to make between "Why you want to ask," "Who you want to ask," and "The number," as in Figure 7.18.

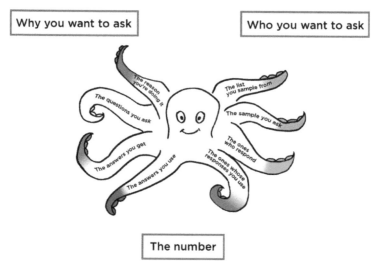

FIGURE 7.18

The Survey Octopus has tentacles about the choices you make in surveys.

Since then, I've discussed the various errors that arise from the choices in creating a survey. Here they all are, in the order that they appeared in the chapters thus far:

- **Chapter 1, "Goals":** Lack of validity happens when the questions you ask do not match the reason why you are doing the survey and what you want to ask about.

- **Chapter 2, "Sample":** Coverage error happens when the list that you sample from includes some people who are outside the defined group that you want to ask or excludes some people who are in it.

  Sampling error happens when you choose to ask some of the people on the list you sample from rather than everyone.

  Non-response error happens when the people who respond are different from the people who don't respond in ways that affect the result.

- **Chapter 3, "Questions"** (also the error for **Chapter 4, "Questionnaire"**): Measurement error is the difference between the true value of the answer and the answer you get.
- **Chapter 6, "Response":** Adjustment error happens when you make less-than-perfect choices about whose answers to include and how to weight them.

  Processing error covers all the mistakes that you make when cleaning the data and calculating the final results, other than the ones included in adjustment error.

And now, our final error.

  Total Survey Error is the consequence of all the individual survey errors.

Now let's see what they all look like when you attach them to the Survey Octopus in Figure 7.19.

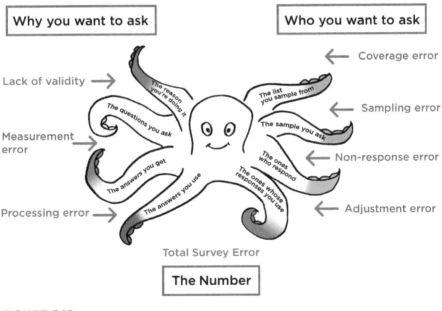

FIGURE 7.19
The Survey Octopus with all the errors.

I think that long ago, when we started to think about whether to do a survey, I pointed out that surveys are not an easy method to get right—and now you can see how the various choices along the way are about making sure that your Total Survey Error is kept as low as possible.

The idea of the Survey Octopus is to show that the errors are related to each other. One mistake that I see far too often is to spend all the money on a large sample to try to reduce sampling error—but meanwhile skimping on the interviewing and question testing that would reduce measurement error.

I know that you won't have fallen into that trap, but instead you'll have tried hard to make good choices all the way—thus keeping your Total Survey Error to a minimum and ending up with the number at the end that you can use with confidence to make decisions.

At this point, you will know

It's the end—you know everything.

OK, just kidding. What I hope you know is that making good choices along the way will result in keeping your Total Survey Error as low as possible.

And also, did I mention iteration? I hope you decided to go for frequent Light Touch Surveys, where you learn from each one and get better at them, rather than one Big Honkin' Survey.

If you do still have to do the Big Honkin' Survey, I hope you decided to iterate at the various stages. In other words: two or three rounds of interviewing, and some extra usability tests, and a really solid pilot test before your fieldwork will help to keep that Total Survey Error as low as it can go.

Three ways to talk about the Survey Octopus

You've also met the Survey Octopus and all its associated errors. If your team and stakeholders are willing to engage with cartoon-like tentacles, have fun with the Survey Octopus.

If you want a more formal presentation using the same terms, then try the one in Figure 7.20.

If you want to go for the full academic language—perhaps if your stakeholders are scientists, or you like references—then the diagram in Figure 7.21 from leading survey methodologists will now be easy for you. Compare the boxes with the tentacles in the Survey Octopus, and you have the translations.

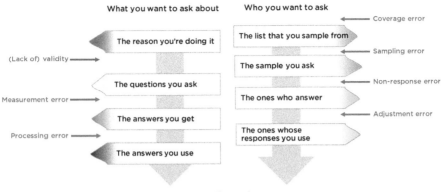

FIGURE 7.20
Total Survey Error without the Survey Octopus.

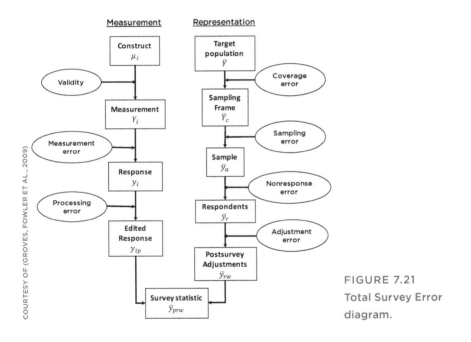

COURTESY OF (GROVES, FOWLER ET AL., 2009)

FIGURE 7.21
Total Survey Error diagram.

Hints:

- The Construct is "What you want to ask about" in the Survey Octopus.
- The Survey Statistic" is what I've talked about as "the number."
- You can ignore the little italic letters until you decide to dive into the mathematics.

Why you want to ask

Who you want to ask

The number

CHAPTER 8

The Least You Can Do™

In this final chapter, we'll think about The Least You Can Do™. Steve Krug has a chapter with the same name in his book *Rocket Surgery Made Easy: The Do-It-Yourself Guide to Finding and Fixing Usability Problems*. He explains The Least You Can Do™ like this:

> When you're deciding how to fix a usability problem, the question you should always be asking is "What's the smallest, simplest change we can make that's likely to keep people from having the problem we observed?"

One day when I was tired, I thought about the many challenging concepts in surveys and thought: "What's the Least You Can Do™?"

Steve said it was OK for me to borrow his trademarked phrase, and I'm adapting it like this:

> What's the smallest, simplest thing to do from each chapter that will make sure that we get good results?

Then I realized that "small and simple" really depends on how far along you are in the survey process and how much time you've got. So I've started with some things you can do in an hour at various steps in the process.

If you're starting from scratch, there's a plan to turn around a Light Touch Survey in a day, and then a suggestion about what to do when you have a whole week to play with.

The survey process has seven steps

The full survey process in Figure 8.1 has seven steps. You've seen that the steps are not really separate, but instead the issues somewhat overlap because of the Survey Octopus. For example, when thinking about Goals at the start, you've also got to think about the decisions that you'll make right at the end.

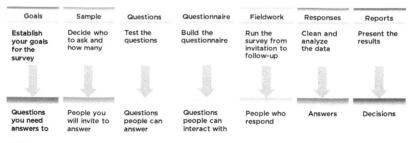

Goals	Sample	Questions	Questionnaire	Fieldwork	Responses	Reports
Establish your goals for the survey	Decide who to ask and how many	Test the questions	Build the questionnaire	Run the survey from invitation to follow-up	Clean and analyze the data	Present the results
Questions you need answers to	People you will invite to answer	Questions people can answer	Questions people can interact with	People who respond	Answers	Decisions

FIGURE 8.1

The survey process in seven steps.

What to do when you've only got an hour

The bad news is that when you've only got an hour, you simply don't have time to do all seven steps in the survey—but I'm hoping that you have made some progress on your survey already. If so, try using that hour to do at least one of these:

If you haven't yet identified your Most Crucial Question (MCQ): Review the questionnaire to see which question(s) are candidates for MCQ. Think about the decision(s) you plan to make on the basis of this survey. Is there a clear relationship between the decisions and the questions in the survey? Note: this may mean that you find out that a survey is not the right method at this point. That's OK: the effort going into drafting the questionnaire isn't wasted; you can use it as the basis for some interviews.

If you haven't yet got a questionnaire: Do a couple of interviews with people in your defined group on the topics you want to cover. I'm allowing 20 minutes of the hour to set them up and 20 minutes each for the interviews. You'll learn a lot about how people think about the topics, and you'll find question writing is a lot easier.

If you've got a questionnaire: Testing! Find two or three people in your defined group and get them to try answering the questionnaire. If you don't have time for separate cognitive interviewing for the questions, followed by separate usability testing of the questionnaire, then you can combine the two by asking people to "think aloud" during the usability test.

If you can't find anyone in your defined group, then you will get some value by asking anyone who hasn't been involved in creating the questionnaire to usability test it for you. It's not quite as good as asking someone from the defined group, because they won't necessarily know how people in your defined group think about the topics, but at least you'll get independent feedback.

When you have responses and need to deal with them: Get a random sample of no more than 100 of the responses. Do as much cleaning, coding, and thinking on that sample as you can in the hour. Now you have an estimate of how long it will take you to do the entire data set, so you can decide whether the effort is necessary, or maybe you can go ahead and make the necessary decisions.

When you've dealt with your responses: Look back at the decisions that you or your stakeholders want to take. Did you get enough from your responses to make the decision now? Have you made sure that the initial hoped-for decision is in the report?

What to do when you've got a day

You can do a survey in one day of your own time, as in Table 8.1. If you need to work with other people, get buy-in from stakeholders, or involve anyone else and then invite them to work with you on the same plan, or split the time according to their schedules.

Plan to restrict yourself to a Most Crucial Question, plus a representativeness question, and a small sample of fewer than 100 people.

TABLE 8.1   A SCHEDULE FOR A SURVEY IN A DAY

The Schedule	
9 a.m.	Goals and sample
	• Decide on your Most Crucial Question.
	• Define your group of people and decide on your representativeness question.
10 a.m.	Questionnaire
	• Build your questionnaire, including writing your invitation and thank-you page.
	• Get someone to do a quick usability test. Ask them to "think aloud" so that you get a little bit of cognitive interviewing at the same time.
11 a.m.	Fieldwork part 1
	• Do your pilot test: send invitations to 10 people, with the request that they respond by 1 p.m.
noon	LUNCH
1 p.m.	Fieldwork part 2
	• Iterate your questionnaire based on your pilot.
	• Send out the questionnaire to the larger sample, with the request that they respond by 3 p.m.
2 p.m.	Responses part 1
	• Some responses will be back. Start your data cleaning.
3 p.m.	Responses part 2
	• Decide what descriptive statistics you want to use.
	• Read all open box responses, possibly sorting them according to one of the other answers.
4 p.m.	Reports
	• Create the report you want to deliver.

For better results, you could split your day of effort across two elapsed days so that you can send out the questionnaire to the larger sample on one morning and resume on the afternoon of the next day with your data cleaning and analysis. That gives your defined group of people a whole day to reply and is more respectful of different work and life patterns.

What to do when you've got a whole week

Did that sound a bit too pressured? Let's try a timetable in Table 8.2 for doing a survey in a week.

Keep it tight—no Big Honkin' Surveys! But you can be a little more relaxed, and perhaps allow up to five questions plus one or two representativeness questions.

If you're looking at that timetable and thinking it seems like a very intense week, you're right.

In terms of the amount of effort, this is close to what I do quite often when working on a survey—but in terms of elapsed time, I usually aim to split the activities across three weeks, with the breaks timed like this:

- Monday and Tuesday morning: as below, but give people in the pilot a week to reply.
- Tuesday afternoon a week later through to Wednesday afternoon: as below, but give people in the main sample a week to reply.
- Thursday and Friday a week later again: as below.

If you need to make some adjustments to the plan, don't compromise by cutting out the pilot study. It's far better to do the pilot study and compromise on the fieldwork than to skip the pilot study and risk making a mess of the fieldwork.

TABLE 8.2 A SCHEDULE FOR DOING A SURVEY IN A WEEK

	Morning	Afternoon
Monday	Goals and sample • Set goals for your survey. • Decide on your Most Crucial Question. • Define your group of people and decide on your representativeness question. • Decide on your sampling method.	Questions and questionnaire • Write your questions. • Build your questionnaire, including the invitation and thank-you page. • Get someone to do a quick usability test. Ask them to "think aloud" so that you get a little bit of cognitive interviewing at the same time. • If you are narrowing down from a list of people, get hold of the list and check it for quality.
Tuesday	Fieldwork part 1 • Do your pilot study. Get your questionnaires out by noon and ask for replies by the end of the day.	Responses • Some responses will be back. Start your data cleaning. • Think about changes you want to make based on the pilot.
Wednesday	Iteration • Review responses from the pilot. • Iterate and re-test the questionnaire.	Fieldwork part 2 • Send out a questionnaire to the larger sample with responses closing on Thursday evening.
Thursday	Responses • Watch responses to see whether there are any issues with questionnaire in the field.	Responses • Some responses will be back. Start your data cleaning. • Decide what descriptive statistics you want to use. • Read all open box responses, possibly sorting them according to one of the other answers.
Friday	Responses • Finish dealing with your responses.	Reports • Create the report you want to deliver.

The checklist for everything

When you can answer the questions under each heading, you're
ready to move onto the next step.

Goals (from Chapter 1)

Checklist question	Is finished when...
Who do you want to ask?	You have a clear definition of a group of people and know exactly who is and isn't in the group.
What do you want to ask them?	You have a single Most Crucial Question.
What decision will you make?	You have agreed on a method of scoring or counting the answers to your Most Crucial Question, and you have a draft of the presentation or other method of sharing the results.

Sample (from Chapter 2)

Checklist question	Is finished when...
How did you find your sample?	If you've chosen "narrow down," you have a list and you have investigated its quality. If you've chosen "in the moment," you have thought about how to intercept people and are ready to test the idea in your pilot study. If you've chosen "snowball up," you have decided on a method of starting the snowball.
How many people do you need to respond?	You have agreed on the number of responses to aim for.
What response rate do you expect to get?	You have an expected response rate from a previous similar survey or from the pilot test of this survey.
Have you decided on a representativeness question?	You have a small number of questions that are appropriate to the topic of this survey and that allow you to compare the results of this survey with other data about your defined group of people that you already have.
Do you know the Burning Issues?	You have completed interviews with people in your defined group, identified issues, and ideally triangulated with results from other types of research.

Questions (from Chapter 3)

Checklist question	Is finished when...
Do your questions use familiar words in familiar ways?	You have completed cognitive interviews with people in your defined group.
Do people have answers for your questions?	You have iterated the questionnaire based on what you found in the cognitive interviews.
Do they feel comfortable with revealing their answers to you?	You have completed another round of cognitive interviews and checked that the problems are sorted out.
	(Question writing is challenging—sometimes it feels like it is never entirely finished, but you have done all the iterations you can manage in the time available.)

Questionnaire (from Chapter 4)

Checklist question	Is finished when...
Have you got your privacy policy sorted out?	The PIA is written and checked against existing privacy policies, and any issues are thought about and resolved. Revised privacy notices are published or ready to go.
Have you chosen your mode and questionnaire tool?	You have created a draft questionnaire.
For electronic questionnaires only: Does your questionnaire work correctly from invitation to thank-you page?	At least one person who did not build the questionnaire has tested it on a variety of browsers and with typical assistive technology.
Can people from your defined group use your questionnaire?	You have completed usability testing with at least three people, amended the questionnaire accordingly, and usability tested again with different people.

Fieldwork (from Chapter 5)

Checklist question	Is finished when...
Have you decided on whether or not you are offering any follow-up?	Your approach is decided and cross-checked with PIA.
Have you run your pilot test?	Pilot test: • Is run from start to finish. • Responses are analyzed. • Draft presentation or other method of communicating the results is sorted out. Make sure that appropriate changes are made to the questionnaire. Changes to the goals and sampling method should also be considered and made as appropriate.

Responses (from Chapter 6)

Checklist question	Is finished when...
Have you backed up your data and created a research log?	Trick question: This is never finished until your survey is completed in every detail. But if you haven't even started—begin now. Do a backup and update the research log on every day when you make any changes to your data set.
Have you done basic data cleaning, such as redacting personal data and checking ranges?	You are sure that all follow-up actions have gone to whoever is doing them, and appropriate personal data is redacted.
Did you have to exclude any responses and why?	You know that all exclusions are documented in the research log.
Did you choose to do any weighting and why?	If you are weighting, the weights are applied and the details of what you did are in the research log.
Did you check that your responses were representative?	Answers to the representativeness questions are checked and look acceptably in line with the results you expected.

continues

Checklist question	Is finished when...
Have you paid appropriate attention to all open answers?	The bare minimum: You have read and thought about every answer. After that, it depends on your goals, so you may have decided to: • Send answers to whoever can take action • Smooth and group answers to make them appropriate for numerical analysis • Code one or more aspects of the answers into categories • Do some combination of the above, or something else
Did you find anything out that surprised you or that was unexpected?	One of the reasons that we do research of any kind is to learn things that we did not already know. There's almost always something surprising or unexpected: when you find it, you'll know that you have looked hard enough at your responses.

Reports (from Chapter 7)

Checklist question	Is finished when...
What did you find out compared to your goals?	You have thought about what your responses told you and what you hoped to learn and decided on the extent to which you have learned what you hoped.
Did you use any descriptive statistics?	You chose to do a numeric method, so your report will have some numbers in it—and usually some descriptive statistics to help people who read the report to compare and use the numbers.
How did you communicate the results?	You have chosen an appropriate reporting method, or several of them because there are groups of stakeholders with different interests, and you have checked that the people who got the report considered that it is accurate and useful.
Did you triangulate?	You have compared what you learned from this survey with any other data you already have and decided on the extent to which these results confirm, add to, or change earlier results.

The final word is "iterate"

We've come a long way together and tackled many technical concepts, some of which I hope now seem familiar.

You may be inspired to dive into the world of survey methodology and statistics. It's fascinating, filled with generous people who do rigorous work—sometimes over decades.

At the other end, I hope you're also inspired to do lots of little Light Touch Surveys that are quick but useful.

Either way, you'll be iterating: trying something, reflecting on whether it works, and then trying a variation to see whether it works better.

Meanwhile, I'll also be iterating. Join me on my blog at Effortmark. co.uk, or write to me with your comments and questions.

Most of all, have fun.

INDEX

using a spreadsheet, 267–268

word clouds, 271–272

cognitive interviews, 34, 118–120, 189

column charts, 278–281

column headers in data set, 245

comparative survey, 13, 14–16, 33, 132–133, 232

comparisons

before and after an event, 297

for data analysis, 258–261

of results within a survey, 298

satisfaction and, 44–46

concentric donut charts, 278

confidence intervals, 84, 93–94, 287

confidence level, 93–94

confidentiality, 220, 221

Conrad, Fred G., 175–176

context

of person who answers, 115–116

of questions, affecting decision on answer, 114–115

context effect, 114–115

correlation, 38

and causation, 39–40

and Net Promoter Score®, 38, 40–41

cost per response, 147

costs of questionnaires, 146–148

Couper, Mick P., 175–176, 307

coverage error, 68–69, 74–75, 76, 83–84, 304

created answers, 104–105, 109

Cronbach's alpha, 213

cross tabulations, 258

curse words in data set, 243–244

curve of forgetting, approximate, 106–107, 160

curve of prediction, 109

customer lists, 11, 69

D

Damiani, L. P., 88

data

downloading, 133

missing data, 247–249

showing results in report, 295–300

data analysis, 251–261

using charts, 255–258

using comparisons, 258–261

using descriptive statistics, 252–255

data breaches, 123–125

data cleaning, 133, 228, 239–247

backups, 240

column headers, 245

example, 246–247

inappropriate language, 243–244

log page setup, 240–241

personal data, 242–243

repeated or implausible responses, 241–242

start time and time to complete, 242

systemic errors with characters, 245

data protection. *See* privacy

data protection regulator, 125, 126

data set, 238

Datasaurus, 257

date-stamp, of entries in log page, 240

Dawson, Jill, 213

deciding on an answer to question, 99, 110–117, 197–198

decision investigation, 64

decision-making with surveys, 4, 23–24

defined group of people, 3

deciding on, 25

sample of people who will answer, 52–53

M

N

no correlation, 38

non-response error, 59–60, 76–78, 84, 304

non-response rate, 57

normal distribution, 255

North Korea, internet prank, 76–77, 229

NPS®. *See* Net Promoter Score®

nudge ideas, 233

number needed to make decision, 24, 32–33

O

observations

analytics and A/B tests, 27–28, 301

usability tests and field studies, 29–30, 301

Oliver, Richard L., 45

omnibus questionnaires, 179–180

Online Surveys, 234

open answers. *See also* coding open answers

cherry picking, 288

open-box comments, and rating questions, 48

open boxes, 156, 157–158, 162–166, 169

open questions, 155–156

opinion sharing, and response rate, 57–58

opinions, statements in Likert scale, 201–202

order of questions. *See* question order in questionnaires

Ospina-Tascón, G. A., 88

"other" answers, 163–164, 264–266

outliers, 254, 256

Oxford Hip, 213–214

P

p-value, 88, 95

painful answers to questions, 116–117

Pairumani, R., 88

panel management, in survey tools, 131–133

panels of people, for sample, 72

paper. *See* mode of questionnaire, choosing

Passives, 41

people survey, 49

perceived effort, 54–57, 218, 224, 226

perceived reward, 54–55, 57–60, 218, 224, 226

percentage scoring method, 207

personal data in data set, 242–243

person's response, 238

Peterson, G., 89

Pettit, Annie, 25

Phan, N., 205

phone. *See* mode of questionnaire, choosing

Picture-in-Picture Video, 262–263, 264

pie charts, 276–278, 296

pilot tests

as advisable method with surveys, 11, 34

iterate up, 64

before launching questionnaire, 227–229, 231

The Least You Can Do™, 313–314

pivot tables, 258–260

pop-up survey invitation, 2

posters, 3, 61, 291

PowerPoint slides, 292

Pratchett, T., 102

prediction

asking about future behavior, 109–110, 202

NPS® using correlation for, 40–41

presentation, 31–32, 228, 294. *See also* delivery of findings

Presentation Zen, 294

Presser, Stanley, 15, 16, 205

privacy

building into questionnaire, 123–128

choosing a survey tool, 129–130

cleaning data, 242–243

responses dependent on trust, 55–56, 112–113

Privacy Impact Assessment (PIA), 124–127

privacy notice (public document), 125, 127–128, 129, 136

private lists, for sample, 70–71

prize draws, 54–55

process of surveys, 5–7, 310, 315–318

processing error, 273, 305

professional association membership, 70–71, 81

Promoters, 41

prompted recall, 108

The Psychology of Survey Response (Tourangeau, et al.), 99

public lists, for sample, 71–72, 131

punch cards, 156–157, 261

purchased panels, for sample, 72

Q

qualitative research, 4, 267, 288

quantitative vs. qualitative, 4

in matrix for choosing the right method, 26–30, 34, 301

question momentum, 181

question order in questionnaires, 179–186

beginning question, 181–182

ending with thank-you, 184

introduction pages, 185

omnibus questionnaires, 179–180

required questions, 185–186

screening out people, 183

unintrusive topics, 180–181

questionnaires, 153–192

building, tips for, 12

checklist, 316

closed questions, 155–156, 158–162

defined, 2

delivery of, and response rates, 53

drop-downs, 157–158

getting back completed ones, 221–222

images in. *See* images in questionnaire

The Least You Can Do™, 311–314

mode selection. *See* mode of questionnaire, choosing

open questions/boxes, 155–156, 162–166, 169

order of questions. *See* question order in questionnaires

other interaction devices, 169–170

problems with, 154–155

response formats, 155–157, 166–169

screenshots of, 191

testing, 187–191

questions, 97–122

challenging the ideas, 22–24

checklist, 316

as column headers in data set, 245

cutoff date, 22

time, checking start time and time to complete in data set, 242

time available for survey, 33, 311–314

timestamp, of entries in log page, 240

Timmus Limited, 232

tools available for survey, 33

top box scoring method, 207

topic, for Likert scale, 200

topic/subtopic slide format, 292–293

topics in questionnaires, unintrusive, 180–181

Total Survey Error, vii, 4–5, 305–306, 307

Tourangeau, Roger, 99, 175–176, 307

tracker, 14, 15

translation of languages, 133

Trello, 225

triangulation, 30, 82, 162

Tripadvisor®, 184

true population, 93

trust
  creation of, 223
  effect on response rate, 54–55
  invitation and trustworthiness, 222–225

Tukey, John W., 255

Tullis, T., 93

U

UCLA tests for Likert scales, 213

UK Government
  Department for Digital, Culture, Media & Sport, 171
  Essex County Council, 177
  Government Digital Service (GDS), 137, 158

uncertainty in surveys, 93

understanding questions, 99, 100–103, 197–198

University of Chicago
  National Data Program for Social Sciences, 115
  NORC, 72

University of Surrey, UK, CAQDAS project, 271

U.S. Bureau of Labor Statistics, 80

U.S. Census Bureau, 3, 8, 80, 82

Usability Testing for Survey Research (Geisen and Bergstrom), 191

usability tests
  advantages of, 10
  as advisable method with surveys, 29, 34, 301
  The Least You Can Do™, 311, 314
  Picture-in-Picture Video, 262–263, 264
  of questionnaires, 189–191

V

validity
  face, 63
  matching of goals and questions, 35–36

variance, 254

verbal rating scale, 205

Vickers, A., 95

visual analog scale, 204, 205

visual clutter in charts, 277, 282–283

voting trolley, 151, 232

W

Wachter-Boettcher, Sara, 117

Wasserstein, R. L., 92

waves (intervals) in LISS, 179

REFERENCES

Allen Miller, S. and C. Jarrett (2001). *Should I Use a Drop-Down? Four Steps for Choosing Form Elements on the Web.* 48th Society for Technical Communication Conference, Chicago, Illinois, US.

Allport, F. H. and D. A. Hartman (1925). *The Measurement and Motivation of Atypical Opinion in a Certain Group.* American Political Science Review 19: 735–760.

Amrhein, V., S. Greenland and B. McShane (2019). *Scientists Rise Up Against Statistical Significance.* Nature Publishing Group. www.nature.com/articles/d41586-019-00857-9 retrieved 12 April 2021.

Anscombe, F. J. (1973). *Graphs in Statistical Analysis.* The American Statistician 27(1): 17–21.

Bartlett, A. (2014). *Burn Your Select Tags.* EpicFEL. www.youtube.com/watch?v=CUkMCQR4TpY retrieved 12 April 2021.

Benedek, J. and T. Miner (2002). *Measuring Desirability: New Methods for Evaluating Desirability in a Usability Lab Setting.* Usability Professionals Association Conference, Orlando, Florida.

Bojko, A. (2013). *Eye Tracking the User Experience: A Practical Guide to Research.* Brooklyn, New York, Rosenfeld Media.

Brooke, J. (1996). "SUS: A "Quick and Dirty" Usability Scale." in *Usability Evaluation in Industry.* P. W. Jordan, B. Thomas, B. A. Weerdmeester and A. L. McClelland. London, Taylor and Francis.

Burnside, R., G. Bishop and T. Guiver (2005). *The Effect of an Incentive on Response Rates and Timing in an Economic Survey.* Canberra, OECD Statistics Directorate.

Cheng, K. (2012). *See What I Mean: How to Use Comics to Communicate Ideas.* Brooklyn, NY, Rosenfeld Media.

Couper, M. P., F. G. Conrad and R. Tourangeau (2007). *Visual Context Effects in Web Surveys.* Public Opinion Quarterly 71(4): 623–634.

Dawson, J., R. Fitzpatrick, A. Carr and D. Murray (1996). *Questionnaire on the Perceptions of Patients about Total Hip Replacement.* The Journal of Bone and Joint Surgery. British volume 78(2): 185–190.

Dillman, D. A. (2000). *Mail and Internet Surveys: The Tailored Design Method.* New York; Chichester, John Wiley.

Dillman, D. A., J. D. Smyth and L. M. Christian (2009). *Mail and Internet Surveys: The Tailored Design Method*. Hoboken, N.J., Wiley & Sons.

Ellis, P. D. (2010). *The Essential Guide to Effect Sizes: Statistical Power, Meta-Analysis, and the Interpretation of Research Results*. Cambridge, Cambridge University Press.

Fine, C. (2010). *Delusions of Gender: The Real Science Behind Sex Differences*. London, Icon Books.

Garner, J. K., M. Alley, A. F. Gaudelli and S. E. Zappe (2009). *Common Use of PowerPoint Versus the Assertion/Evidence Structure*. Technical Communication 56(4): 331–345.

Geisen, E. and J. R. Bergstrom. (2017). *Usability Testing for Survey Research*. Cambridge, MA, Morgan Kaufmann / Elsevier.

Groves, R. M., F. J. Fowler, M. P. Couper, J. M. Lepkowski, E. Singer, and R. Tourangeau (2009). *Survey Methodology*. Hoboken, N.J., Wiley.

Hernández, G., G. A. Ospina-Tascón, L. P. Damiani, E. Estenssoro, A. Dubin, J. Hurtado, G. Friedman, R. Castro, L. Alegría, J.-L. Teboul, M. Cecconi, G. Ferri, M. Jibaja, R. Pairumani, P. Fernández, D. Barahona, V. Granda-Luna, A. B. Cavalcanti, J. Bakker, f. t. A.-S. Investigators and t. L. A. I. C. Network (2019). *Effect of a Resuscitation Strategy Targeting Peripheral Perfusion Status vs Serum Lactate Levels on 28-Day Mortality Among Patients with Septic Shock: The ANDROMEDA-SHOCK Randomized Clinical Trial*. JAMA 321(7): 654–664.

James, J. M. and R. Bolstein (1992*). Large Monetary Incentives and Their Effect on Mail Survey Response Rates*. Public Opinion Quarterly 56(4): 442–453.

John, L. K., A. Acquisti and G. Loewenstein (2011). *Strangers on a Plane: Context-Dependent Willingness to Divulge Sensitive Information*. The Journal of Consumer Research 37(5) (February 2011): 858–873.

Krosnick, J. A. and S. Presser (2009). "Question and Questionnaire Design" in *Handbook of Survey Research (2nd Edition)*. J. D. Wright and P. V. Marsden, Elsevier.

Krug, S. (2010). *Rocket Surgery Made Easy: The Do-It-Yourself Guide To Finding and Fixing Usability Problems*. Berkeley, CA, New Riders.

Likert, R. (1932). *A Technique for the Measurement of Attitudes*. Archives of Psychology 140: 55.

Medvec, V. H., S. F. Madey and T. Gilovich (1995). *When Less Is More: Counterfactual Thinking and Satisfaction Among Olympic Medalists*. Journal of Personality and Social Psychology 69(4): 603–610.

Menn, L. (2011). *Psycholinguistics: Introduction and Applications*. San Diego, Plural Pub.

Meyer, E. and S. Wachter-Boettcher (2016). *Design for Real Life*. A Book Apart.

Oliver, R. L. (2010). *Satisfaction: a Behavioral Perspective on the Consumer*. Armonk, N.Y., M.E. Sharpe.

Peterson, G. (2012). *Unintended Mobile Respondents*. CASRO Technology Conference. New York.

Peterson, G., J. Griffin, J. LaFrance and J. Li (2017). "Smartphone Participation in Web Surveys." in P. P. Biemer, E. D. de Leeuw, S. Eckman, B. Edwards, F. Kreuter, L. Lyberg, C. Tucker, B. T. West (eds), *Total Survey Error in Practice*. Hoboken, New Jersey, Wiley: 203–233.

Pettit, A. (2016). *Anatomy of a survey question: This is why questionnaire design is not a 20 minute task*. Retrieved 31 March 2021 from web.archive.org/web/20160716204613/http://web.peanutlabs.com/ anatomy-of-a-survey-question-this-is-why-questionnaire-design-is-not-a-20-minute-task/

Phan, N., C. Blome, F. Fritz, J. Gerss, A. Reich, T. Ebata, M. Augustin, J. Szepietowski and S. Ständer (2011). *Assessment of Pruritus Intensity: Prospective Study on Validity and Reliability of the Visual Analogue Scale, Numerical Rating Scale and Verbal Rating Scale in 471 Patients with Chronic Pruritus*. Acta dermato-venereologica 92: 502–507.

Pratchett, T. (1990). *Diggers: The Second Book of the Nomes*. London, Corgi Books.

Reichheld, F. F. and R. Markey (2011). *The Ultimate Question 2.0: How Net Promoter Companies Thrive in a Customer-driven World*. Boston, Mass., Harvard Business Press.

Rey, L., C. Quintana-Orts, S. Mérida-López and N. Extremera (2019). *Being Bullied at School: Gratitude as Potential Protective Factor for Suicide Risk in Adolescents*. Frontiers in Psychology 10(662).

Reynolds, G. (2012). *Presentation Zen: Simple Ideas on Presentation Design and Delivery*. Berkeley, CA, New Riders.

Saldaña, J. (2013). *The Coding Manual for Qualitative Researchers*. Los Angeles and London, SAGE.

Schuman, H. and S. Presser (1996). *Questions and Answers in Attitude Surveys: Experiments on Question Form, Wording, and Context*. Thousand Oaks; London, Sage.

Schwarz, N., H.-J. Hippler, B. Deutsch and F. Strack (1985). *Response Scales: Effects of Category Range on Reported Behavior and Comparative Judgments*. Public Opinion Quarterly 49(3): 388–395.

Sinclair, S., C. D. Hardin and B. S. Lowery (2006). *Self-stereotyping in the Context of Multiple Social Identities*. Journal of Personality and Social Psychology 90(4): 529–542.

Singer, E. and C. Ye (2013). *The Use and Effects of Incentives in Surveys*. The ANNALS of the American Academy of Political and Social Science 645(1): 112–141.

smith, s.e. (2009). *Beyond the Binary: Forms*. Retrieved 31 March 2021, from meloukhia.net/2009/12/beyond_the_binary_forms/.

Spiegelhalter, D. (2019). @d_spiegel "This paper motivates the call for the end of significance. A 25% mortality reduction, but because P=0.06 (two-sided), they declare it 'did not reduce' mortality. Appalling. https://jamanetwork.com/journals/jama/article-abstract/2724361" Retrieved from https://twitter.com/d_spiegel/status/1110477993317679104 12 April 2021.

Stigler, S. M. (1980). *Stigler's Law of Eponymy**. Transactions of the New York Academy of Sciences 39 (1 Series II): 147–157.

Suchman, L. and B. Jordan (1992). "Validity and the Collaborative Construction of Meaning in Face-to-face Surveys" in *Questions about Questions: Inquiries into the Cognitive Bases of Surveys*. J. M. Tanur. New York, Russell Sage Foundation: 241.

Sudman, S., N. M. Bradburn and N. Schwarz (1996). *Thinking About Answers: The Application of Cognitive Processes to Survey Methodology*. San Francisco, Jossey-Bass Publishers.

Thurstone, L. L. (1928). *Attitudes Can Be Measured*. American Journal of Sociology 33: 529–554.

Tourangeau, R., L. J. Rips and K. A. Rasinski (2000). *The Psychology of Survey Response*. Cambridge, U.K.; New York, Cambridge University Press.

Tukey, J. W. (1977). *Exploratory Data Analysis*. Reading, Mass., Addison-Wesley Pub. Co.

Tullis, T. and B. Albert (2008). *Measuring the User Experience: Collecting, Analyzing, and Presenting Usability Metrics*. Amsterdam; Boston, Elsevier/Morgan Kaufmann.

Vickers, A. (2010). *What Is a P-value Anyway: 34 Stories to Help You Actually Understand Statistics*. Boston, Addison-Wesley.

Wachter-Boettcher, S. (2015). *Personal Histories*. Retrieved 19 December 2016, from http://www.sarawb.com/2015/01/13/personal-histories/.

Wasserstein, R. L., A. L. Schirm and N. A. Lazar (2019). *Moving to a World Beyond "p < 0.05"*. The American Statistician 73(sup1): 1–19.

ACKNOWLEDGMENTS

When I signed the contract to write this book in 2010, I was convinced that I had learned from the nine years it took to write my previous book: *Forms that Work*, co-authored with Gerry Gaffney. This one would be different!

I was right: This one was different. It took me 11 years. I'd like to thank everyone at Rosenfeld Media for their support and patience over all that time, especially Lou Rosenfeld and Marta Justak.

Why so long? Several reasons.

First of all, I did not know as much about surveys as I thought I did when I signed the contract. In my work as the forms specialist, I'd learned a lot about how people answer questions, but I rapidly realized that I needed to know a lot more about the other aspects of surveys, such as sampling and fieldwork, and about how user experience (UX) professionals use surveys in their work. I did interviews and ran workshops over several years and in many countries. I want to thank UX professionals, market researchers, and survey methodologists who participated in my interviews or who came to workshops, including the STC Seattle chapter, SAPOR in Raleigh, Interactions in Dundee, UX-LX in Lisbon, GOR in Cologne, OZCHI in Australia, JBoye in Aarhus, UX New Zealand in Wellington, LibDesign in Prague, and many events in the UK. One key source of inspiration has been my sister Ann Turner, who explained to me the importance of not asking a question until you know what you're going to do with the answer.

Secondly, I realized that I needed to learn about survey methodology, as well as about surveys. I'm grateful to Alex Johnson of Kantar Operations who had hired me in the late 2000s to work on the user experience of specific question types in market research surveys. Zoë Dowling, PhD, market researcher and survey methodologist, was part of our team, and has been an inspiration to me and eventually became a reviewer of this book: thank you, Zoë. She arranged for me to be invited to the Internet Survey Methodology workshops over several years, where I was able to learn directly from leading experts, such as Professors Mick Couper, Ger Snijkers, Fred Conrad, and Vasja Vehovar. I would like to thank them and so many others who patiently answered my newbie questions—and my reading list grew longer and longer.

Thirdly, there was the problem of statistics. Surveys are a quantitative method, and I embarked on a Diploma in Statistics in 2010. I also read as many "statistics for beginners" books as I could find. I'm not sure any of it helped, and I'm very grateful to James (Jim) Lewis, PhD, who was the technical reviewer of this book from a statistical point of view.

At a low point in 2013, I realized that I needed help and contacted Jane Matthews, who agreed to become my life coach. We ended up working together in many ways. She has taught survey courses with me and spent countless hours helping me work out technical ideas and many other things too numerous to mention. Jane: thank you so much. I definitely could not have finished this book without you.

By early 2015, I worked out that I needed a unifying concept for the book: Total Survey Error. I was accepted at the Total Survey Error conference in Baltimore in the fall of that year, when the Survey Octopus had its first public outing in a highly memorable week that included a chance to see Whitney Quesenbery, UX expert and a reviewer of this book; Professor Kathryn Summers, PhD, who has patiently tested several drafts with her students; and Ginny Redish (Janice Redish, PhD), who has been a stalwart supporter and reviewer of many drafts over the years. Their support and encouragement have been invaluable.

By 2016, I had my structure, I had my unifying concept, and I had my shelves of reference books and my collection of papers. I was making consistent progress at last. I thought I would finish in 2017.

Instead, I found myself in the hospital with acute myeloid leukemia and endometrial cancer in February 2017. It's impossible to adequately express my gratitude to the wonderful National Health Service and the vast number of people who mended me, and to my brother Martin Sankey for his donation of stem cells to give me a new immune system. Although my recovery has been remarkable, I ended up in the hospital again in 2018 with double pneumonia— most likely, because my fragile immune system was not quite able to cope with an infection. Once again, the National Health Service got me back to health, but this book had to be set aside.

I was able to start working again a little bit in 2019. Since then, it's been relatively quick and easy. By that September, I was sufficiently recovered to get the majority of the chapters sorted out. Many thanks to Naintara Land for detailed testing and ideas especially for the "Sample" chapter, and to Amy Hupe (reviewer) and Will Myddleton (tester).

In 2020, I finally worked out what I wanted to say about Likert scales and statistical significance—two topics that Steve Krug was especially firm about in the many hours we spent together scrutinizing every word. Thank you, Steve: the book is much better for your help. Alongside that, Jean Fox, user researcher and survey methodologist, also reviewed the manuscript in detail, and I'd like to thank her, too.

Over the years, there have been so many people who have contributed in some way to this book. I wish I had the space to acknowledge everyone by name. I take full responsibility for any errors and omissions that have slipped through despite all their efforts.

Most of all, I'd like to thank my husband Malcolm. I asked him what he thought his contribution was and he said "washing up." I prefer to focus on the constant supply of delicious healthy meals and his verdict on this book: "It's not really my sort of thing."

 **Rosenfeld**®

Dear Reader,

Thanks very much for purchasing this book. There's a story behind
it and every product we create at Rosenfeld Media.

Since the early 1990s, I've been a User Experience consultant, conference
presenter, workshop instructor, and author. (I'm probably best-known
for having cowritten *Information Architecture for the Web and Beyond*.) In
each of these roles, I've been frustrated by the missed opportunities to
apply UX principles and practices.

I started Rosenfeld Media in 2005 with the goal of publishing books
whose design and development showed that a publisher could practice
what it preached. Since then, we've expanded into producing industry-
leading conferences and workshops. In all cases, UX has helped us
create better, more successful products—just as you would expect. From
employing user research to drive the design of our books and conference programs, to working closely with our conference speakers on
their talks, to caring deeply about customer service, we practice what we
preach every day.

Please visit 🐘rosenfeldmedia.com to learn more about our **conferences**, **workshops**, **free communities**, and **other great resources** that
we've made for you. And send your ideas, suggestions, and concerns my
way: louis@rosenfeldmedia.com

I'd love to hear from you, and I hope you enjoy the book!

Lou Rosenfeld

Lou Rosenfeld,
Publisher

RECENT TITLES FROM ROSENFELD MEDIA

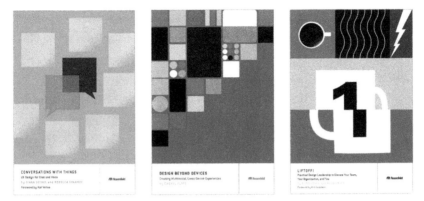

Get a great discount on a Rosenfeld Media book:
visit rfld.me/deal to learn more.

SELECTED TITLES FROM ROSENFELD MEDIA

View our full catalog at rosenfeldmedia.com/books

ABOUT THE AUTHOR

Caroline Jarrett is the forms specialist, advising organizations on how to make forms easier to fill in and how to improve websites and business processes that include forms.

Her research on topics like "How do people answer questions?" led her to explore the literature on survey methodology, the concept of Total Survey Error, and advising her clients on how to improve their surveys, as well as their forms.

Caroline has an MA in Mathematics from Oxford University, an MBA and a Diploma in Statistics from the Open University, and is a Chartered Engineer.

Caroline is co-author of *Forms that Work: Designing Web Forms for Usability* (Morgan Kaufmann/Elsevier) and of *User Interface Design and Evaluation* (The Open University/Elsevier).

Caroline's website is Effortmark.co.uk. Find her on Twitter as @cjforms.